# sugarbaby

CONFECTIONS,

CANDIES, CAKES

*& other*

DELICIOUS RECIPES

*for*

COOKING

WITH SUGAR

**Gesine Bullock-Prado**     photographs by *Tina Rupp*

Stewart, Tabori & Chang   New York

Published in 2011 by Stewart, Tabori & Chang
An imprint of ABRAMS

Copyright © 2011 Gesine Bullock-Prado
Photographs copyright © 2011 Tina Rupp
Props featured in this book were either the author's own or provided courtesy of Simon Pearce.

Library of Congress Cataloging-in-Publication Data:
Bullock-Prado, Gesine.
Sugar baby / by Gesine Bullock-Prado.
p. cm.
ISBN 978-1-58479-897-2 (alk. paper)
1. Cooking (Sugar) 2. Cookbooks. I. Title.
TX819.S94B85 2010
641.6'36--dc22

2010037768

UK Edition ISBN: 978-1-58479-943-6

Editor: Natalie Kaire
Designer: Alissa Faden
Production Manager: Tina Cameron

The text of this book was primarily composed in Walbaum, Gotham, and Archer.

Printed and bound in the U.S.A.
10 9 8 7 6 5 4 3 2 1

Stewart, Tabori & Chang books are available at special discounts when purchased in quantity for
premiums and promotions as well as fundraising or educational use. Special editions can also be created to
specification. For details, contact specialsales@abramsbooks.com or the address below.

ABRAMS
THE ART OF BOOKS SINCE 1949
115 West 18th Street
New York, NY 10011
www.abramsbooks.com

FÜR

*Meine Süße Schwester*

# contents

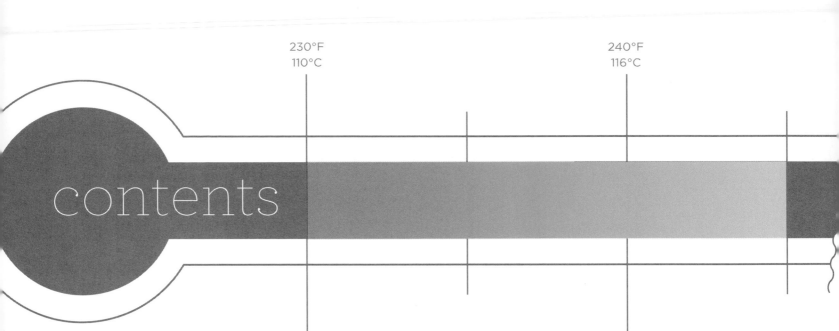

230°F
110°C

240°F
116°C

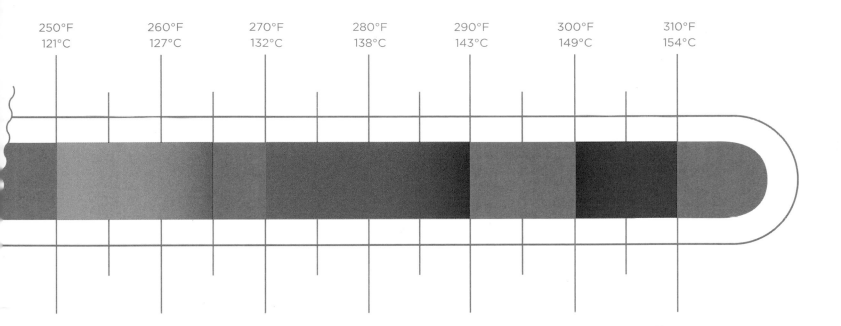

| 250°F | 260°F | 270°F | 280°F | 290°F | 300°F | 310°F |
| 121°C | 127°C | 132°C | 138°C | 143°C | 149°C | 154°C |

SECTION IV

## HARD-BALL STAGE

*page 122*

250°F–265°F
(121°C–129°C)

*Sugar Concentration:*
92%

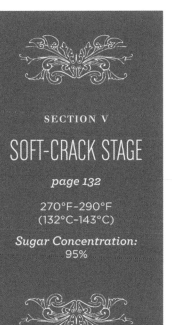

SECTION V

## SOFT-CRACK STAGE

*page 132*

270°F–290°F
(132°C–143°C)

*Sugar Concentration:*
95%

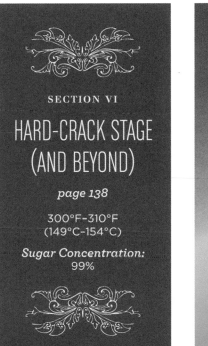

SECTION VI

## HARD-CRACK STAGE
## (AND BEYOND)

*page 138*

300°F–310°F
(149°C–154°C)

*Sugar Concentration:*
99%

SECTION VII

## PUT IT
## ALL
## TOGETHER

*page 166*

# INTRODUCTION

*Allow me to introduce my little friend, Sugar. Reader, meet Sugar. Sugar, meet Reader. I figured you'd have a few questions before we got started, so:*

**READER:** Is this a baking book?

> **SUGAR:** No. Well, yes. There are some recipes that require baking, but this is a book about cooking sugar, not about baking with sugar.

**READER:** What on earth do you mean by "cooking sugar"?

> **SUGAR:** If you've made toffee or hard candy or caramel, you've cooked sugar. By putting sugar in a pot over a flame, you're subjecting those sweet little granules to a chemical transformation that is magical. At least it is to me. Often you add some water, maybe a little corn syrup (don't get your knickers in a twist—we'll talk about the bogeyman of sweeteners in due time), sometimes butter or cream, usually a pinch of salt, and on occasion a healthy dose of local honey. I'll even throw some maple at you, and—if you're good—a touch of agave nectar to keep things interesting. As you heat the sugar, either alone or with some ingredient friends, it starts sloughing off moisture. The more moisture it loses, the hotter it becomes. The hotter it becomes, the harder it gets: from simply melting, to transformation into ropey syrup, to metamorphosis into chewy caramel, to transmogrification into hard candy.

**READER:** So this is a candy book?

> **SUGAR:** No. Well, yes. There are candy recipes here, but cooking with sugar goes far beyond candy. Sugar work, in my opinion, encompasses culinary staples like pastry cream and chocolate mousse and the oft-feared-but-ever-so-delicious Parisian macaron. This book will also give you ideas! For instance, there's a recipe tucked away among these soon-to-be-sticky pages with their pretty color pictures that you can use to make delicious caramels. You have every right to make the recipe as-is and go no further; there's nothing wrong with making caramels for caramels' sake. However, what if I told you that you could take what you've just learned and make a caramel buttercream? Because you can. Then I bet you'd be inclined to shovel some of that buttercream in between a few layers of delicious chocolate cake, or sandwich it between two crispy Parisian meringues . . . . Well, I'll give you the recipes to make these pastry dreams come to fruition.

**READER:** But isn't it hard to work with sugar?

**SUGAR:** Who says? Not I. Sure, you can screw it up, but I've had more baking disasters than sugar disasters. And I'll say this for cooking sugar versus baking: All you need is an open flame. When I moved into my present house I, of all people, didn't check to see if the oven worked. It didn't. Neither did my stand mixer. But the stovetop did. So when I had to make sweet treats, I had plenty of things up my sleeve with which to impress the sugar deprived.

**READER:** Isn't it dangerous?

**SUGAR:** It can be if you aren't careful. I'll show you the sugar-burn scar I have on my back as proof. (You'll have to wait until the caramel chapter for that story.) But as with driving, you can work with sugar safely if you know the rules of the road. Sugar, as it cooks, gets hot. Hotter than boiling water. You just have to be prepared with the proper gear—like oven mitts, safety goggles, and a hard hat. Just kidding. The hard hat would be utterly useless against a sticky onslaught of freshly churned marshmallow. And you can leave out the safety goggles, unless you insist on keeping the mixer on high when you start pouring hot sugar into it. Think of it this way: Would you reach into the oven with your bare hands to take out a pan of chocolate chip cookies? Of course not. Just be aware of the fact that hot sugar is, in fact, hot.

**READER:** Isn't sugar bad for you?

**SUGAR:** Yes. I'm not going to lie. But here's my philosophy: Sugar in moderation is okay as long as it is beautifully and lovingly prepared.

There are solid links between things like high fructose corn syrup and the rise in obesity, and you can't tell me that hiding sugar in foods that have no business containing it doesn't aid us in getting plump. It's just common sense: The more sugar you eat, the fatter you'll be. But it's also common sense that you can't have a decent celebration without dessert. And a dessert will contain sugar, no matter the form—except in this case it's not hidden; it's the guest of honor. Sugar is a glorious treat, and when you spin a wondrous confection from your own kitchen, the glory is all yours. So celebrate food and life; just be respectful of yourself and mindful of the things you consume.

**READER:** Are the recipes complicated?

**SUGAR:** No. They may seem long at times, but not because there's more stuff to do—I simply want you to have enough information to make things perfectly. So I like to explain things as clearly as I can, giving you guidance that I hope is illuminating as well as entertaining. Some recipes are more involved than others; I can't say Parisian macarons are easy or that you'll get them right the first time, but they certainly aren't impossible, and they're well worth the effort.

READER: So all I need is a pot and some sugar?

SUGAR: Essentially, yes. Make sure the pot you're using has a heavy bottom and, preferably, is made of stainless steel, as aluminum pots tend to be of inferior material and often react adversely with ingredients. If you have a copper pot, you're way ahead of the game.

You will, however, be doing yourself a colossal favor by buying a few additional things, such as a candy thermometer. (Don't tell anyone, but I've used a digital meat thermometer to make marshmallows when I was in a bind, so if that's all you've got and you're desperate to dive in, go to it. Just promise me that at your earliest convenience you'll get yourself the real deal.) It also helps to have a stand mixer for some things, like making marshmallows, but a hand mixer will do in a pinch. I have a list of things for you to think about getting on pages 14–15, so consult that to see what you might already have around the house so you can get started. You can also check my website, www.sugarbabycookbook.com, for extra tips and tricks.

READER: So why do specific temperatures matter so much?

SUGAR: Water boils when it heats up to 212°F (100°C). It can't get much higher on the thermometer. Sugar, on the other hand, gets a hell of a lot hotter, but since it contains moisture when it first starts out on your stovetop, it takes a bit of time to get to the molten stage while it's sloughing off those vestigial bits of $H_2O$. But trust me, it'll get there. And with each stage of heat comes a very specific chemical reaction that brings with it a special goodness quite unlike the last. This is also why candies have a stupendous shelf life. The hotter the sugar gets, the less moisture a confection contains, the harder it gets, and the longer it can be stored. I can't say I've personally witnessed a sweet treat lasting longer than a few moments after I've laid eyes on it, but I'm sure there's a candy bowl somewhere in the darkest recess of the universe filled with ancient gummi bears and Swedish fish that look exactly as they did when the sugar within was first heated—just a little dustier.

READER: Will playing with hot sugar be fun?

SUGAR: Hell, yes!

# SUGAR—THE PREQUEL!

*A Brief History of the World (As It Pertains to Sugar)*

Honey was the first of the confectionery heroes. Egyptians, Greeks, and Byzantines all have tales of honey goodness nestled in their zany stories—its name is even carved in cuneiform writing as early as 2100 BCE in Sumerian and Babylonian stone texts. It's the ambrosia of the gods, the nectar in which Cupid dipped his arrow before aiming, and the name on the signpost to Israel: "Exit at the Land of Milk and Honey." Honey plays a role in the tale of Noah's ark, being a main ingredient in asure, that celebratory concoction made when the poor guy finally hit land. (A dish made of beans, barley, dried fruit, and honey isn't really the gold standard of desserts nowadays, but see what *you'd* ingest after 150 days on a leaky boat with the world's remaining animal population.) Honey, it seems, was a sweet universally enjoyed, at least by the rich. It was added to wine, used as a preservative coating for nuts and fruits, and, in the oldest known cookery book, *Apicius*, was showcased in a dessert made of nut-filled dates, sprinkled with salt and pepper, then fried in honey.

The Abnaki tribe of my home state, Vermont, not only relished the bounty of beehives but also tapped maple trees and enjoyed their sap in all manner of applications. When Europeans first made their way to the lands of the Algonquin and Cree, they were introduced to a practice called *sinzibuckwud*, which means "drawing from wood." Discovering that the result was as delicious as the notoriously difficult-to-cultivate sugar cane, Europeans began transplanting sugar maples back to their homelands. However, it seems that sugar maples like the climes of subfreezing at night and tolerable during the day that spawned them, and thrive only in the Americas.

Sugar grew as a native reed in India. Emperor Darius of Persia took some time out from his pillage of that region in 510 BCE to sample the local produce and remarked that in India there is "the reed which gives honey without bees." Presumably, he took the secrets of cane production back home and kept them under lock and key, because nary another peep is heard about the sweet stuff until the seventh century CE. It was the Arabs who, in their own empire-building skirmishes into Persia, grabbed the sugar cane and ran with it. They spread the love of the sweet cane throughout their travels and gave us one of the loveliest words in the English language: "candy," from the Arabic word *qandi*, meaning "made of sugar." You can probably guess the instigator of sugar's next wave of expansion. That's right: blood, entrails, carnage! The Crusaders waged holy war and, in between, satisfied their sweet teeth in the Mideast, bringing sugar cane back to Europe.

The Venetians first imported sugar, but by the fifteenth century were refining their own. The process, it turned out, was terribly expensive. Only the stupidly rich enjoyed it, including Henry III of

France, who was treated to cutlery, dishes, and table linens made of spun sugar.

Columbus is ultimately responsible for bringing sugar production and consumption to a larger population—partly due to the growing conditions in the warmer climes of the West Indies where he initially brought the plant, but primarily due to the slave trade, which made production of such a labor-intensive crop significantly cheaper. Despite its expanded production, however, sugar was still costly, and due to its exclusivity or its ability to mask unpleasant tastes or both, it was viewed primarily as medicinal. (Something I've been telling everyone as long as I can remember—yet neither my mother nor my dentist Jedediah would ever believe me.)

In time, sugar's exclusivity vanished. In fact, my own ancestral history is saturated with sugar. Quite frankly, it's in my blood. My grandmother Nanny raised seven children during the Depression; she lost her husband to heart disease when my father was only six and she worked three jobs to keep her family fed. Nevertheless, sugar was always a sweet part of their lives despite their relative poverty. Nanny would throw sugar-pulling parties on birthdays; all she needed was a couple cups of sugar and a stove. She'd boil the sugar to hard crack, something she could do by sight—she probably didn't have money to waste on a thermometer anyway. When the sugar got to just the right stage, she'd pour it on a slab and divide it among the children at the party. The kids would pull the sugar, with Nanny watching over them as the sugar cooled and took on new shapes and textures from the pulling. At just the right moment, when it was cool enough to keep its shape but still warm enough to slice, she'd cut the candy into little hard squares. During the holidays, she'd spend a little more on some dye to transform the sugar into brightly colored candy canes.

I've asked my father, "Wasn't Nanny worried she'd send the neighborhood children home with third-degree burns?" But Dad doesn't recall there being any worry about scarring, or lawsuits—he just remembers the joy of the sugar-pulling parties. During the same period, my Aunt Sis would bribe neighborhood kids with a chance to get into the movies free if they'd bring her a cup of sugar. The local theater had a matinee special: If you were sixteen or older and bought a ticket, you could bring along as many kids under sixteen as you could muster (and chaperone) for free. If a kid wanted to tag along with Aunt Sis, they had to bring her a cup of sugar an hour before show time. She'd make peanut brittle with the sugar just in time for the matinee and the kids would follow her like ducklings, bags of crunchy nut brittle in their hands, to see a movie.

When I was born into my family of candy magicians, every granule of sugar history was distilled in my DNA, from ancient history to my own ancestral dance with the delicious stuff. I swear I popped out of the womb screaming for a piece of candy, a natural-born sugar baby. Now that I'm old enough to write my own sugar story, I make sweet treats every day. So join me, and let's go make a little sweet history together.

# WHAT YOU'LL NEED

## TO GET STARTED

*It's true that many of these recipes require far less equipment than you'd need for traditional baking, but there are a few items that you'd be lost without.*

① **First, there's the candy thermometer.** You can choose from a wide variety these days, and I tend to use more than one type depending on the sugar work I've got on the agenda. My main man is the traditional Taylor flat candy thermometer that you'll find easily in cooking supply stores, and even some well-stocked grocery stores. The Taylor is sturdy and reliable. But I also recommend having an instant-read digital thermometer on hand. I find myself grabbing for the digital not because it is proudly advertised as "instant" but because it works beautifully when you have very low levels of sugar in the pot, so low that the safety cage around the Taylor thermometer won't allow the bulb to hit your syrup and get a reading.

② **Second, you need a good pan: specifically, a heavy-duty pan.** Very specifically, I use a 4-quart stainless-steel All-Clad saucier for the majority of my work. A saucepan is probably better for the job—its deep, straight sides make clipping on a thermometer effortless—but I got a saucier as a wedding present and it does the job just as well. I actually prefer the saucier for things like crème anglaise and pastry cream because the sloping sides make getting into the corners with a whisk much easier.

Do not use an aluminum pan for any cream-based sauces, as they tend to discolor the sauce. And don't use enamel pans for cream-based products, as the invisible cracks in the enamel can harbor bacteria.

The key, no matter the shape, is that you use a large, heavy-duty pan with a thick bottom to ensure that the sugar doesn't burn. If you have a copper pot, you're way ahead of the game, since copper distributes heat quickly and evenly. However, you must only use your copper sugar pot for sugar work and clean it exclusively with vinegar and water. Don't dry with it a dishtowel; this could deposit grease and fat into your otherwise clean pan.

While high-quality stainless-steel pots are expensive, copper pots are painfully so. I've managed to find a few at reasonable prices at flea markets and antique shops, so keep your eyes peeled. You'll also want a pan big enough to accommodate your piping-hot ingredients when they boil. Sugar likes to get a bit raucous and at high heat, will climb up a pan like a hungry bear in search of honey. There are times when a recipe calls for very little sugar and you may want to opt for a smaller pan so you can get enough depth for a thermometer reading, but if you want a good all-around pan, a 4-quart saucepan will do you right in most situations.

③ **The third item you'll want around is a wooden spoon.** You can use metal spoons or heat-resistant rubber spoons and spatulas for stirring sugar, but a wooden spoon is less reactive and sugar crystals don't stick to its surface as readily.

④ **The fourth thing that you'll want to have if you're going to get hot and heavy with sugar is a stand mixer.** You'll be so damn happy you have one if you're at all inclined to make pastry cream, marshmallow, or nougat, because I guarantee that simultaneously beating egg whites by hand and pouring molten sugar is not only going to make you cramp and sweat, it could also very well send you to the burn unit. And with recipes like nougat, the hot sticky stuff is going to be spending some quality time getting beaten. On those occasions, a stand mixer is your best friend.

⑤ **There are also tools for the stages when you'll be manipulating painfully hot sugar.** A few things will make your life easier, such as a couple bench scrapers and a pair of sugar gloves. I keep two bench scrapers handy, one for each hand, when I need to keep hot and flowing sugar in check. Sugar gloves are a little tricky to find; I get mine online. They usually run about $8 and are well worth it to keep your hands clean and relatively cool. Another option—and this is just between us—is a pair of dishwashing gloves. They don't fit very tightly so I put rubber bands at the cuffs to keep them on, and I spray them with nonstick spray to keep the hot sugar from sticking, but they do work in a pinch and usually provide a nice degree of insulation that allows you to start manipulating hot sugar faster than you could with the less-insulated sugar glove or, God forbid, your bare hands. One caveat is that dishwashing gloves usually have ridged patterns on the palms and fingers, so you'll want to take them off once you're at a stage where you can comfortably handle the sugar; otherwise you run the risk of leaving weird marks on your finished product as the sugar starts to set.

⑥ **A marble slab is always handy when you need to pour sugar syrup onto a surface before you can work it by hand.** Marble and other stone surfaces can handle the high heat of sugar syrups; they are naturally cool and quicken the setting process, and when sprayed with nonstick spray they are very—well, nonstick. I've used both verdigris (green) Vermont marble and white Vermont marble and have found that the verdigris is the best of the stones because it cools the sugar the most quickly. I didn't believe it when I first heard about its candy superpowers; I even checked the temperatures of both marbles with a laser thermometer to see if the verdigris was naturally cooler. It wasn't. However, the green in the marble is produced when copper carbonate invades the stone and, as copper is a super-conductor of heat, it makes sense to this amateur geologist that the copper present in the marble acts as a heat sponge. Another advantage of using that dark-green slab is that it won't show the psychedelic hues of any dyes you've added to your candy while it's on the board. But while stone is a fantastic surface, it isn't a necessity. Stainless-steel surfaces work almost as well or, barring that, you can use the back of a metal sheet pan as a work surface if you have nothing else that's suitable.

⑦ **Lastly, while not an utter necessity, a scale is incredibly handy when you're working with sugar.** If you're serious about sweets, you know that precise measurement is key. A scale is the only tool that will guarantee your measurements are correct. I use dry measure in most of my recipes, but some require a scale. Consider it. You won't regret the purchase. I promise.

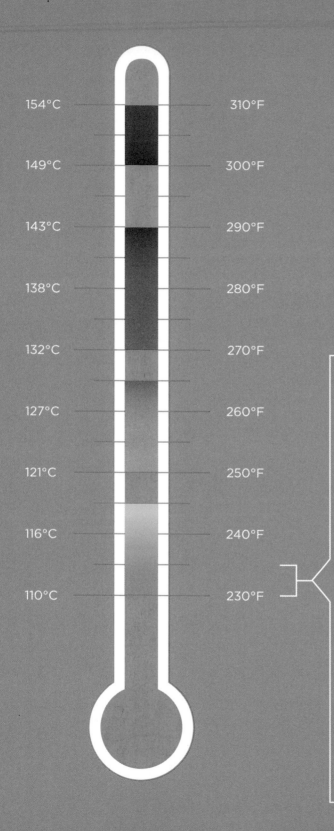

| 154°C | | 310°F |
| 149°C | | 300°F |
| 143°C | | 290°F |
| 138°C | | 280°F |
| 132°C | | 270°F |
| 127°C | | 260°F |
| 121°C | | 250°F |
| 116°C | | 240°F |
| 110°C | | 230°F |

# SIMPLE DISSOLVE TO THREAD STAGE

*230°F–235°F (110°C–113°C)    Sugar Concentration: 80%*

When dropped into a glass of cold water, sugar will simply dissolve. Starting at 230°F (110°C), sugar dropped into water will form a soft thread that will not hold a shape and will dissipate.

At these temperatures, syrups are formed, not tactile confections. In some instances, the syrup itself is the finished product. In other instances, the hot syrup is an integral element in the formation of a more complicated pastry component (macaron shell, pâte à bombe, Italian meringue). When combined with proteins (eggs and cream) in making a custard on the stovetop, such as crème anglaise or pastry cream, sugar delays the coagulation of the protein structures and allows the custard thicken properly. Sugar acts as crowd control, fanning out among the protein molecules that want to clump together and congeal. In meringues, sugar stabilizes the mixture by, again, dispersing the proteins and creating that signature shiny-white, stiff meringue.

At this stage of heating, sugar becomes the great enforcer, bullying ingredients into behaving deliciously when things start getting hot.

# ROCK
# CANDY

*I love rock candy.* It's pure sugar. That's it. It doesn't pretend it's anything more than an unadulterated cavity maker. Just look at it: Instead of itsy-bitsy granulated morsels that can easily hide, rock candy is a series of gigantic, in-your-face sugar crystals. It's the badass of candies, and yet it's beautiful, too. When I am reincarnated—and you know I'm coming back as something sweet—I want to come back as rock candy.

Approach making rock candy as a lab experiment; it's kind of like shoving toothpicks into an avocado seed, setting it in a jar of water on your windowsill, and waiting months for it to sprout. Rock candy doesn't take as long as the avocado but it *is* a week-long process—and well worth the time.

IIIIIIIIIIIIIIIIIIIIIIIIIIII *Makes 2 large rock candies or up to 20 miniature rock candies* IIIIIIIIIIIIIIIIIIIIIIIIIIII

| sugar | 4 cups | 800 g |
|-------|--------|-------|
| water | 2 cups | 480 ml |

① Dissolve the sugar in the water by gently heating the two in a saucepan over medium-low heat. Once all the sugar has melted, take the syrup off the heat and allow to cool very slowly and completely. Alternatively, place the sugar and water in a microwave-safe container and stir, making sure to saturate the sugar with the water. Microwave for 3 minutes on high. Stir. Nuke for 3 more minutes and stir. The sugar has probably melted by now but make sure, and nuke for a few more minutes. Allow to cool completely. Run the solution through a fine sieve.

② Divide the cooled syrup into two tall glasses. Cut two lengths of cotton or wool cooking string that are just a wee bit shorter than the height of the glasses and dip one into the mixture in each glass. Make sure the strings

are saturated. Remove the strings, roll them in extra granulated sugar, and let them dry completely on a piece of wax or parchment paper, at least overnight and for up to 2 days, depending on the humidity. Alternatively, pour the entire batch of syrup in a large, shallow casserole dish and, depending on the size of the vessel, dip as many toothpicks as you can reasonably expect to fit into that surface, allowing for a 2-inch perimeter for each toothpick when it's suspended in the drink. Remove the toothpicks and let them dry completely, as above, at least overnight and for up to 2 days.

✱ **A Note from the Sugar Baby:** This is my first warning about sugar and moisture but certainly not my last. Moisture is the bane of sugar work—perfectly executed brittle on a rainy day can turn into a sticky, malleable mess in under an hour. The whole point of heating sugar is to evaporate the moisture hidden within the granules; the hotter the sugar gets, the more moisture is sloughed off. In the case of rock candy,

we're only heating the sugar to melt in water. Plenty of moisture there, right? So what's the big deal about drying the sugar-saturated string before dipping it back into the drink? Well, it's a big deal because no sugar granule wants to stick to a soggy string. And you'll find it virtually impossible to dry your string on a humid day. But unlike brittle or caramel, you *can* do something to save the day when that sticky little string refuses to dry. Place your sugar-saturated string(s) on a parchment-lined sheet pan and let them dry out in a very low-heat oven, about 200°F (90°C) to 220°F (105°C), for about 20 minutes. Pinch the string with dry hands to make sure it's no longer tacky to the touch before dipping it back into the sugar mixture. For more rock candy troubleshooting tips, go to www.sugarbabycookbook.com.

③ Resubmerge the now dry strings into the sugar water, weighing each end down with a non-lead fishing weight, a washer, or something equally heavy to keep the string straight. Tie the top end of each string to a pencil placed across the lip of the glass so that the string suspends gently in the liquid. If you've chosen the shallow-dish method, secure a piece of parchment or plastic wrap tautly across the top of the dish with a rubber band and poke the toothpicks through so they are suspended in the liquid and held tightly in place by the parchment or plastic.

④ No matter your method, let your experiment sit for *at least* 7 days. I usually keep my experiment going for a few weeks for maximum rock-candy goodness, and I've found the process is much speedier in the cool, dry winter months. It's worth gently wiggling your strings or sticks every few days to keep the ends from adhering to the bottom of the glass or dish.

GF: In the food world, it doesn't stand for "girlfriend." It means "gluten free," girlfriend. And you'll find that most of the recipes in this book are just that (gluten free, that is, not girlfriends—but if you're in the market for a girlfriend, making something from this book for a nice lady person might get you closer).

Gluten allergies have become rampant. Allergies in general, for that matter. I can't remember anyone in elementary school having any food ailment—or if they did, they suffered their gastrointestinal discomforts in silence. But once I started to bake professionally, the litany of allergies for young ones and older folks alike made for a long list of allergen-free treats I had to have on deck. Thankfully, I've always had a healthy arsenal of gluten-free desserts on call, not for any particular reason other than I liked them. So whether you've got a slight wheat aversion or full-blown celiac disease, know that this book is going to be a very handy guide to allergen-free treats.

⑤ Remove the strings or sticks when you're satisfied with the amount of crystal growth. Store in an airtight container for up to 1 month.

**Option!**
If you're feeling particularly fancy, replace the 2 cups (480 ml) water with 2 cups (480 ml) coffee to produce java-infused bonbons.

# SIMPLE
# SYRUP

*How plain and simple is a plain simple syrup?* Take a cup of sugar, pour it into a cup of water, heat the mixture until the sugar is dissolved, and voilà! Simple syrup. You may ask yourself, "Why bother?" Well, have you ever wondered how fancy pastry shops keep their cakes so moist? No? Okay, let's try this: Have you ever wondered how to keep your own cakes moister, longer? If so, then simple syrup is the stuff for you. Once the syrup is cooled, simply brush a bit of it on top of each layer of cake. You don't want to soak it through and make it soggy; just dip a pastry brush into the syrup and gently apply a small amount.

You may add extracts—lemon, ginger, peppermint, lavender, almond, and the like—to the simple syrup, not only to moisten your cakes but also to heighten their flavors. If you're so inclined, you can also replace the water with coffee. I use coffee syrup on chocolate cakes, since coffee is a lovely enhancer for cocoa flavor. The list could go on, but you get the idea: This stuff is versatile.

And it's not just for cakes. At Gesine Confectionary, my former pastry shop in Montpelier, Vermont, we always kept a bottle of simple syrup at the coffee station for sweetening iced coffees or fresh-brewed iced tea. No more stirring and stirring, waiting for those pesky granules to dissolve and infuse your icy drink with sweetness. A couple pumps of plain-and-simple and you're ready to rumble.

|||||||||||||||||||||||||||||||||||||||||||||||||||||||||||||| *Makes 2 cups (480 ml)* ||||||||||||||||||||||||||||||||||||||||||||||||||||||||||||||

① In a microwave-safe container, microwave the sugar and water for 5 minutes. Stir to make sure all the sugar is dissolved. Nuke for a few more minutes, until all the sugar is dissolved into the water. Allow to cool before using.

| | | |
|---|---|---|
| sugar | 1 cup | 200 g |
| water | 1 cup | 240 ml |

② If you're making this on your stovetop, simply heat the water and sugar in a heavy saucepan over medium heat, stirring occasionally, until the sugar is dissolved. Again, cool before using.

③ The yield can easily be doubled, tripled, or quadrupled, as the ratio is always 1 cup (200 g) sugar to 1 cup (240 ml) liquid. Store in refrigerator until needed.

**Options!**

OPTION 1: **COFFEE SIMPLE SYRUP**

For a delicious variation, replace the water with an equal amount of coffee and follow instructions for simple syrup above.

OPTION 2: **LEMON SIMPLE SYRUP**

In the summertime, I'll squeeze piles of lemons and make a pitcher of lemon simple syrup. The ratio remains the same: 1 cup (240 ml) lemon juice to 1 cup (200 g) sugar. One thing I add to the syrup is the rind of the lemon—the quality of the juice is deeply enhanced by cooking with the zest. Using a Microplane, zest the rind into the juice. Heat the zest along with the juice and the sugar according to the instructions for simple syrup above. Allow the zest to steep in the syrup until it's completely cooled, pour the syrup through a fine sieve to remove any bits of zest, and refrigerate.

I whip out the lemon syrup to make homemade lemonade whenever the summer heat creeps into my bones. The syrup alone tends to be too sweet and concentrated, so I just add water and ice to taste. Often I add sparkling water for a nice fizz. Sometimes I'll add a few sprigs of mint to jazz it up. And at cocktail hour, a generous splash of vodka will put some swagger into your sunset.

OPTION 3: **LIME SIMPLE SYRUP**

Follow instructions above for lemon simple syrup, replacing the lemon juice with an equal amount of lime juice and the lemon zest with lime zest. Great in spritzers and margaritas.

OPTION 4: **LAVENDER SIMPLE SYRUP**

Making lavender syrup is easy—what's not so easy is keeping the stuff around. Lavender Italian sodas were so popular at our bakery in Montpelier that we had trouble matching supply to demand! Add 4 tablespoons (25 g) crumbled dried lavender to the pot before you start heating the water and sugar according to the instructions above for plain simple syrup. Allow the lavender to steep in the syrup until it's completely cooled, pour the syrup through a fine sieve to remove any dried lavender bits, and refrigerate.

It takes very little of the syrup to animate a drink; lavender packs a potent punch. A few spoonfuls added to sparkling water make a lovely lavender spritzer that lends a whisper of Provence to my day. My friend Ann makes a sublime lavender martini by combining lavender syrup, lavender liqueur, and vodka. She even rims the glasses with lavender sugar (she mixes dried lavender and granulated sugar in an airtight container and waits patiently until the lavender has infused the sugar with its aromatics). And for a luxurious aperitif, add a squirt of lavender syrup to the bottom of a champagne glass and pour in some bubbly.

OPTION 5: **A MELLOW JITTER (COFFEE SYRUP WITH VODKA)**

What we have here is essentially a homemade Kahlúa. This is a delightful way to mellow a caffeine buzz—or to put a little buzz into your vodka mellow. Combine ¼ cup (60 ml) coffee simple syrup with a shot (or two, or three—I'm not your keeper) of vanilla vodka, and pour over ice.

OPTION 6: **DOMAINE DE CANTON GIN(GER) FIZZ**

Domaine de Canton is a ginger liqueur, and it's delicious. This is a lemony-sweet cocktail with just a hint of ginger. Warning: This isn't for the hard-core martini drinker who can't stand a froufrou libation, but the tonic water does give the drink a hint of bitter to make it an adult beverage built for fun. Into a cocktail shaker filled with ice, pour 2 ounces (60 ml) Hendrick's Gin, 1 ounce (30 ml) Domaine de Canton ginger liqueur, and 1 ounce (30 ml) lemon simple syrup* (page 22), and shake shake shake! Pour into two Collins glasses filled with crushed ice. Pour 5 ounces (150 ml) tonic water into each glass, give a good stir, and add a lemon wedge to each glass. Cheers!

*If you want an extra ginger kick, add 1 teaspoon (2 g) grated ginger to infuse the lemon syrup while you cook it, and strain the ginger pieces out along with the lemon zest.

OPTION 7: **MARGARITA**

I don't know why tequila gets such a bum hangover rap. It's the nectar of the gods, in my book. A margarita on the rocks, with salt on the rim and a little tequila floater to give it that punch of extra goodness—there's nothing better on a summer night. In a cocktail shaker filled with ice, combine 2 ounces (60 ml) tequila (Gold Patron, baby!), ½ ounce (15 ml) Cointreau, and 2 ounces (60 ml) lime simple syrup (page 22), and shake shake shake! Gently moisten the lips of two margarita glasses and dunk them, one at a time, in a saucer of coarse kosher salt. Fill each glass with ice and divide the contents of the shaker between them. Add a wedge of lime to each, and if you're feeling a little racy, top each glass with an extra splash of tequila.

*I've already told you that you need to get yourself a candy thermometer.* Yes, you can do the water method, but I'm advising you: Go get a thermometer—now. There are plenty of options out there; that's why I have a drawer full of them. There's the flat, traditional Taylor thermometer with a trusty black handle and a clip on the back. This is the thermometer I use the most. I do have two problems with it, though. The first is that I use it so much that the writing wears off and I can barely read the numbers. The second is that it has a gap at the bottom to keep the working end of the gauge from touching the bottom of the pan. This is a handy feature, as you want to get the temperature reading from sugar itself and not the pot. But sometimes there's so little sugar syrup in the pot that the wee nubbin that's meant to be suspended in the drink is hovering just above it. That's not going to help you. In those cases, I use a digital instant-read candy thermometer. Most are just a long spike with a bulb at one end (containing the working parts) and the temperature display on top. You'll have to hold the thermometer in the sugar yourself to make sure it doesn't rest on the bottom of the pot, unless you can find the kind that has a really convenient clip and an adjustable reading display. The good news is that since this is an instant-read, you don't have to sit over a steaming cauldron and melt your hand off, because it's pretty fast and usually comes with an alarm that starts beeping when you get close to temperature. I must warn you, though, that the "instant" part is a bit of a misnomer. While the digital does read temperature faster than a traditional candy thermometer, it still takes a few seconds to go through its paces and get to the right mark.

There's a third option, but I would advise against it: the laser-gun thermometer. I have one of these. It looks like a phaser from a 1980s sci-fi movie. You even pull a trigger, and it has a little button that lets loose a red laser beam so you can see exactly where the temperature is being read on the surface. And therein lies the problem. It reads the surface temperature, and what we want is the temperature in the middle. Surface temperature can be considerably cooler than the interior, and that can throw you off quite a bit in the world of sugar. So save your money and get the old-fashioned kind for a couple of bucks.

I suggest you calibrate your new thermometer by putting it in boiling water—I always do. Boiling water temperature is 212°F (100°C) at sea level (this temp goes down as the elevation goes up). If your thermometer reads the temperature correctly, you're golden. If it's slightly off, just keep that in mind and do a little math when you're working with it. I also check periodically to see if the thermometers I've been using for a while are still true. Harry Potter wouldn't be bubkes without the right wand, and so it goes with the sugar wizard and the thermometer.

HARRY POTTER WOULDN'T BE BUBKES *without the* RIGHT WAND, AND SO IT GOES *with the* SUGAR WIZARD *and the* THERMOMETER.

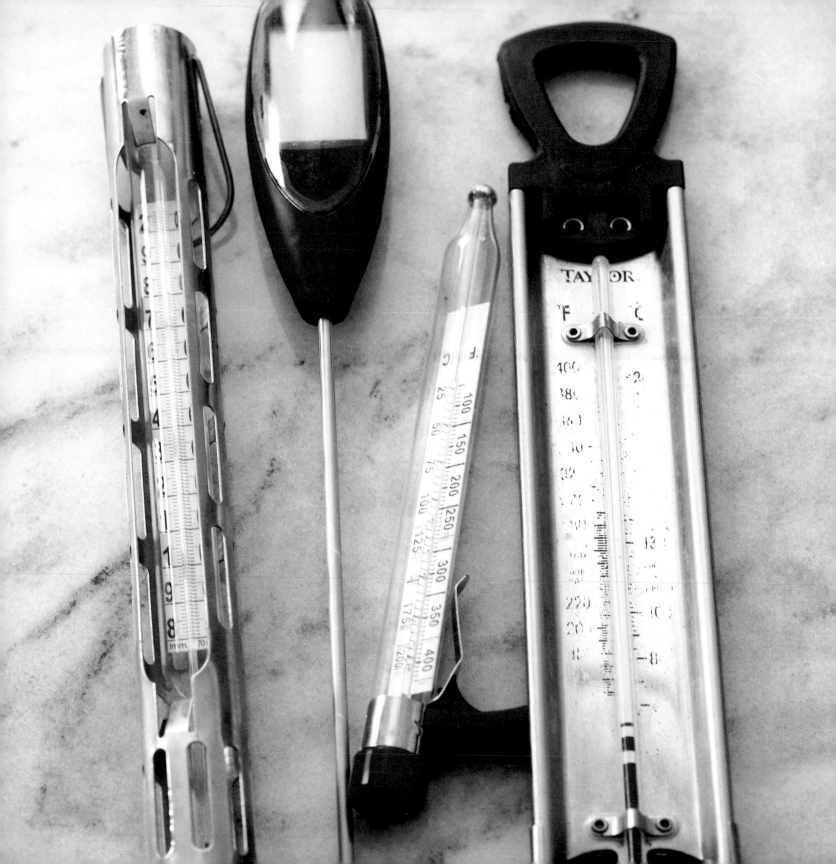

# CONFITURE DE LAIT/
## *dulce de leche/*
# HAMAR PÅLEGG

*This sweet caramelized milk is a nutty-brown delicacy tailor-made for all lactose-tolerant sugar babies—it's no surprise that many a culture has their own version of and name for the glorious goo. The French (of course!) have their* confiture de lait, *or "milk jam." The Argentines have their "sweet milk,"* dulce de leche. *How the Argentines differ from the French is that they make life incredibly convenient by skipping the whole ingredients list, poking a few holes in a can of sweetened condensed milk, and simmering it over medium-low heat in a water bath for about 3 hours. The hardest parts about this recipe are (1) waiting, and (2) remembering to make sure the can stays submerged in simmering water almost to the top of the can—otherwise it will overheat and just might explode! Oh, and (3) not burning your hand on the can when you get around to opening it. But it's the Norwegians who had me with their version,* Hamar pålegg, *or "cold cut from Hamar." Any Norwegian municipality that considers a milk-caramel spread something akin to a cold cut is my kind of town. Where are my passport and my duffel? I think I've just found my new home.*

|||||||||||||||||||||||||||||||||||||||||||||||||| *Makes approximately 2 cups (480 ml)* ||||||||||||||||||||||||||||||||||||||||||||||||||

| milk | 8 cups | 2 L |
|---|---|---|
| sugar | 2½ cups | 500 g |
| salt | 1 teaspoon | 6 g |
| vanilla bean paste | 1 tablespoon | 15 ml |

① Fill a large stockpot a little more than halfway with water.

② In a very large heatproof bowl that's still small enough to rest inside the stockpot, combine all the ingredients and whisk them together well.

③ Place the bowl gently in the stockpot so it is surrounded almost three-quarters up the sides by water. Place the stockpot over high heat, gently and constantly stirring the contents of the floating bowl until the sugar has dissolved. Reduce the heat to medium or medium-low until the water is barely simmering.

④ Cut a round of wax or parchment paper and place it directly on top of the simmering milk to keep a skin from forming.

✪ **A Note from the Sugar Baby:** Yes, hot milk forms a skin. We've all seen it and wondered how the hell to avoid it. First, let me tell you why it happens. The skin is formed from solid proteins that have congealed as the milk evaporates over heat. This is true of milks with fat, but non-fat milk, since it contains no fat, will not form a skin.

The skin won't disintegrate back if you stir it; you'll have to skim it off (though this can still leave small bits behind). Constantly stirring the milk keeps the proteins from binding together to form the skin, though in the case of *confiture de lait*, this would require you to stand over the stove for hours. The solution is to create what's called a "cartouche," a parchment cover that sits directly on top of the milk, which slows the evaporation and prevents that pesky lactose epidermis from forming.

⑤ Continue to simmer (the lower the heat the better) for a minimum of 3 hours and up to 7 hours, until the milk caramel reduces by half, thickens to the point that it coats the back of a spoon, and is a golden brown. This is an exceedingly long time, and you must monitor the water level in the stockpot, making sure it doesn't dip below halfway down the bowl containing the evaporating milk. Try setting an alarm to go off every half hour, and check the water level, and let it take as long as it takes.

⑥ Transfer the mixture to a large, heavy-bottomed saucepan and simmer, stirring constantly, over medium-high heat. (I use a large, heatproof plastic spatula to stir this mixture—it has enough "give" to scrape along the edges, as the caramel thickens more along the sides than in the center.) Stir vigorously and constantly for 15 to 20 minutes, until the caramel thickens to the point that it "ribbons" (when you insert and remove a spoon, a ribbon of caramel appears on the surface and then disappears back into the mixture).

⑦ Allow the milk caramel to cool completely. Feel free to use it as a spread or a sauce on just about anything. Personally, I like to fill a pastry bag full of the stuff and squirt it into Salted *Dulce de Leche* Cupcakes (page 216). It can be stored in an airtight container in the refrigerator for up to 2 weeks.

**Options!**

OPTION 1: **SWEETENED CONDENSED MILK (*DULCE DE LECHE*)**

① With a can opener, puncture two holes into a can of condensed milk, but do not take off the entire lid. You want air to flow freely so that the can doesn't explode during cooking but you still want to take advantage of a secure lid to keep water from penetrating the caramel.

② Place the can in a deep saucepan and fill the saucepan with enough water that it reaches three-quarters of the way up the side of the can.

③ Heat over medium-high heat until the water comes to a simmer.

④ For a pourable dulce de leche, cook for 2 hours. For a more firm dulce de leche, cook for at least 4 hours. Keep an eye on the water levels at all times, adding water about every half hour to insure that the can is submerged three-quarters of the way.

OPTION 2: **GOAT'S MILK *CONFITURE DE LAIT***

You may replace the milk in the *confiture de lait* recipe above with an equal amount of goat's milk. Aside from the fact that those suffering from lactose intolerance digest goat's milk more easily, it's available in both regular and sweetened condensed forms, so you have the choice of making this unsurpassed delicacy either way. Goat's milk has a distinct musky flavor, and as it evaporates with the sugar, the caramel develops a darker caramel flavor. It's divine.

# G'S GELÉE
# SHOTS

*A champagne gelée—ooh la la!* Sounds so fancy! If it sounds too fancy for you, how about calling it a sparkling gelée shooter? Because that's essentially what it is. To make this dessert a presentational triumph, suspend fruits inside the setting gelée. For a more homey kick, replace the champagne with hard apple cider. Either way, it's a spirited dessert.

|||||||||||||||||||||||||||||||||||||||||||||||||||||| *Makes 1 large gelée or 6 ramekins* ||||||||||||||||||||||||||||||||||||||||||||||||||||||

| | | |
|---|---|---|
| champagne | 2 cups | 480 ml |
| sugar | ½ cup | 100 g |
| unflavored gelatin | 1 packet | 7 g |
| fresh berries or other fruits, or fruit gummis | to taste | |

① In a medium saucepan over medium heat, combine 1½ cups (360 ml) of the champagne and the sugar. Allow to simmer until the sugar has completely dissolved.

② Pour the remaining champagne into a small bowl and sprinkle the gelatin evenly over the liquid. Allow the gelatin to bloom, which usually takes about 1 minute. It should look soggy.

③ Remove the champagne mixture from the heat, scrape the gelatin mixture into the still-hot champagne, and stir until the gelatin has completely melted.

④ Pour the liquid gelée mixture into a 6-cup (48 oz) gelatin mold or divide evenly into 8-ounce ramekins and tap the ramekins firmly on a tabletop to release any air bubbles.

⑤ If you are planning on suspending anything in your gelée such as a heavy fruit or fruit gummis, fill the gelatin mold or each ramekin halfway and allow to set in the refrigerator; this will take up to 1 hour. Leave the remaining gelatin at room temperature. If it solidifies, gently reheat over low heat until it becomes fluid, then cool completely (otherwise, it will melt the set gelatin when you pour it over the first layer). Place your desired ingredient(s) on top of the set gelée, pour the unset gelatin evenly over the suspended ingredient(s), and refrigerate until the second layer is set. If you wish to add something lighter, such as small berries, fill the dish or the ramekins halfway and add the ingredient(s)— they'll float to the top. Refrigerate until the gelée is set, then fill with the remaining mixture and refrigerate overnight.

✱ **A Note from the Sugar Baby:** I have one warning for you: Do not add fresh pineapple, kiwi, figs, guava, papaya, passion fruit, or ginger root to the gelée. All of these otherwise wonderful things contain the enzyme bromelain, which will break down the gelatin and turn the gelée runny. Cooking those fruits to 158°F (70°C) deactivates the bromelain, so canned pineapple and most commercial purées should be okay, since they are typically heat-pasteurized.

# LEMON
# GELATO

*My mother was formidable.* She was German *and* an opera singer, which translates into loud and occasionally scary—with an accent. So I was a kid who pretty much toed the line for fear of Helga's wrath. With one exception: when I was in pain. And in the summer of 1981 I was in agony, reeling from the unbearable twinges of an almost-ready-to-drop-but-not-quite-there baby tooth. We were in Germany, visiting my aunt, and one of her neighbors just happened to be a dentist. I hated dentists more than I hated the nagging bicuspid torment—even Mom couldn't begin to terrify me into the dentist's chair. So she bribed me. With Italian *gelato al limone.* As many scoops as I wanted.

So I sat in Dr. Seitz's pneumatic chair and let him manhandle my tooth. But the nanosecond he wiggled it from its perch, I demanded my gelato. Lemon. Seven scoops.

It was well worth the pain.

*Makes 4 servings*

| | | |
|---|---|---|
| half-and-half | 2 cups | 480 ml |
| salt | pinch | |
| zest of 4 lemons | | |
| Greek-style yogurt | 6 ounces | 180 ml |
| Simple Syrup (page 21) | 1 cup | 240 ml |
| freshly squeezed lemon juice (from approximately 4 large lemons) | 1 cup | 240 ml |

① In a large saucepan over medium-low heat, bring the half-and-half and salt to a simmer. Add the lemon zest. Turn off the heat and allow the zest to steep until the half-and-half has cooled completely.

② Whisk the yogurt into the half-and-half mixture. Pour the mixture through a sieve into a clean bowl. Stir in the simple syrup and lemon juice. Cover and cool in the refrigerator overnight.

③ Process the mixture according to the instructions on your handy-dandy ice cream machine. Or to make this more of a granita (Italian-style flavored ice), after the mixture has refrigerated until cool, at least 2 hours or overnight, freeze it for 1 hour in a roasting pan or large bowl. Remove it from the freezer, and using two forks, scrape the mixture to break up the ice. Freeze for 3 to 4 hours longer, until completely frozen. Serve!

# CRÈME
# ANGLAISE

*Crème anglaise is the mother of pastry sauces—if you know your anglaise, you've already got a handle on* crème pâtissière *(pastry cream), sabayon, ice cream, crème brûlée, and pot de crème.* Use her as a sauce on a dessert or as the creamy sea in the buoyant beauty *Île Flottante* (page 174). Dredge slices of brioche in her and fry up the breakfast food that puts the French in toast, *pain perdu* (page 33). Or just dip a spoon into a bowl of this English cream and enjoy it as the sweetest, most sublime, and most arterially congestive soup you've ever savored. This recipe is easily doubled, tripled, or quadrupled. You simply need to find the corresponding pot large enough to hold your batch.

|||||||||||||||||||||||||||||||||||||||||||||  *Makes 1¾ to 2 cups (420 to 480 ml)*  |||||||||||||||||||||||||||||||||||||||||||||

① In a large, heavy saucier over medium heat, bring the half-and-half to a simmer.

✱ **A Note from the Sugar Baby:** For cream sauces like crème anglaise or pastry cream, I always use a saucier pan. The sloping sides allow for much easier whisking and help prevent the cream from thickening and hiding in the corners, thereby creating a more consistent sauce.

② Meanwhile, in an electric mixer fitted with the whisk attachment, beat the egg yolks, sugar, vanilla paste, and salt until light and fluffy.

③ With the mixer running on medium speed (to reduce any splashing), slowly pour ¼ cup (60 ml) of the hot half-and-half mixture along the side of the bowl into the egg mixture, to temper the eggs. Mix for 30 seconds, then pour the remaining half-and-half mixture very slowly down the side of the bowl into the whisking egg mixture.

④ Beat until all the ingredients are well combined. The mixture won't thicken much at this point; it will be quite watery and probably a little foamy. Transfer the liquid back into the saucier, taking

| half-and-half | 1 cup | 240 ml |
|---|---|---|
| egg yolks | 4 | |
| sugar | ¼ cup | 50 g |
| vanilla bean paste | 1 teaspoon | 5 ml |
| salt | pinch | |

care to scrape down the sides of the mixing bowl.

⑤ Place the saucier over medium-low heat. Whisk constantly and vigorously until the mixture thickens and coats the back of a spoon. You may attach a thermometer to the side of the pan to ensure that the temperature rises above 160°F (71°C) to kill all potential bacteria. However, the thermometer bulb will impede efficient whisking and will allow cream to thicken in that area. So if this allays your fears at all, know that I've taken the temperature of a finished anglaise 5 minutes after I've transferred it into a container for cooling and the temperature still read above 160°F (71°C).

POT DE CRÈME

⑥ Use immediately or store in an airtight container for up to 2 days.

## Options!

### OPTION 1: *PAIN PERDU*

As I said earlier, crème anglaise is the batter that makes *pain perdu* happen. Get your hands on a loaf of brioche or an equally luscious sweet bread, like challah. (Even better, bake some.) I've also used leftover Christmas Panettone (page 197) for the best French/Italian breakfast mash-up I've ever eaten.

Simply cut your bread into slices about 1 inch (2.5 cm) thick. Pour the crème anglaise into a shallow pan (I find a pie plate works beautifully). Lay the pieces in the sauce just long enough for the cream to soak in. Flip each slice so that both sides are coated.

Place 2 tablespoons (30 ml) butter in a hot pan and when the butter has melted, fry the cream-soaked pieces of bread over medium to medium-high heat until both sides are golden brown. Enjoy with luscious maple syrup or sprinkled with a touch of confectioners' sugar for breakfast, or serve with a scoop of ice cream for a delectable dessert.

### OPTION 2: FRENCH/AMERICAN BUTTERCREAM

I was teaching a class at King Arthur Flour, demonstrating how to make Italian buttercream, when one of my students asked me, "Have you ever made custard icing? It's similar but less sweet." I hadn't. I'd never even heard of it. I, the woman-child who lives for creamy fillings, had gone my entire life without getting acquainted with what sounded like my frosting soulmate. Of course I made up for lost time by going home and experimenting immediately. And oh. My. Goodness. Where had this stuff been all my life? This is the cake filling I'd been longing for since I learned the word "cake" (in utero, of course). I use it in the Red Sox Nation Tortes (page 201), my alternative to Boston cream pie.

There are a few differences in the base cream from the crème anglaise. First, have 1 pound (455 g) unsalted butter ready at room temperature to transform this cream into a spreadable love fest. Then, replace the yolks with whole eggs and the half-and-half with whole milk, and add ¼ cup (30 g) of cornstarch to the eggs and sugar. Continue as you would with the anglaise: Whip the eggs, sugar, and cornstarch until fluffy, then add the hot milk.

Because we've added cornstarch to the mixture, it will thicken far more during the whisking than traditional crème anglaise. You'll be looking for very thick, smooth custard. Once you've gotten the right consistency, transfer the finished custard back into the mixer and beat on high with a paddle attachment until the bowl is cool to the touch. Add your softened (not melted) butter a chunk at a time until it's all incorporated. You'll notice the mixture thickening considerably. If you add too soft a butter or you don't let the cream cool enough, the icing won't thicken. If you've gotten yourself in this situation, just place the bowl in the fridge for 10 to 15 minutes and start mixing again.

### OPTION 3: POT DE CRÈME

Pot de crème has to be the most genteel comfort dessert known to humanity. It's a warm, elegant pudding traditionally cooked and presented in an adorable little ceramic pot with a lid. As in the buttercream above, the egg yolks in the crème anglaise recipe are replaced by whole eggs; otherwise the ingredients remain the same. The difference is that after the crème is heated and thickened to the point of coating the back of your spoon, you divide the mixture among your little pots, making sure to skim off any foam that's on the surface that might mar the finished product after it's baked (it should be smooth and glossy when finished). I double the anglaise recipe for 4 portions.

Preheat the oven to 350°F (175°C). Fill your pot de crème pots (or ramekins, if you don't have the sweet little things) halfway (using only half your anglaise) and place the pots in a large, high-walled, ovenproof pan. (A deep hotel pan is perfect; otherwise I use a large, oblong glass baking dish.) Carefully add hot water to the pan, so that the water reaches halfway up the pot de crème containers but none of the water sloshes into the pots de crème themselves.

Pull an oven rack out as far as it will safely go and still hold the weight of your baking pan, and carefully transfer the pan to the rack. (If you feel confident you can transfer the dish and your little pots into the oven once they are filled, be my guest. I know from experience and unsteady hands that I've never managed this without an accident.) Fill each pot de crème with the remaining crème mixture. If you have official pot de crème pots, put the lids on now. If you don't, cover the entire pan with aluminum foil.

Bake for 25 minutes, or until the custard is set; the time will vary depending on the size of your containers. Serve immediately.

For chocolate pot de crème, add ¼ cup (60 ml) bittersweet chocolate morsels to the crème just as you've taken it off the heat. Let the mixture sit for 5 minutes, then whisk until the chocolate is completely melted and incorporated. Divide among the pots as you would for the standard version.

OPTION 4: **CRÈME BRÛLÉE**

The difference between the base cream in crème anglaise and crème brûlée is that whole eggs replace the yolks, just as in the American buttercream and the pot de crème. The initial procedure is also the same. Whisk until the mixture is thick enough to coat the back of a spoon.

The baking procedure is exactly the same as for pot de crème, only using a shallow ramekin because you want that larger surface area to caramelize the sugar at the end. Bake at 350°F (175°C) for 25 minutes, or until the crème has set. Allow to cool to room temperature and then refrigerate until chilled.

To finish, sprinkle granulated sugar in an even layer over the entire surface of the custard. Caramelize the sugar by gently passing a kitchen torch over the sugar until it starts to brown and bubble, using even strokes and making sure

not to burn the sugar, but melting it enough to form a hard outer layer that you have to break through to get to the creamy goodness within.

OPTION 5: **OLIVE OIL CREEMEE**

Ray and I spent Holy Saturday eating our way through Chicago. We stopped for lunch at the Purple Pig. We settled at the sumptuous marble bar and ordered wine while we perused the pork menu, rubbernecked as the waiters brought around splendid bacon-infused temptations. Despite all these glorious porky delights, it was a Taylor tabletop soft-serve machine that hypnotized me throughout the meal.

A Vermonter by choice, I've unabashedly adopted the local obsession with the seasonal soft-serve, the creemee. And most creemees of note are dispensed from a Taylor. The season wouldn't hit Vermont for a few more months and yet here, sitting directly across from me and taking up a large portion of the bartender's workstation, was a top-of-the-line and resplendently gleaming soft-serve delivery system. Pork-infused lunch be damned—I wanted dessert, stat.

While Vermont specializes in the delicious and very locally inspired maple creemee, the Purple Pig was feeling its influences from elsewhere: Italy, to be exact. And on that day, I sampled my very first olive oil ice cream. I resolved to bring this wonderful delight back to the Green Mountains and the creemee-loving masses.

For two generous servings of ice cream: Make a double batch of crème anglaise, but in the first step, add ¼ cup (60 ml) olive oil to the half-and-half. Once the sauce has begun to thicken, set the saucepan in a large bowl of ice and continue whisking until the sauce has cooled completely. Add 1 cup (240 ml) whole milk and continue whisking.

Pour the cooled mixture into an ice cream maker and proceed per the manufacturer's instructions. For a lovely dessert pairing, try a Strawberry Basil Napoleon (page 187)—it will mesh beautifully with the olive oil flavors. For a chocolate ice cream variation, replace the olive oil with ½ cup (40 g) cocoa powder.

CRÈME BRÛLÉE

# CRÈME
# CARAMEL

*Crème caramel is a kissing cousin to crème anglaise, a sexy little custard cooked in a caramel bath and upended so that the amber syrup flows around it to form a pool of luscious sweetness. This dessert minx also goes by the alias "flan."*

|||||||||||||||||||||||||||||||||||||||||||||||||| *Makes 4 servings* ||||||||||||||||||||||||||||||||||||||||||||||||||

| FOR THE CARAMEL | | |
| --- | --- | --- |
| lemon juice | 1 drop | |
| sugar | ¾ cup | 150 g |
| water | 3 tablespoons | 45 ml |
| ice water | 1 large bowl | |
| FOR THE CUSTARD | | |
| whole milk | 2 cups | 480 ml |
| salt | ¼ teaspoon | 1.5 g |
| vanilla bean paste | 1 teaspoon | 5 ml |
| sugar | ½ cup | 100 g |
| eggs | 4 | |
| berries, for garnish | to taste | |
| whipped cream, for garnish | to taste | |

### PROCEDURE FOR THE CARAMEL

① In a heavy-bottomed saucepan over medium heat, combine the sugar, water, and lemon juice, stirring constantly with a wooden spoon. The sugar will melt and caramelize quickly, so keep stirring and adjusting the heat; you want the sugar to melt evenly and to have a golden brown color. Make sure your lighting is very good, because it can be hard to see the exact hue of your caramel.

② When the color reaches a dark amber, immediately remove the saucepan from the heat and gently place it over the ice water to stop the caramelization process. Take care not to splash any water into your caramel.

③ Immediately spoon a small amount of caramel into each of four 8-ounce ramekins and swirl to create an even layer. Set aside.

### PROCEDURE FOR THE CUSTARD

① Preheat the oven to 350°F (175°C).

② In a large saucepan over medium-low heat, bring the milk, salt, and vanilla paste just to a simmer.

③ In the bowl of an electric mixer on medium speed, beat the sugar and eggs.

④ Slowly pour the hot milk mixture along the side of the bowl and into the eggs. Whisk until well combined.

⑤ Return the sauce to the saucepan over medium heat and whisk until the mixture thickens to the point that it just coats the back of a spoon.

⑥ Strain the custard mixture. I prefer to strain the custard into a large measuring cup with a spout to make pouring easier.

⑦ Place the ramekins in a deep baking dish (I use a casserole dish or a deep brownie pan) and place the baking dish on a sheet pan. At this point you can proceed on a kitchen counter-top if you have steady hands, or you can choose to pull an oven rack out far enough to use that as a work surface. In the latter case, you have to work quickly to keep the temperature of the oven from dipping too low. If this is how you choose to proceed, increase the oven tempera-ture to 375°F (190°C), and once you're done fill-ing the ramekins and the water bath, turn the temperature down to 350°F (175°C).

⑧ Pour the custard mixture evenly into the rame-kins, to just below the tops.

⑨ Pour hot water in the baking dish to cre-ate a bath for the ramekins. The water should reach about three-quarters up the outside of the ramekins. Pour the water slowly so that it doesn't splash into the custard. Carefully place the baking dish inside the oven.

⑩ Bake for 30 to 40 minutes, until set.

⑪ Remove from the oven and allow to cool com-pletely at room temperature. You can keep the ramekins in the water bath—they will cool more slowly, but it's safer than pulling hot ramekins from scalding water with clunky oven mitts. Transfer the ramekins to the refrigerator to chill for several hours.

⑫ To unmold the crème caramel, slowly and evenly run a very thin paring knife along the inside edge of each ramekin, keeping the knife flat against the edge to keep from cutting into the custard. Place a plate on top of each ramekin and invert the two together so that the ramekin is sitting upside down on the plate. Gently shake the ramekin, keeping it close to the plate, until it slides out.

⑬ Serve with berries and whipped cream.

# VANILLA
# PASTRY CREAM

*Have you heard about the lady who married the Eiffel Tower?* That's just crazy, right? Everyone knows you don't marry inanimate objects unless you can eat them. For instance, if I could marry pastry cream, I would. It's delicious. It's versatile. It's gotten me out of baking jams. It's opened up the world of pastry for me. If you learn one thing, learn to make pastry cream. And learn to make it well. You won't be disappointed.

||||||||||||||||||||||||||||||||||||||||||| *Makes approximately 2¼ cups (540 ml)* |||||||||||||||||||||||||||||||||||||||||||

| | | |
|---|---|---|
| egg yolks | 6 | |
| sugar | ½ cup | 100 g |
| cornstarch | 4 tablespoons | 32 g |
| vanilla extract | 1 teaspoon | 5 ml |
| salt | pinch | |
| milk | 1 cup | 240 ml |
| heavy cream | 1 cup | 240 ml |

① Place the egg yolks, sugar, cornstarch, vanilla extract, and salt in the bowl of an electric mixer with a whisk attachment. Beat the mixture on high until light and fluffy.

② Meanwhile, in a heavy saucier, mix the milk and cream together. Place the saucier over medium-high heat and bring the mixture to a rolling boil.

③ Decrease the mixer speed to medium and carefully pour the hot milk mixture down the side of the bowl. You need to lower the speed to prevent splashing, but you must add the milk mixture while the egg mixture is in motion to prevent the hot liquid from scalding the eggs. (Note: Keep the saucier on hand—you'll need it again. You want it perfectly clean when you

transfer the unthickened pastry cream back into it—make sure there's no browned milk sludge on the bottom of the pan.)

④ Once all the milk mixture is incorporated, slowly increase the mixer speed and let it run for about 1 minute. Stop the mixer, scrape down the sides and bottom of the bowl to ensure that all vestiges of egg, cornstarch, and sugar are completely incorporated, and transfer the contents of the mixing bowl to your clean saucier.

⑤ Before you take your liquidy pastry cream back to the stove to thicken, make sure you have a clean bowl and a fine sieve at the ready. You're going to be pouring the finished mixture through the sieve and into the bowl the moment the mixture is done.

⑥ Return to the stove with your saucier. Clip a candy thermometer to the side of the saucier if you're anxious about the temperature reaching 160°F (71°C)—the official temperature for killing pesky bacteria—but I can assure you it will, and then some.

⑦ Over medium-high heat, vigorously whisk the mixture until it has thickened, 4 to 5 minutes. You may break a sweat, but don't ever stop whisking, and make sure your whisk is getting to the bottom and along the sides of the sauce-pan—this stuff can burn easily.

(8) You'll notice that you're stirring for an awful long time before you see much change. But I warn you, it will happen, and all at once. Most often the thickening begins in earnest at the edges of the pan; get to that thickening portion with your whisk and stir it into the thinner portion.

(9) Once the pastry cream has thickened enough to coat the back of a spoon and then some—it should be the consistency of mayonnaise—take the saucier off the heat and pour the pastry cream through the sieve into a clean bowl. (You may get lucky and have smooth and luscious pastry cream—if so, feel free to forego the siev-ing. Otherwise, why not take every precaution to make it super smooth?) Use a rubber spatula to speed the process along by pressing the pas-try cream through the sieve. Once you've got every last drop in your bowl, give a quick stir for good measure.

(10) Take a piece of plastic wrap that's larger in diameter than your bowl and place it directly on the surface of the pastry cream. Make sure that every last bit of pastry cream is touching the plastic; otherwise it will form a skin. Transfer the bowl to the refrigerator to cool completely. (While you wait, you can daydream about what you want to create with your gorgeous pastry cream. Pumpkin éclairs, anyone?)

(11) Once your pastry cream is cool, you'll notice that it's considerably thicker than when you saw it last. This is normal. Pastry cream keeps for about 2 days in the refrigerator.

## Options!

### OPTION 1: FLAVORS

Pastry cream is unbelievable in its natural state. It's a damn shame to mess with it—but I do! For an Asian-inspired delicacy, add 4 tablespoons (12 g) matcha (powdered green tea) just after you've sieved the stuff and right before you give it a final stir. For a coffee infusion, add 1 table-spoon (3 g) espresso powder to the milk and cream when you first heat it. Or add ½ cup (120 ml) ganache for a gorgeous chocolaty custard, ½ cup (120 ml) lemon curd for a citrus zing, or ½ cup (120 ml) pumpkin purée for a warm autum-nal variation. For each of these, stir the flavor addition in during the last step.

You can also experiment with fruit purées and other fruit flavorings. I keep an array of Ital-ian soda flavorings handy—especially banana—for those occasions when I need a splash of unusual yet natural flavor. Add ½ cup (120 ml) purée or Italian soda flavor to the pastry cream just before refrigerating, whisking briskly to dis-tribute the flavor evenly.

### OPTION 2: LIGHTENING

Pastry cream is often "lightened," which is a cir-cuitous way of saying "add whipped cream." Per 1 cup (240 ml) chilled pastry cream, fold in ½ cup (120 ml) chilled whipped cream for a lighter, airier texture. Conversely, if you like to layer cakes with sweetened whipped cream, consider adding a touch of pastry cream.

### OPTION 3: FILLING

Pastry cream is a workhorse. You can use if for so much more than the inside of a cream puff. (But goodness, it sure is tasty in a cream puff.) Take three layers of vanilla cake and smooth chilled pastry cream between them. Top with chocolate ganache, and you've made a Boston cream pie. Or fry up a Berliner doughnut and fill the inside with pastry cream. Add ganache to a pastry cream and you have a chocolaty filling for any cake.

Do you like banana cream pie? Coconut cream pie? Chocolate cream pie? Well, hell, any cream pie? Then go make a yummy pie shell and while it's cooling, make some pastry cream. There are some wonderful flavored syrups: Fabri and Monin are both brands I love—they use natural flavors and their syrups taste phenomenal. Add just enough—about ¼ cup (60 ml)—banana- or coconut-flavored syrup to your pastry cream, and over a layer of bananas or toasted coconut, add 2 cups (480 ml) flavored pastry cream directly to your baked and cooled pie shell. Take an additional 2 cups (480 ml) pastry cream and fold in 1 cup (240 ml) whipped heavy cream; with this you can pipe lovely designs on top of the pastry cream layer. If you have puff pastry on hand, you can make Napoleons with your lightened pastry cream.

With Vanilla Pastry Cream

Make Pumpkin Éclairs, page 204

OPTION 4: **FROZEN CUSTARD**

If you want to make frozen custard, follow the instructions for Pastry Cream through step 9. Instead of step 10, pour the mixture through a sieve into a bowl that's sitting atop another bowl filled with ice and stir until the pastry cream is completely cold. Add 1 cup (240 ml) whole milk and combine well. Transfer the mixture to an ice cream machine and process according to manufacturer's instructions. Best vanilla-custard ice cream ever!

OPTION 5: **BAKE!**

That's right—bake with pastry cream. I add ½ cup (120 ml) to my apple pie filling. Really! It's phenomenal. If I'm making a strudel, 1 cup (240 ml) pastry cream added to the filling makes it creamy and luxurious. The great thing about pastry cream is that although you can't use it after 2 days for applications like adding it to whipped cream or as a layer in a cake, you *can* bake with it for up to 1 week. It lends creaminess to pastries, it can elevate any humdrum pie filling, and it's what makes bread pudding absolutely divine. So don't despair if you've forgotten the pastry cream in the fridge; it's got endless uses in your oven.

# FRUITY
## *Bavarian*
# CREAM

*This is a lazy person's Bavarian cream, using pastry cream that's been in the fridge with no other use.* This is also very close to something called "diplomat cream." It's a fantastic alternative for cake filling, or is delicious served by itself as a quasi-mousse dessert.

||||||||||||||||||||||||||||||||||||||| *Makes 3½ cups (840 ml) filling or 6 dessert servings* |||||||||||||||||||||||||||||||||||||||

① Place the purée and water in a small microwavable bowl. Sprinkle the gelatin over the purée and allow it to bloom for several minutes (until it all looks soggy).

② Microwave the gelatin for 20 seconds on high and then stir. Continue to microwave in 20-second intervals until the gelatin has dissolved completely.

③ Add a heaping spoon of the whipped cream to the gelatin mixture and stir to temper the gelatin. (Tempering simply means adjusting the gelatin to a cooler temperature so that it doesn't seize when you add it to the final mixture.)

④ In an electric mixer fitted with the paddle attachment, beat the pastry cream until it becomes loose and creamy.

⑤ Using a plastic spatula, fold the remaining whipped cream into the pastry cream. Quickly fold the gelatin mixture into the lightened pastry cream until it is evenly distributed. Use as a filling in a layer cake or divide among 6 serving glasses for individual mousses.

| | | |
|---|---|---|
| fruit purée | ¼ cup | 60 ml |
| water | 1 tablespoon | 15 ml |
| unflavored gelatin | 1 teaspoon | 2.5 g |
| heavy cream, whipped to stiff peaks | 1 cup | 240 ml |
| Pastry Cream (page 38), completely chilled | 1 batch | |

⑥ Chill individual mousses in the refrigerator overnight before serving. If you are using the Bavarian cream as a cake filling, place the finished product (the assembled cake) in the freezer for a few hours or overnight to allow the gelatin to set completely. Three hours before serving, place it in the refrigerator to thaw.

# LEMON
# CURD

*"Curd" is such an unfortunate word.* It really does an incredibly delicious treat such a disservice. The English slather the citrusy stuff on scones. I love to add it in between layers of coconut cake, or I'll fill a sweet tart shell with a few cups of it and top it with meringue for the best lemon tart you'll ever taste. Another option is to eat it by the spoonful. I won't judge.

||||||||||||||||||||||||||||||||||||||||||||| *Makes 2½ cups (600 ml)* |||||||||||||||||||||||||||||||||||||||||||||

| lemon juice (from about 3 large lemons) | ½ cup plus 2 tablespoons, divided | 120 ml plus 30 ml, divided |
|---|---|---|
| organic agave nectar | 1 cup | 240 ml |
| egg yolks | 6 | |
| unflavored gelatin | 1 teaspoon | 2.5 g |
| unsalted butter | 2 tablespoons | 28 g |
| zest from the above lemons | | |

① In a heatproof metal bowl, combine the ½ cup (120 ml) lemon juice, agave nectar, and egg yolks.

② In a separate bowl, sprinkle the gelatin on top of the remaining 2 tablespoons (30 ml) lemon juice until it blooms, or, in other words, looks soggy. Set aside.

③ Place the bowl with egg mixture over a simmering pot of water and whisk until it has thickened enough that it ribbons when you pull out the whisk. Remove from the heat; immediately add the gelatin and whisk until it's completely melted. Add the butter and zest and whisk until fully incorporated. The temperature will have risen above 160°F (71°C) by this time—I've checked—but if you're nervous, work with a thermometer for your own peace of mind.

✸ **A Note from the Sugar Baby:** Like pastry cream, lemon curd takes a good long while to thicken. But it gives you some warning signs that it's about to turn. First, it starts to get foamy and lightens in color from a deep, egg-yolk yellow to a light, butter yellow. Just keep whisking. Then the foam starts to dissipate. Keep whisking. Then it thickens. STOP!

④ Transfer the curd to a bowl. Take a piece of plastic wrap that's larger in diameter than the bowl and place it directly on the surface of the curd. Make sure the plastic touches the entire surface of the exposed curd; otherwise a skin will form. Refrigerate for a few hours until it's completely cool. Store in an airtight container in the refrigerator for up to a week.

✸ **A Note from the Sugar Baby:** You'll notice I use gelatin, which isn't a necessary addition to curd if you are planning to use it as a simple spread on scones. However, I like to use it as a filling in pastries, and the addition of gelatin gives me a measure of assurance that the curd will set up firmly so that it stays neatly within the confines of the pastry instead of oozing out.

# SUGARING WITH THE SUGAR BABY

Making maple syrup is more of a North Country adventure than an actual recipe.

First, get a giant maple tree. Second, tap the tree in April, just as the days get above 40°F (8°C) but making damn sure it falls below 32°F (0°C) at night. Third, hang buckets from the tap and collect sap. Fourth, boil your gallons of syrup down to a thimbleful of syrup and pray you don't overheat the stuff or it'll be useless.

That's sugaring in a nutshell. "Sugaring" is the term used by insane Northern folk who, just as winter breaks, spend their days collecting gallons of sap and boiling those gallons down to just a few cups. To be exact, you need forty to fifty gallons of sap to make one measly gallon of syrup.

Let's say you manage to collect that much sap. So your ingredients are:

50 gallons of sap

You'll notice that in a lineup, sap could pass for water. It's clear, it's free flowing without a hint of syrupy thickness, and it's barely sweet. Which leads me to wonder, as I so often do when I think about how food creations came to be, who the hell thought to boil down this innocuous stuff until it became liquid pancake gold? You do get some sense of the impulse to do something when you first tap a maple in prime sugaring season. Drill a little pilot hole at a slight angle, and a good maple will instantly start oozing sap; you feel compelled to either plug the hole or find something in which to collect the bounty. So now you have to follow some procedure to transform what could very well be water into New England wine.

I was in this very position in the spring of 2010 when my husband, Ray, and I tapped our first maples. We have a handful of two-hundred-plus-year-old trees on our property and, being the good Vermonters we're trying to be, we had to tap those puppies. The weather wasn't complying with us when we first drilled our tap holes; it wasn't warming up sufficiently in the afternoon to heat the tree "just so" in order to get her running. So we went on a short weekend trip and left our beloved friend and native Vermonter Agnes in charge of our peculiar pack of hounds and what seemed to be a dormant pack of maple trees. "Don't worry much about the sap, Agnes. We've barely seen a few drops in the buckets."

Naturally this kind of flippant statement could only lead to a perfect storm of sap weather, leaving Agnes on a desperate hunt for ever larger buckets in the barn, in the shed, in the stables, and, finally, in the bakery. When we returned to Vermont, and I swear we were only gone three days, Agnes introduced us to the new members of our family: fifty gallons of sap collected in all manner of containers waiting patiently in my bakery cooler. Presenting our liquid offspring, Agnes added, "And you have to boil it off right away because it sours fast. Like milk. Just worse."

Here's where the procedure comes in. The rule of thumb in sugaring is that you boil sap until you reach a temperature of *exactly* 7.1°F (3.9°C) over the boiling point at your particular elevation (or if you have a fancy-schmancy sugar-concentration reader, it's 66–67 percent sugar concentration). You see, the temperature of boiling water is 212°F (100°C) at sea level; this temperature gets lower, however, as elevation increases and atmospheric pressure decreases. So you may think the correct temperature for perfect maple syrup is 219.1°F (103.9°C)—but where I live, it's 217°F (102.8°C). I know this because I boiled my first batch to 219.1°F (103.9°C) and as it cooled, it started to form a mountain range of crystals perfectly suitable for a family of sea monkeys but not at all the stuff of maple syrup. Thankfully, I am the Sugar Baby that I am and I just made maple candy with the disaster (after I stopped crying).

In the end, after harvesting about a hundred gallons of sap, we were left with a Nutella jar full of maple syrup. But my oh my, what delicious maple syrup it was.

# SWISS
# BUTTERCREAM

*There's no cake, no Parisian macaron complete without this luscious stuff, and the varieties are endless—vanilla bean, caramel, blackberry, maple, and more.* There are two ways to make the real deal. This is the first way, the Swiss way. The second is the Italian way (page 63). Both results are wonderful—it's simply a matter of procedural preference. I also believe that Swiss buttercream gives you a bit more assurance in terms of killing any food-borne buggers that could be hiding in your raw egg whites, since you heat the egg whites to 160°F (71°C).

|||||||||||||||||||||||||| *Makes enough to fill and lightly cover 1 (10-inch/25-cm) cake* ||||||||||||||||||||||||||

| | | |
|---|---|---|
| egg whites | 10 | |
| sugar | 2 cups | 400 g |
| salt | pinch | |
| vanilla bean, seeds scraped from the pod | 1 | |
| vanilla extract | 1 tablespoon | 15 ml |
| unsalted butter, slightly cooler than room temperature, cut into small pieces | 2 cups | 455 g |

① In the bowl of an electric mixer, add the egg whites, sugar, salt, vanilla bean seeds, and vanilla extract. Place the bowl over a bain-marie (a simmering saucepan of water). Clip on a candy thermometer and whisk constantly until the sugar has completely dissolved (I stick two fingers in and rub to see if I feel any granules) and the temperature has reached 160°F (71°C). Immediately transfer the bowl to the mixer and whisk on high until the mixture holds soft peaks and the bowl no longer feels hot to the touch.

✪ **A Note from the Sugar Baby:** At the end of step 1, you've got meringue. The same holds true for Italian meringue, when you're on the road to making buttercream but you've only reached the point of whipping the egg whites and the sugar together to form peaks. If you stopped right now, you could fill a pastry bag, pipe soft white mountains onto the top of a pie, and use a kitchen torch or your broiler to brown the edges of the fluffy cloud of sweet egg white. You can even forget the butter and ice the outside of your cake with this stuff. You can also bake the meringue at 250°F (120°C) for a few hours and come out with crunchy, chewy, airy baked sweetness. I just wanted you to know that you've officially made something at this point. This could be a destination, but really it's only a stop on our journey.

② Start adding bits of butter, a few tablespoons at a time. You may be thinking a pound of butter seems a bit excessive. And you're right. Because there *is* a chance that this will come into its whipped glory without using all the butter. So add slowly. The buttercream will start to appear as if it's separating; this is perfectly normal and is the stage before it transforms. Keep whipping and watching; before your very eyes, the buttercream will magically turn a perfect fluffy consistency. (If either the bowl or the buttercream still feels at all warm, put the bowl in the freezer for 2 minutes and then whip on high again. If it doesn't come together, add a few more knobs of butter.)

③ Use buttercream immediately, or refrigerate for up to 1 week or freeze up to a month. If you refrigerate or freeze it, you'll have to rewhip it before you use it because it will have hardened. You'll notice that once you start whipping, it looks as if it's fallen apart. It has. Just keep whipping until it gets back into shape. It'll happen.

### Options!

OPTION 1: **MAPLE BUTTERCREAM**

Replace the sugar with maple sugar and proceed exactly the same way with the recipe. Maple sugar is not the easiest thing to purchase—I live in maple country and it's still not a breeze to find it. But if you can get your hands on a cup of maple in its granulated form, I heartily recommend giving this a try. And yes, you can substitute maple syrup for the sugar, but it's not quite the same taste. Remember, though, maple is much sweeter than sugar cane. You'll want to pair this with a cake that's a little mellow.

OPTION 2: **FLAVORS!**

Add ½ cup (120 ml) fruit purée after you've reached fluffy perfection to add color and flavor. You can futz with the amount, but beware—adding too much will destroy the balance between sugars, proteins, and fats and will break down the buttercream.

Add an extract of any variety at any point in the process, or add 2 teaspoons (2 g) instant espresso or matcha (powdered green tea) for a delightful infusion.

Add ¼ cup (60 ml) lemon curd or ganache to bring a headier flavor to your buttercream. (But don't overdo it or you'll upset the balance.)

OPTION 3: **PIPING**

Buttercream is the cake decorator's right-hand man. If you keep it at the perfect temperature—not warm and not cold, but just right—you'll be piping roses and leaves and filigree all the live-long day.

# BITTERSWEET
*Pudding*

(POPS)

*When I was old enough to babysit, I didn't do it for the money; I did it for the food.* I'd get the little stinkers to bed by reading bedtime stories so fast you could hear a sonic boom, and then I'd eat that poor family out of house and home. I only babysat at homes with a guaranteed score, and I find it curious that I was ever asked to babysit more than once because I never left without demolishing every last edible morsel from inside the freezer. The Stewart family was especially hard hit, since they always carried the full line of Jell-O Pudding Pops and I had no problem polishing off every last box. I'd apologize for my foolish youthful behavior, but I cannot honestly say that I'm sorry. Or that I wouldn't do it again now that I'm full-grown.

|||||| *Makes approximately 2½ cups (570 g) pudding, 7 rocket pops, or 14 individual brûlées* ||||||

| agave nectar | ½ cup | 120 ml |
| --- | --- | --- |
| dark cocoa powder (I use Callebaut Extra Brute) | ½ cup | 40 g |
| heavy cream | 1 cup | 240 ml |
| salt | ½ teaspoon | 3 g |
| coffee | 1 cup | 240 ml |
| cornstarch | 1 tablespoon | 8 g |
| egg yolks | 3 | |
| vanilla extract | 1 tablespoon | 15 ml |

✪ **A Note from the Sugar Baby:** Agave nectar is a sweetener produced primarily in Mexico and is derived from the agave plant. Yup, the same plant that produces nature's other sublime nectar—tequila!—yet the nectar tastes nothing like the liquor. As a matter of fact, light agave nectar has a rather neutral flavor, perhaps with just a hint of caramel, so it's a perfect sweetener for both hot and cold beverages. Its consistency is very much like honey but not as viscous; it pours as quickly as Heinz 57. One benefit of agave nectar is that although it's been found to be about one and a half times sweeter than table sugar, it has a much lower glycemic index. Be aware, however, that agave nectar isn't a sweetener that can replace sugar or corn syrup in every recipe; its chemical composition doesn't lend itself well to higher-temperature sugar work, but it can be useful at lower temperatures in baked goods.

① In a medium saucepan over medium heat, whisk together the agave nectar, cocoa powder, heavy cream, and salt until the mixture comes to a simmer. Remove from the heat.

② In a separate bowl, whisk together the coffee and cornstarch. While whisking constantly (especially if the coffee is still warm), add the egg yolks one at a time and then add the vanilla extract.

③ Return the pan containing the cocoa mixture to the stove. Pour the egg mixture into the cocoa mixture, whisking constantly over medium heat. Clip on a candy thermometer and whisk whisk whisk. In all likelihood, the temperature has already exceeded 160°F (71°C), so you're safe, bacteria-wise. Now keep whisking for about 5 minutes, until the pudding thickens and the temperature reaches 200°F (93°C) to 210°F (100°C).

④ Transfer the pudding to a large bowl and serve family style, or use it in other crafty ways like a filling for a glorious crêpe cake (see page 238). Alternatively, pour the pudding into seven popsicle molds and freeze overnight for a luscious, chocolaty summertime treat. You can also pour the pudding into fourteen individual 2-ounce (60 ml) serving cups and cover each with plastic wrap, making sure that the wrap touches the entire surface of the pudding to prevent a skin from forming, and refrigerate for a few hours. You can serve the pudding straight from the fridge or with a dollop of whipped cream. However, I like to sprinkle a spoonful or two of sugar over the top and take a kitchen torch to the sugar to caramelize it into a brûlée crust.

# DARK
## *Chocolate*
# MOUSSE

*In my shop, Gesine Confectionary in Montpelier, Vermont, I used to make this mousse in tall cylinder cake molds, metal rings that were only about 2 inches in diameter but 4 inches tall.* They were beauties. I'd fill up a serving tray with them and I had to slide them into the pastry case ever so carefully. They were so damn tall that they could easily tip over, so any miscalculation on my part would result in severing the top half of the mousse. We called them chocolate towers, of course. This is the coveted recipe.

||||||||||||||||||||||||||||||||||||||||||||||  *Makes 8 servings*  ||||||||||||||||||||||||||||||||||||||||||||||

① In a saucepan over low heat or in a microwave, melt the butter, making sure not to let it brown.

② Transfer the melted butter to a large metal bowl and place the bowl over a bain-marie (simmering water in a saucepan). Attach a candy thermometer. Making sure you have a whisk ready to go, add the egg yolks, 2 cups (480 ml) of the cream, ¼ cup (50 g) of the sugar, and the vanilla extract. Whisk like the dickens, checking to make sure the temperature has passed 160°F (71°C)—it will likely reach about 220°F (105°C) due to the constancy of the heat during whisking, but you want to make sure you get to at least 160°F (71°C) to kill any potential bacteria. Sometimes the custard mixture appears to be "breaking," as if the butter is separating from the cream. Don't panic; it'll be fine. Keep whisking until the custard mixture thickens to the point that it coats the back of a spoon.

③ Take the custard off the heat and immediately add the chocolate pieces, making sure all the chocolate is coated with hot custard. Let the chocolate enjoy the warm bath for a few minutes; then, with a clean whisk or a wooden

| unsalted butter, cut into small pieces | 1 cup | 225 g |
|---|---|---|
| eggs, separated | 8 | |
| heavy cream | 4 cups, divided | 960 ml, divided |
| sugar | ½ cup, divided | 100 g, divided |
| vanilla extract | 1 tablespoon | 15 ml |
| bittersweet chocolate pieces | 1 pound | 455 g |
| salt | ¼ teaspoon | 1.5 g |

spoon, stir until the chocolate is completely melted and incorporated into the custard. If you weren't able to chop the chocolate into small enough pieces, you might be left with some chunks. If so, transfer the custard back to the bain-marie and stir constantly until every last piece is melted. Set the custard aside. Keep the bain-marie going.

④ In the clean bowl of a stand mixer, combine the egg whites, the remaining ¼ cup (50 g) sugar, and the salt. Place the bowl over the bain-marie, with the candy thermometer attached (make sure you've cleaned it very well since you used it last—even a tiny amount of fat introduced into the egg whites will keep them from whipping). Whisk (with a clean whisk!) the egg whites constantly until the sugar is completely melted and the temperature reaches 160°F (71°C).

⑤ Immediately transfer the bowl to the stand mixer and, with the whisk attachment, beat the mixture on high until it achieves soft peaks. Don't overbeat the egg whites. You don't want lumpy and dry—you're going for soft, shiny peaks.

⑥ With a rubber spatula, transfer about one quarter of the beaten egg whites into the chocolate custard and stir vigorously to combine the two. Transfer the remaining egg whites into the custard, and this time gently fold the egg whites into the custard, using the flat rubber spatula in sweeping motions like a gentle oar and turning the bowl as you go. This is to maintain as much of that airy texture in the egg whites as possible. At this stage, don't be panicked if there are still bits of egg white not fully incorporated. Set the mixture aside.

⑦ Clean your mixing bowl and whisk attachment and add the remaining 2 cups (480 ml) cream. Whip until the cream is very stiff, but be careful not to overbeat—if the cream starts to churn, you get butter instead of fluffy whipped cream. (In the event you go overboard, all is not lost. You can save the day by adding about ¼ cup (60 ml) heavy cream and whisking gently. The hard knots of clotted cream will relax and you'll be able to reverse the problem.)

⑧ Gently fold the whipped cream into the custard mixture until there are no white streaks of either egg white or whipped cream remaining.

⑨ Distribute the mousse evenly into 8 single-serving bowls to chill, for 4 hours or overnight, before serving. Or use the mousse as part of a beautiful finished dessert. I've got some ideas for you starting on page 176 with the I Heart Mousse Cake.

# FRUIT
# MOUSSE

*I'm never out of ideas when it comes to creating a new flavor of mousse.* Of course it's never really a new flavor—someone's always tried it before. But once you get the hang of making the stuff, the options are endless. And once you realize that you can use mousse as a filling in a cake, in a pie, between macarons, or as individual cakes, you'll be hard-pressed to tear yourself away from making a rainbow of fruity mousses.

|||||||||||||||||||||||||||| *Makes enough for 1 (10-inch/25-cm) cake or 12 individual servings* ||||||||||||||||||||||||||||

① Place the gelatin in a microwave-safe bowl and cover it with ¼ cup (60 ml) water, making sure each particle of gelatin is saturated; it should look like wet sand. (If there are dry particles peeking through before you microwave the gelatin, you'll scorch it.) Microwave the gelatin mixture on 50-percent power for 20 seconds at a time, swirling the bowl between each heating, until the gelatin is completely melted. Be careful not to overheat because this can kill the efficacy of the gelatin. You want to time the melting of the gelatin so that it is still liquid when you incorporate it into the cold whipped cream mixture; it's tough to fold in gelatin that has already solidified. You'll end up with chunks. Alternatively, heat the water just to boiling and pour it over the gelatin.

② In a medium saucepan, gently heat the purée and stir in the gelatin mixture. Set aside.

③ In a heavy saucepan over low heat, combine the sugar and ⅓ cup (75 ml) water. Stir until the sugar has completely dissolved. Wash down the sides of the pan with a damp pastry brush. Clip on a thermometer, stop stirring, and heat the syrup to 234°F (112°C).

| | | |
|---|---|---|
| unflavored gelatin | generous 1 tablespoon | generous 7 g |
| water | ¼ cup plus ⅓ cup | 60 ml plus 75 ml |
| mango purée (or any other fruit purée you like) | 1 cup | 240 ml |
| sugar | 1 cup | 200 g |
| egg whites | 5 | |
| salt | pinch | |
| heavy cream | 1½ cups | 360 ml |
| mascarpone cheese | ½ cup | 115 g |

④ Meanwhile, whisk the egg whites with the salt until foamy. When the sugar reaches the correct temperature, lower the speed of the mixer to medium and carefully pour the hot sugar syrup down the side of the bowl. Once all of the syrup has been added, increase the speed to high and whip until the meringue is a shiny, bright white and maintains a stiff peak when you lift the whisk attachment. Transfer the meringue to a metal bowl and set aside.

⑤ Using the same mixing bowl the meringue was in (you don't have to clean it), add the heavy cream and mascarpone and whip until they achieve soft peaks.

⑥ Combine the whipped cream and meringue, gently folding the two together.

⑦ Add ½ cup of the cream-meringue mixture to the purée, and whisk to lighten.

⑧ Quickly add the gelatin-purée mixture; make sure the gelatin mixture isn't too warm or the cream-meringue mixture will break and deflate. But also make sure that the gelatin hasn't cooled so much that it's begun to harden—it should be fluid so you're not left with nibs of Jell-O in the mousse. Work quickly to ensure a smooth, silken texture.

⑨ Pour the mousse into a 10-inch (25-cm) cake pan or into 12 separate serving glasses and chill until set. You can also freeze the mousse; remove it from the freezer 2 hours before serving and allow it to thaw in the refrigerator. If you want to make something really beautiful and mango-rific, try the Mango Mousse Cake on page 181 for a dessert even your tweener will remember.

With Fruit Mousse!

Make Mango Mousse Cake, page 181

# DARK CHOCOLATE
## *Fudgy*
# FROSTING

*This is a spreadable frosting when it gets to exactly the right temperature and consistency.* Unfortunately, I tend to forget the frosting altogether while I'm running around the kitchen, and there's a definite point beyond which the frosting just doesn't want to be spread. But I'm not one to let a perfectly good fudge frosting go to waste. What I like to do is take a heaping spoonful of the frosting, roll it in a ball in my hands and then flatten it just enough to cover the top of a cupcake. Manhandling the frosting brings on a nice sheen, and by rolling and flattening as symmetrically as you can, you'll have a very clean (and delicious) topping for your latest cupcake invention. Personally, I top my chocolate *dulce de leche* cupcakes with this shiny marvel. If you'd like to do the same, go to page 216 for further instructions.

IIIIIIIIIIIIIIIIIIIIIIIIII *Makes enough to frost 1 (10-inch/25-cm) round cake or 8 large cupcakes* IIIIIIIIIIII

① Place all the ingredients except the vanilla paste in a heavy saucepan over low heat, stirring until the sugar has completely melted.

② Clip on a candy thermometer, stop stirring, and heat to 234°F (112°C). Remove the pan from the heat and allow the frosting to cool slightly.

③ Add the vanilla paste and beat with a wooden spoon until the frosting thickens enough to spread on a cake. If the frosting becomes too thick, add 1 tablespoon (15 ml) of cream and stir.

| | | |
|---|---|---|
| unsweetened chocolate, finely chopped | 2 ounces | 60 g |
| sugar | 1¼ cups | 250 g |
| coffee | ½ cup | 120 ml |
| salt | ¼ teaspoon | 1.5 g |
| corn syrup | 2 tablespoons | 30 ml |
| unsalted butter | 1 tablespoon | 14 g |
| vanilla bean paste | 1 teaspoon | 5 ml |

# CANDIED
# CITRUS PEEL

*One of our favorite customers at Gesine Confectionary, Dr. Carol, used to bring small batches of candied citrus to the bakery.* You might think, "Coals to Newcastle" but not once did those precious crystallized bits get dismissed. When your day is filled with dark chocolate and heavy cream, a small bite of ever-so-vaguely sweet and tart can cut through the fat blob setting up camp in your stomach. Just what the doctor ordered.

|||||||||||||||||||||||||||||||||||||||||||||||||||| *Makes about 1 pound (455 g)* ||||||||||||||||||||||||||||||||||||||||||||||||||||

| | | |
|---|---|---|
| 10 lemons or 6 oranges | | |
| water | 6 cups | 1.4 L |
| sugar | 7 cups, divided | 1.4 kg, divided |
| lemon juice | 1 teaspoon | 5 ml |
| citric acid (optional) | 1 teaspoon | 5 ml |

① Cut the lemons or oranges into quarters. Remove the fruit from the rind. Using a spoon, scrape the white pith off of each rind so you are left with a clean quarter-slice of peel. Cut each peel lengthwise into strips ¼ inch (6 mm) wide and set aside.

**You're thinking, "Citric acid? Sounds dangerous, as if it will cause grievous harm if ingested!** Not to worry. Citric acid is merely a powder extracted from citrus fruits. It's what makes the sour and bitter in lemons and oranges. I like to use it in citrusy confections to give them a little oomph, but you can just as easily leave it out. And since it's a little hard to come by, I wouldn't blame you if you never used it. But if you're game, you can purchase it at baking supply shops or online.

There are other ingredients that you might not find at the corner store either. For instance, when I use chocolate, I use Callebaut or Valrhona. Those are my tried-and-true favorites. For cocoa powder, I use Callebaut Extra Brute or Valrhona. That's it. Period. In larger cities, Whole Foods and other well-stocked stores will carry large hunks of those chocolates and will often carry the cocoa powders

as well. Or perhaps you have a restaurant supply store nearby that also carries such ingredients, like the drool-worthy Surfas in Los Angeles. Otherwise, you'll find the ingredients at www.pastrychef.com. They carry my chocolate and cocoa powder. They also have citric acid, glycerin, sugar gloves, glucose syrup, vanilla bean paste, and a host of other goodies. If you're on the prowl for unusual (or usual) fruit purées, go to www.lepicerie.com. They have a rainbow of flavors to choose from.

For Italian soda flavors, I order from www.baristaproshop.com. For ingredients like almond flour, almond paste, coconut chips, and every nut on the planet, I depend on www.nutsonline.com. They offer both small-portion and bulk quantities and their customer service is unparalleled. For great spices and spice mixtures, like the Afrika line, I depend on the gorgeous selection at www.flavorbank.com.

② In a stockpot, blanch the peels by soaking them in simmering water for 40 minutes. Fish the peels out and place them in ice water. Blot the peels with a paper towel.

③ Pour the water out of the stockpot and refill it with 6 cups (1.5 L) water, 6 cups (1.2 kg) of the sugar, and the lemon juice. Place the pot over medium heat, stirring occasionally, until the sugar has dissolved. Raise the heat to high and bring the syrup to a boil. Clip on a candy thermometer and continue cooking, stirring occasionally, until the temperature reaches 200°F (93°C), 20 to 30 minutes.

④ Add the peels and continue boiling for 40 minutes. Remove the pot from the heat but leave the peels in the syrup to rest overnight (8 hours). Don't discard the syrup! Just leave the peels in until I tell you to take them out!

⑤ After the overnight soak, bring the mixture back to a boil until the temperature reaches 226°F (108°C). This can take half an hour! Remove the pot from the heat and let the peels and the poaching syrup soak overnight again (8 hours).

⑥ For the last time (I promise), bring the syrup and peels to a boil until the temperature reaches 230°F (110°C)—yup, it takes about half an hour. Let the concoction sit for 8 hours again. Here's the thing: **don't take the peels out after the 8 hours until you . . .**

⑦ . . . reheat the syrup until it liquefies. *Then* fish the peels out with a slotted spoon and allow them to dry on metal cooling racks set over parchment-lined sheet pans. This allows the excess moisture to drain off and the peels to dry evenly. Let the peels become dry but still slightly tacky, so that the remaining sugar crystals adhere to them. Again, this can take up to 8 hours, or considerably longer if you're in a humid climate. You've been patient this long—just let the peels do their thing. Even if they take a whole day.

⑧ Spread the remaining 1 cup (200 g) sugar and the citric acid (if you're using it) on a large plate, and give a good stir to make sure the citric acid is evenly distributed. Roll the peels in the sugar, making sure each strip is evenly coated. Place your finished beauties on a piece of parchment. Add more sugar and citric acid if you start running low. You may also want to sieve the sugar in the event you start to see clumps. Dry the peel for a few hours and then, at long last, you can take a bite! Store in an airtight container in a cool, dry place for up to a month.

✻ **A Note from the Sugar Baby:** Under what circumstances, you ask yourself, would you go through all this trouble to make citrus peel? I understand it's not often that you've found yourself in the deep throes of a citrus-peel craving, and that you identify it primarily with that red-headed stepchild of holiday confectionery, the fruitcake. But there are two things that wouldn't be half as wonderful without it: panettone and stollen. (I'll give you these recipes on pages 197 and 210, respectively, so you can appreciate the beauty of a homemade candied peel in a holiday staple.)

**Option!**

### CANDIED GINGER

Candied ginger differs from candied citrus peel in that you want to candy the interior and not the exterior. So you peel 1 pound (455 g) of large, fresh ginger root, discard the peel, and cut the tender insides into ¼-inch (6-mm) cubes. Then proceed with the above instructions, exactly as you would with citrus peel. I use candied ginger in The Best Ginger Cookies Ever (page 230) and I like to have small uniform pieces, like a spicy alternative to chocolate chips. But that's just me. Some people use a mandoline and thinly slice the ginger for candying. For another delicious way to bake with candied ginger, check out the Gingered Drop Scones on page 183.

# SACHERTORTE
# GLAZE

*Sachertorte is a magnificent layer cake that's so damn good it has spawned a war between two pastry greats in Vienna since the 1800s: the Hotel Sacher and the confectionery haven Demel, who both claimed the dessert as their invention.* Legal wrangling ensued as to who owned the rights to sell the "original" Sacher. Expert witnesses testified under oath that a second layer of apricot marmalade was *never* applied to the original two-layer chocolate sponge cake. And imagine the horror when it was revealed in court that margarine had been substituted for butter in one of the litigant's cake recipes. Scandal!

Notice that all the wrangling was about the innards of the cake? If it were I, I'd have sued for the rights to the fabulous chocolate glaze and let those whiners keep their marmalade-encrusted interior, because it's the chocolate glaze on a Sacher that is consistently sublime. It is shiny. It is decadent. It is fudgy. That's right. The icing for a fancy-schmancy Austrian dessert, originally created for a prince, has the same culinary origins as down-home American fudge. No wonder it's so tasty. Use it as a glaze on any cake you think could use a pretty sheen and a powerful chocolate punch. Just don't get in a lawsuit over it.

|||||||||||||||||||||||||||||||||||||| *Makes enough to cover 1 (10-inch/25-cm) torte* ||||||||||||||||||||||||||||||||||||||

| | | |
|---|---|---|
| sugar | 2 cups | 400 g |
| water | 1 cup | 240 ml |
| salt | ⅛ teaspoon | 1 g |
| bittersweet chocolate, finely chopped | 8 ounces | 240 g |
| unsalted butter | 1 cup | 225 g |
| salt | ½ teaspoon | 3 g |

① In a heavy-bottomed saucepan, combine the sugar, water, and salt. Over medium heat, stir until the sugar has completely melted. Add the chocolate and stir until it is melted.

② Clip on a candy thermometer, stop stirring, and raise the heat to medium-high. Heat to 234°F (112°C). Immediately remove from the heat and allow to cool, undisturbed, for about 5 minutes, to allow the glaze to thicken.

③ Pour the glaze over your layer cakes, dunk the tops of your cupcakes, or douse your petit fours. Just don't scrape the bottom of the pan, to avoid any burnt bits from separating and marring the pristine sheen of your chocolate-covered delicacy. For more ideas, check out Nanny's Torte on page 199.

# VUNDERFOOL
## *Ice Cream*
# FUDGE

*When I was a kid, if we didn't go to Germany to visit my grandmother in the summer, Omi came to these fair United States armed with one word of English vocabulary: "Wonderful!" Actually, it came off as "vunderfool" but we got her gist. Never did she put her single word to use as prolifically as she did at the Gifford's ice cream parlor in Arlington, Virginia. Omi was partial to banana splits drizzled with rich fudge. After each bite she'd mutter "vunderfool."*

||||||||||||||||||||||||||||||||||||||||||| *Makes approximately 3 cups (720 ml)* |||||||||||||||||||||||||||||||||||||||||||

① In a medium bowl, stir together the cocoa powder, brown sugar, and granulated sugar until they are well combined.

② Place the cream, butter, and salt in a saucepan and heat on low until the butter is melted.

③ Carefully add the cocoa mixture to the cream mixture, whisking constantly until you've eradicated any lumps. Clip on a candy thermometer and continue whisking constantly over medium-low heat until the sugar dissolves, the mixture thickens and is smooth, and the temperature reaches 225°F (110°C).

④ Pour the fudgy sauce into a heatproof jar, taking care not to scrape the sides or the bottom of the pan in the event you dislodge burnt cream, and either allow to cool or serve immediately over some tasty vanilla ice cream. If you somehow manage not to consume the entire batch in one sitting, store the fudge in the refrigerator in a microwave-safe screw-top jar. When you plan on serving the fudge again, take the cap off and microwave on 50-percent power for 30 seconds

| | | |
|---|---|---|
| unsweetened cocoa powder | 1¼ cups | 105 g |
| light brown sugar, firmly packed | 1 cup | 220 g |
| granulated sugar | ¾ cup | 150 g |
| heavy cream | 1¼ cups | 300 ml |
| unsalted butter | 1 cup | 225 g |
| salt | ½ teaspoon | 3 g |
| vanilla ice cream (your choice!) | | |

at a time, gently stirring in between each blast until the mixture has reached the right ice-cream-topping consistency and is comfortably warm and cozy. Alternatively, place the jar, cap off, in a simmering pot of water, making sure the water only reaches halfway up the jar (because if you walk away and the water starts boiling, you don't want hot water in your gorgeous fudge). Heat until you're happy.

simple dissolve to thread stage

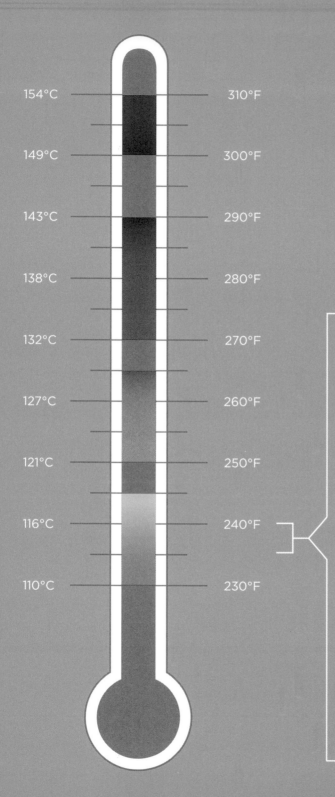

| | |
|---|---|
| 154°C | 310°F |
| 149°C | 300°F |
| 143°C | 290°F |
| 138°C | 280°F |
| 132°C | 270°F |
| 127°C | 260°F |
| 121°C | 250°F |
| 116°C | 240°F |
| 110°C | 230°F |

# SOFT-BALL STAGE

*235°F–240°F (113°C–116°C)    Sugar Concentration: 85%*

When dropped into cold water at this stage, hot sugar syrup will form a soft, pliable ball. When you remove the sugar, it won't maintain a permanent shape and will flatten in your hand.

Whipped eggs that receive a baptism from soft-ball sugar transform into an ethereal cloud. That touch of sweet heat manages to kill bacteria, sure, but it also imparts a stabilizing force to the eggs that makes for especially pointy meringue peaks. It's this temperature that is also the domain of fudge, giving a firmness and silken architecture without any discernible chew.

# SEVEN-MINUTE
# FROSTING

*Seven-minute frosting is straight out of* Leave it to Beaver. It's an icing that's so homey, so fifties, so sweet and plush that you can't help but smile at its innocence. This isn't the kind of stuff you toil over to make sure every last millimeter of the cake you're icing is smooth and presentable. No way. You want peaks and valleys; you want this to swirl and twirl willy-nilly. You want to be able to take a big swipe out of the frosting and leave little or no evidence of your crime.

|||||||| *Makes approximately 10 cups (2.5 L), enough to fill and cover 1 (10-inch/25-cm) cake* ||||||||

| sugar | 1½ cups, divided | 300 g, divided |
|---|---|---|
| corn syrup | ¼ cup | 60 ml |
| water | ⅓ cup | 75 ml |
| egg whites | 6 | |
| salt | ½ teaspoon | 3 g |

① In a heavy saucepan over medium heat, combine 1¼ cups (250 g) of the sugar, the corn syrup, and the water. Heat, stirring continuously, until the sugar has completely melted. With a damp pastry brush, wipe down the sides of the pan to prevent stray sugar crystals from forming. Attach a candy thermometer, stop stirring, and heat the mixture to 235°F (113°C).

② In the meantime, in the bowl of a stand mixer fitted with the whisk attachment, beat the egg whites and salt. Gradually pour in the remaining ¼ cup (50 g) sugar and beat until you achieve soft peaks.

③ When the sugar in the saucepan has reached 235°F (113°C), with the mixer on medium speed, pour the hot sugar in a slow stream down the side of the bowl into the beating egg whites. Whisk on high until the frosting is very thick and shiny, about 10 minutes. Slather this goodness on a layer cake or a petite cupcake. Use immediately.

**Options!**

OPTION 1: **FLUFF**
Seven-minute frosting is really just spreadable marshmallow, i.e., Fluff. And the first thing any red-blooded American will make with Fluff is a sandwich built for a king, if that king is Elvis. White bread, peanut butter, sliced bananas, and Fluff.

OPTION 2: **MAPLE FROSTING**
For maple frosting, replace traditional white granulated sugar with maple sugar or an equal amount of maple syrup. If you are using the maple sugar, proceed as you would with the traditional version by adding water along with corn syrup to the saucepan. If you are using maple syrup, reduce the amount of water to 2 tablespoons (30 ml) and proceed per the recipe.

# QUICK
# FUDGE

*Fudge is notorious for being finicky and a big time-waster.* But there's one way to make it without the fuss, and that's with Seven-Minute Frosting (page 60).

|||||||||||||||||||||||||||||||||||||||||||||||  *Makes 24 pieces*  |||||||||||||||||||||||||||||||||||||||||||||||

① In a large saucepan over medium-low heat, combine the sugar, salt, butter, and evaporated milk and simmer until the sugar has melted. Increase heat to medium-high. With a damp pastry brush, wipe down the sides of the pan to prevent stray sugar crystals from forming. Attach a candy thermometer and allow the mixture to boil and reach 235°F (113°C).

② Remove from the heat and immediately stir in the frosting, vanilla bean paste, and chocolate. Keep stirring until the chocolate is completely melted and incorporated.

③ Pour the fudge into a buttered 9-inch (23-cm) square pan and allow to set overnight. Cut into pieces and serve. Store in an airtight container in a cool, dry place for up to a week.

| | | |
|---|---|---|
| sugar | 2½ cups | 500 g |
| salt | 1 teaspoon | 6 g |
| unsalted butter | ¼ cup, plus extra for the pan | 55 g, plus extra for the pan |
| evaporated milk | 5 ounces | 150 ml |
| Seven-Minute Frosting (page 60) | 2 cups | 480 ml |
| vanilla bean paste | 1 teaspoon | 5 ml |
| bittersweet chocolate, finely chopped | 2 cups | 260 g |

**Option!**

**PEANUT BUTTER FUDGE**
For peanut butter fudge, replace the bittersweet chocolate with ¼ cup (60 ml) smooth peanut butter.

# ITALIAN
# MERINGUE

*This is the second method of making meringue; it requires you to pour hot sugar syrup into whisked egg whites.* Some pastry chefs believe that Italian meringue is marginally more stable than Swiss and that it holds up better to heat. There's no definitive proof to resolve this matter, but I tend to work with Italian meringue more often than not. Bottom line is, there are two ways and now you know them both.

||||||||||||||||||||||||||||||||||||||||||||| *Makes 2½ to 3 cups (600 to 720 ml)* |||||||||||||||||||||||||||||||||||||||||||||

| sugar | 1 cup | 200 g |
|---|---|---|
| water | ⅓ cup | 75 ml |
| egg whites | 5 | |
| salt | pinch | |

**All egg whites are not created equal.** When I see a recipe that calls for a specific number of egg whites, I look at my bowl of fresh eggs courtesy of our backyard hens. Kiki lays dark-brown monster eggs, Bertie lays extra-large tan eggs, Moussie lays very long, large, robin's-egg-blue eggs, and Helga's are light-green, oblong golf balls. Moussie's very first attempt was the size of an ostrich egg and it's no surprise that she refused to lay another for two weeks. Four hens laying four very different-size eggs means that each egg will contain a yolk and a white that are totally different sizes and weights from the others'. Obviously, a recipe that simply calls for "five egg whites" sometimes doesn't cut it.

So I go by the baker's weight standard for eggs: 1 egg white equals 1 ounce (30 g), and 1 yolk equals 0.6 ounce (18 g). If you find yourself with eggs in a variety of sizes, weigh them for complete accuracy.

① In a small saucepan, combine the sugar and water. Make sure that the sugar is saturated with the water and that there aren't any dry clumps remaining before you start heating it up. Stir the water and sugar over low heat until the sugar has completely dissolved. With a damp pastry brush, wipe down the sides of the pan to prevent stray sugar crystals from forming. Turn the heat up to medium-high, clip on a candy thermometer, and heat to 240°F (116°C).

② Meanwhile, put the egg whites and salt into the bowl of an electric mixer fitted with the whisk attachment. When the sugar gets to 230°F (110°C), start the mixer on medium-high so that the egg whites start to lighten and get foamy before you add the sugar syrup.

③ Once the syrup reaches temperature, carefully carry the saucepan to your work table and ratchet the speed of your mixer down to medium. With the mixer running, slowly pour the sugar syrup down the side of the bowl. (By pouring the sugar down the side of the bowl instead of straight into the egg whites, you keep them from turning into sweet scrambled eggs. This also prevents the hot sugar from splashing onto your person. Safety first!)

④ Turn the mixer to high and whisk until the meringue is light and fluffy and holds a stiff peak. Transfer the meringue to a pastry bag fit with an open star tip and pipe perky peaks onto pie or ice cream.

### Option!

#### ITALIAN BUTTERCREAM
Turn the mixer down to medium speed and add 2 cups (455 g) softened unsalted butter a small bit at a time—just like making Swiss Buttercream (page 44). Add the butter slowly and pay attention to the changes in the texture of the buttercream. If you notice that it's beginning to curdle, stop adding butter and increase the mixer speed to high. You've probably added enough butter, and if you allow the buttercream to mix on its own for a few minutes, it's very likely that it will start to come together into a creamy frosting. This makes 3½ to 4 cups (840 to 960 ml).

With Italian Meringue
Make Red Sox Nation Tortes, page 201

I'll watch over a pot of boiling water, but I tend to abandon saucepans of boiling sugar. The worst that can happen with water is that it will evaporate and your pan will be left over the flame with no water buffer to dissipate the heat. You can scorch a great pan and you can disembowel a mediocre one. Complete evaporation also creates a very distinct smell—you know the one. The same smell that emanates from parked vans the world over.

Sugar left unmonitored, however, can wreak havoc not only on a pan but on an entire recipe. Precise temperature is queen in sugar work. If you're going for soft-ball and walk away in a huff because it's taking so damn long, I'll guarantee you'll be facing hard crack the next time you check your thermometer. But there is a way to go back in time (so long as you haven't reached caramelization, i.e., the sugar has gone to the dark side). As with cream that has been slightly overwhipped, you can add a bit more of the base ingredient to get your recipe back on track. With sugar that's gone over temperature, you can add a bit of clean, cold water to bring down the temperature and then continue boiling until you've hit the correct mark with the mercury.

# PÂTE
## *à*
# BOMBE

*So you're asking yourself, "What the hell do I do with all the yolks?"* Well, you could make a crème anglaise. Or you could whip up some *pâte à bombe*. It's terribly simple and heart-breakingly sinful. Just as with Italian meringue, you pour hot sugar syrup into the whisking eggs, but this time it's the yolks that get the sweet treatment. It's delicious enough to eat by the spoonful, but it is traditionally used as the base of French buttercream, parfaits, and beautiful mousses. It really is "the bombe."

IIIIIIIIIIIIIIIIIIIIIIIIIIIIIIIIIIIIIIIIIII *Makes approximately 1½ cups (360 ml)* IIIIIIIIIIIIIIIIIIIIIIIIIIIIIIIIIIIIIIIIIII

| egg yolks | 10 | |
|---|---|---|
| salt | pinch | |
| sugar | 1 cup | 200 g |
| water | ⅓ cup | 75 ml |

① In the bowl of a stand mixer fitted with the whisk attachment, whisk the yolks with the salt until the mixture starts to pale and thicken.

② Meanwhile, in a small saucepan over low heat, stir together the water and sugar until the sugar has completely melted.

③ Stop stirring, wash down the sides of the pan with a damp pastry brush, clip on a candy thermometer, and raise the heat to medium-high. Heat until the temperature reaches 240°F (116°C).

④ Transfer the sugar syrup to a heatproof container with a spout (such as a measuring cup). With the mixer running, carefully pour the sugar syrup in a slow, steady stream down the side of

the bowl into the whipping egg yolks. Continue beating until the mixture thickens and cools.

### Options!

#### OPTION 1: LA BOMBE—THE BEST CHOCOLATE BUTTERCREAM EVER

Add chocolate to a *pâte à bombe*, and you'll forget that you've whipped up the stuff as a frosting and just spoon the cocoa deliciousness straight into your pie hole.

This procedure follows the *pâte à bombe* recipe above, with a few differences. As the egg yolks are whisking, in a small saucepan, combine the sugar with 1 teaspoon (5 ml) vanilla extract and ⅓ cup (75 ml) coffee to replace the water. (Feel free to use water, but I enjoy the oomph that coffee imparts to chocolate.) Stir over low heat until the sugar has melted, then raise the heat to medium-high and heat to 234°F (112°C). Transfer the sugar syrup to a heatproof container with a spout and pour it in a slow, steady stream into the whisking egg yolks. Continue beating the mixture.

In the meantime, melt 1 pound (455 g) finely chopped bittersweet chocolate in a metal bowl over a simmering pot of water. Stir continuously until the chocolate has completely melted. Reduce the mixer speed to medium. Using a large rubber spatula, scrape the chocolate into the whipping egg mixture until it is completely incorporated.

Add 2 cups (455 g) softened unsalted butter in small pieces and continue mixing until the frosting is smooth. Allow to thicken and cool before using, about 30 minutes. Makes approximately 3 cups (720 ml).

OPTION 2: **LA BOMBE—THE MOUSSE EDITION**

Instead of adding butter after all that glorious melted chocolate in Option 1, whip 2 cups (480 ml) of heavy cream with ½ cup (115 g) mascarpone until light and fluffy. Stir in ½ cup (120 ml) of the mixture to lighten, then gently fold in the remaining mixture, for an outrageous mousse. Divide the mousse among separate serving dishes and chill, or use as a cake filling. Better yet, make a quick puff pastry crust (page 187), line the bottom of the baked crust with a layer of ganache (page 172), and top it all off with this luscious mousse. Chocolate cream pie made "ooh la la."

# CANDY
# CORN

*My favorite Halloween costume was a death trap: seven feet of chicken wire slathered in papier mâché, festooned in flammable white, orange, and yellow oil paint, made mobile with four shimmying grocery cart wheels, and equipped with a sticky trap door for candy deposits.* I was the envy of every kid at Woodmont Elementary. I was the biggest candy corn on earth.

Sadly, there was no ventilation, it tipped whenever I tried to negotiate a curb, and the built-in mesh window was inches too low for my gangly frame. But I was happy to withstand any discomfort for a giant candy corn, even if it wasn't edible. Luckily, I usually got a few pounds of the real stuff deposited into the bucket attached precariously to the inside of the costume. Today, I bypass trick-or-treating and death-trap costumes and simply make my favorite ghoulish treat at home.

|||||||||||||| *Makes 2½ pounds (1.2 kg), approximately 400 small pieces, or 12 large cobs* ||||||||||||||

| | | |
|---|---|---|
| confectioners' sugar | 3½ cups | 350 g |
| powdered milk | ½ cup | 65 g |
| salt | ½ teaspoon | 3 g |
| granulated sugar | 1½ cups | 300 g |
| corn syrup | 1 cup | 240 ml |
| unsalted butter | ½ cup | 115 g |
| glycerin | 1 teaspoon | 5 ml |
| yellow food coloring | 2 drops | |
| orange food coloring | 2 drops | |

① In a food processor, blend the confectioners' sugar, powdered milk, and salt until they form a very fine powder. Set aside.

② In a large saucepan over medium-high heat, combine the granulated sugar, corn syrup, butter, and glycerin. Stir until the sugar dissolves.

③ Lower the heat to medium. Attach a candy thermometer and allow the mixture to simmer undisturbed for 5 minutes, until the temperature reaches 240°F (116°C).

④ Remove the sugar syrup from the heat and pour it into the bowl of an electric mixer fitted with the paddle attachment. With the mixer on low, pour in the confectioners' sugar mixture until a paste forms. Allow to cool completely.

⑤ Divide the dough into 3 even pieces. Knead 2 drops of yellow dye into one piece and 2 drops of orange dye into a second piece. Leave the third piece white.

# !!!!!!!!!WARNING!!!!!!!!!

You'll notice it's starting to get hot in here. The sugar, that is. I'm not going to lie: The stuff burns like a Mother Hubbard. Take the time when I was poking hot caramel, for instance. You know how they tell you not to pester tigers in a cage? Well, don't pester hot caramel on a stove.

I had made caramel in my favorite saucepan. I'd let it go hard in my favorite saucepan. And then I decided that I really needed to use that particular saucepan and no other saucepan for something else entirely. I decided to put the caramel on low heat to soften it up so I could get it out of my favorite saucepan and store it in another container. I kept the caramel on low heat—I didn't want to burn it. Every once in a while I'd go poke at the caramel to see if it had softened. Poke. Still hard. Poke. Still hard. Poke. Still hard. Poke. Molten, soft caramel and my hand is right in the middle of it. My paw was coated in what I've since decided was over 300°F (150°C) caramel, and instantaneously I couldn't care less about getting to my favorite saucepan—I just wanted to stop the excruciating pain caused by delicious caramel. And like any idiot, I had the reflex to wipe my hand on the back of my shirt to get the sticky, blistering candy glove off—and instead of fabric I hit skin. So now I had a scalding substance on my hand and my back. Brilliant.

This is just a very long way of telling you to be careful. Boiling water is hot. Sugar gets even hotter. So when I say things over and over like "pour the hot sugar down the side of the bowl with the mixer on medium speed," I'm reminding you to be careful. When you're whipping something and simultaneously pouring sugar into the mix, slow the mixer down so that searing-hot blobs of pain don't fly all over your kitchen. Pour the sugar down the side of the bowl so the fiery syrup doesn't scorch the ingredients inside it. And above all:

## DON'T POKE HOT CARAMEL.

⑥ If you're going for the traditional tri-color look, divide each color of dough in half, roll each half into a rough rope approximately 4 feet (1.2 m) long, and place one of each color rope on a long piece of plastic wrap. Line up the pieces, white then orange then yellow, next to each other on the wrap. Gently squeeze them together so they adhere to each other, and press down the length of the rope so you've got a very long, thin rectangle. Do the same with the second ropes. With a sharp knife, cut the ropes into about 400 small triangles. Using an offset spatula, place the triangles on a parchment-lined sheet pan approximately ½ inch (12 mm) apart. Allow to dry, uncovered, in a cool, dry place for a few hours.

⑦ I prefer to go against the grain and use vintage cast-iron cornbread molds in the shape of real corn, because the bigger the candy corn, the better. If you'd like to go this route, spray twelve molds with nonstick cooking spray. Take a piece of white dough and press it into the top of a mold. Place some orange dough in the middle and press it so it abuts against the white very snugly. Then add yellow dough to the bottom and press until the orange snuggles up to the yellow. Continue with the remaining molds and cover with plastic wrap. Give each "corn" another good press on top of the plastic wrap to ensure that the individual colored pieces are fused together and that the candy fills every nook of the mold. Allow to set for 1 hour. Gently turn the mold upside down to release the candy and allow to air-dry in a cool, dry place overnight. Store in an airtight container in a cool, dry place for up to a week.

# MAPLE
# CANDY

*Sugar bomb.* You know exactly what I mean. There's no other way to describe it. Sucking on twenty sugar cubes would have less impact than one solitary piece of maple candy. Don't let those dainty shapes of maples leaves and prim pilgrims fool you into believing that there's anything but total sugar shock awaiting you at the end of the road. But if you can ignore the impending throb of the guaranteed headache, there's that nuance of flavor, that subtle, earthy succulence that makes maple candy the unimpeachable high priestess of sugar indulgence. Just don't eat more than a few, unless you have spectacular medical coverage and a family size bottle of ibuprofen.

*Makes 2 dozen small candies*

① In a heavy-bottomed saucepan over medium heat, stir together the syrup, butter, and salt, and heat until the butter is melted. Attach a candy thermometer, stop stirring, and heat to 235°F (113°C). Meanwhile, spray your molds with nonstick spray, and set aside.

② Immediately remove the pan from the heat but leave the candy thermometer attached. Let the maple rest, untouched, until the temperature drops to 175°F (79°C), 5 to 10 minutes.

③ Beat the maple with a wooden spoon until the mixture starts to lighten and thicken a bit, 3 to 5 minutes.

| grade B maple syrup | 2 cups | 480 ml |
|---|---|---|
| unsalted butter | 1 tablespoon | 14 g |
| salt | pinch | |

④ Immediately pour into your molds. Work quickly, as the mixture will begin hardening.

⑤ Allow to cool completely before turning the candies out of the molds. Store in an airtight container in a cool, dry place for up to a month. Enjoy with caution.

# PEANUT BUTTER FUDGE

*My grandmother Nanny raised seven kids on her own during the Depression.* Seven. On her own. During the Depression. The fact that she was able to do anything in the kitchen seems a miracle, yet she found time to perfect candies and create lasting memories of raucous sugar-pulling parties during a time when nothing should have been sweet. The recipes are simple—there wasn't money for fancy filler ingredients—but they are simply delicious. This is her peanut butter fudge. I like to get fancy on it and pour the fudge over a layer of dense chocolate fudge cake, top the peanut butter with another cake layer, cover all of that with a Sacher glaze, and then stud the sides with chopped roasted peanuts. I'll tell you how to do that on page 199. You'll probably find it hard not to eat this fudge all by its lonesome though. Just imagine having to share it among seven siblings!

*Makes approximately 45 squares*

| | | |
|---|---|---|
| sugar | 2 cups | 400 g |
| evaporated milk | 5 ounces | 150 ml |
| smooth peanut butter | generous ¼ cup | generous 60 ml |

① In a saucepan over low heat, cook the sugar and milk until the sugar has melted.

② Raise the heat to high and bring the mixture to a full boil, stirring constantly.

③ Reduce the temperature to medium-high, keeping the mixture at a continuous rolling boil until the temperature reaches 235°F (113°C). Remove from the heat. Add the peanut butter and allow it to melt into the milk mixture, undisturbed, for 5 minutes.

④ Working quickly, stir the peanut butter into the mixture vigorously to distribute it throughout the fudge. Immediately pour the candy into a buttered 8-by-8-inch (20-by-20-cm) dish and allow to cool completely either in the freezer or at room temperature. Slice into 1-inch (2.5-cm) squares. The recipe can easily be doubled. Store in an airtight container in a cool, dry place for up to a week.

# GESINE'S DAMN GOOD
# PEANUT BUTTER FUDGE

*I could swear I had evaporated milk in the pantry.* I remember the can sitting there, right on the middle shelf next to the jar of Nutella. Why in the fudge couldn't I find it? Then I realized my fatal error. I had sweetened condensed milk, not evaporated milk. Entirely different animal.

Well, damn. I had the peanut butter and the insatiable craving, so what was a Sugar Baby to do? Improvise! So what if I screwed up? It was worth a shot trying to create something divine on my own terms and with pantry staples I knew I'd always have on hand—evaporated milk be damned.

Lo and behold, I experimented. And it was good. It was damn good.

|||||||||||||||||||||||||| *Makes 12 heart-shaped fudge bites or 1 (10-inch/25-cm) round layer* ||||||||||||||||||||

① In a large saucepan over low heat, stir together the sugar, half-and-half, and salt and cook until the sugar has completely melted.

② Increase the heat to medium-high and attach a candy thermometer. This is one of the rare cases where I keep stirring once I've attached the thermometer. Milk easily forms a skin and I like to keep it smooth. So keep stirring until your candy thermometer reads 235°F (113°C).

③ Remove the syrup from the heat and immediately add the butter, peanut butter, and vanilla. Stir with a wooden spoon until the butter and peanut butter have completely melted.

④ I beat this fudge immediately; I don't wait for it to cool and form a skin. Why? Because it turns out exactly to my specifications, with just a hint of crunch, and it's a fantastic workout.

⑤ Stir the fudge vigorously for 15 to 20 minutes, until it loses its shine and starts to firm up considerably. I like to pour my fudge into silicone heart molds for a much sweeter presentation

| | | |
|---|---|---|
| sugar | 3 cups | 600 g |
| half-and-half | 1 cup | 240 ml |
| salt | 1 teaspoon | 6 g |
| unsalted butter | 5 tablespoons | 70 g |
| smooth peanut butter | ¼ cup | 60 ml |
| vanilla extract | 1 teaspoon | 5 ml |

than your humdrum fudge wedge. Or I pour the entire batch into a 10-inch (25-cm) round cake pan that's been sprayed with nonstick spray. I nudge the firming fudge to the very edge of the pan to fill the entire circle. It's probably not going to be perfectly flat or even, but try your best not to end up with too many peaks and valleys. Allow the fudge to set completely, at least 2 hours. Store in an airtight container in a cool, dry place for up to a week.

## *A Note from the Sugar Baby:*

Grainy fudge happens to the best of us. Some actually prefer their fudge with a hint of granular crunch; they think it simply isn't fudge without it. However, some like it super smooth. To ensure that your fudge is the ultimate in silken deliciousness, when you start the initial heating of ingredients, be 100 percent positive that the sugar is completely melted before you bump up the heat and stop stirring. A second precaution is to refrain from stirring the fudge until the temperature has fallen below 140°F (60°C). If you've done all this and your fudge still has a slightly grainy mouthfeel, you can melt the fudge along with a few tablespoons (40 to 50 ml) cream and start again. I know, it's a pain in the butt, but at least you know that you can make it right without wasting ingredients! Either that or make fudge with Seven-Minute Frosting (page 60) instead. Never say I didn't give you options.

# OLD-SCHOOL
## *Chocolate*
# FUDGE

*Fudge isn't easy.* I'm not saying that the procedure is necessarily hard, but it's a finicky little sweet, known to crystallize on the best of candy makers in a most unappealing way. This is a pretty tried-and-true fudge recipe, following the standard tenets of successful fudge making. Just know that if you reach the end of the road and find that your fudge has indeed taken on a bit of a granular crunch, you can always reheat the stuff and start over—or, as I do, learn to appreciate that sugar crunch as an integral component of old-school fudge.

|||||||||||||||||||||||||||||||||||||||||| *Makes approximately 30 squares* ||||||||||||||||||||||||||||||||||||||||||

① In a small bowl, whisk together the sugar and cocoa powder.

② In a large, heavy saucepan over medium heat, whisk together the sugar–cocoa powder mixture, corn syrup, milk, espresso powder, and salt. Stir until the sugar melts.

③ Clip on a candy thermometer and raise the heat to medium-high. Stop stirring and heat to 235°F (113°C). Remove the fudge from the heat and add the butter—just plop it in and don't stir.

④ Let the mixture sit undisturbed until the fudge cools to lukewarm and the temperature drops down to between 110°F and 140°F (43°C and 60°C). Don't stir!

✴ **A Note from the Sugar Baby:** Fudge success is all in *not* stirring until you *gotta* stir. It's a waiting-and-temperature-watching game. Why all the waiting? It's the sugar's fault, of course. Sugar always wants to recrystallize, and agitating the mixture too soon will cause the candy to form large, very discernable chunks of sugar crystals. But here's the irony: You *want* crystals in fudge, because its very structure is based on

| | | |
|---|---|---|
| sugar | 1 cup | 200 g |
| cocoa powder | ½ cup | 40 g |
| corn syrup | 3 tablespoons | 45 ml |
| milk | 1 cup | 240 ml |
| espresso powder (optional) | 1 teaspoon | 1 g |
| salt | ½ teaspoon | 3 g |
| unsalted butter | 3 tablespoons | 42 g |
| vanilla extract or vanilla bean paste | 1 teaspoon | 5 ml |

a microscopic web of sugar granules; the trick is to form just the right kind. That's why you wait. Stir too early, and you wake up seed crystals that, when agitated, grab on to the sugar molecules all around them. It's akin to a tiny snowball starting a journey down a gargantuan hill, collecting bits of snow along the way, and eventually transforming into an ice boulder of epic proportions.

⑤ Add the vanilla extract or paste and beat the mixture with a wooden spoon until the fudge loses its shine and thickens. This can take up to 20 minutes and is one heck of an upper-body workout. Which leads to a confession: I've been known to transfer my fudge to a mixer and beat at medium speed with the paddle attachment until it's ready. I know. I'm a fudge cheater.

⑥ Immediately transfer into an 8-inch (20-cm) square dish sprayed with nonstick spray. Cool completely, cover with plastic wrap, and allow to set for a few hours or overnight. Cut into 2-inch (5-cm) squares. Store in an airtight container in a cool, dry place for up to a week.

### Options!

OPTION 1: **ADD-INS**
Add 1 teaspoon (5 ml) extract just as you start whipping the fudge. My all-time favorite is mint. Orange and raspberry extracts are other lovely choices that go very well with chocolate.

OPTION 2: **MILK CHOCOLATE OR *GIANDUJA***
Here's the thing about chocolate fudge: It's good to go no matter what style of chocolate you prefer, whether it's milk chocolate or that hazelnut-infused delight called *gianduja*. If you love Nutella, have I got a treat for you. You've probably noticed that the original recipe calls for cocoa. If you're going to add milk chocolate or *gianduja*, leave out ½ cup (100 g) of the granulated sugar and proceed per the instructions with ½ cup (120 ml) milk chocolate or *gianduja*.

OPTION 3: **LAYERS**
I've been known to layer fudges from dark to light. My personal favorite is chocolate fudge, followed by Muscovado Fudge (page 76), followed by a layer of peanut butter fudge (pages 70–71). If I go this route, I always add salty nuts to the muscovado layer for texture.

WE NOW INTERRUPT YOUR REGULARLY SCHEDULED PROGRAMMING TO ADDRESS THE ELEPHANT IN THE ROOM: CORN SYRUP.

It's in quite a few of these recipes. I've experimented and tried to replace it. Some things work very well, like glucose syrup and golden syrup, but these ingredients are tough to find outside of Europe. I've also tried alternatives like agave nectar and honey, but the results are never quite the same due to chemical composition (the agave), general taste (the honey), and overall sugar density (both). So I thought I'd ask an expert, because I'm confused by the disparate reports regarding corn syrup. One thing I do know, no matter the type, all sugar consumption must be in moderation. But let's ask Marion Nestle, Professor of Nutrition at New York University and author of *What to Eat*:

GP: From a health standpoint, what's the difference between sugar and corn syrup?

MN: None, really. Sugar (sucrose) is 50 percent glucose/50 percent fructose. High fructose corn syrup (HFCS) is 45 percent glucose/55 percent fructose. The difference is not biologically significant.

GP: Is the corn syrup we find in the baking aisle the same as the high fructose corn syrup found in industrial food products?

MN: Corn syrup used to be 100 percent glucose, or close to it. It is now a mixture of glucose and fructose, but unless the proportions are stated, you really can't know what they are.

GP: Does corn syrup have a chemical property different from granulated sugar, and if so, what about this property makes it a common ingredient in so many traditional American candies? Why not use just sugar when money's not an option?

MN: HFCS is sweeter than either glucose or sucrose, but it also has properties that make it terrific for baking.

GP: Recent studies have confused me regarding corn syrup. I've read that sugar and corn syrup carry with them the same health deficits, that one isn't any less healthy than the other, and that corn syrup is simply used more than sugar in everyday food products because it's cheaper. Therefore, it gets a bad rap.

MN: Correct.

GP: And then there are reports that corn syrup has a negative impact on the manner in which we metabolize sugars.

MN: This is a misunderstanding based on the erroneous name "high fructose." As noted above, HFCS is basically the same as table sugar. Both have the same amount of fructose, and it's fructose—and only fructose—that is metabolized differently.

GP: What about agave nectar? It's been touted as the johnny-come-lately in sugar alternatives. I've read, on one hand, that it has a lower glycemic index than sugar.

MN: That's true, because agave syrup is mostly fructose.

GP: I've also heard that agave nectar is the healthier alternative, and then in the next breath, I'll read an article that states it's the processing of agave that varies, which may cause the syrup to have the same or a lower glycemic index based on how it's been processed.

MN: The amount of fructose varies.

GP: And if it's a liquid sugar, why can't I just replace it with corn syrup and get the same results in my caramels and hard candies? Because I don't!

MN: Neither does anyone else, mainly because agave nectar is mostly fructose, the one you want to avoid in large amounts. Fructose does not bake as well as HFCS.

GP: Is there any sweetener that's better than the others? Honey, beet sugar, cane sugar, turbinado, muscovado, maple sugar, agave nectar, corn syrup, fructose, or candy tabs from the health food store? Or is it all the same as far as our bodies are concerned?

MN: Sugars are sugars. All have four calories per gram and are best consumed in small amounts. Some taste better than others. I am especially fond of the brown turbinado.

GP: And for that matter, what—if any—difference is there between cane and beet sugar?

MN: None. Both are sucrose.

GP: How do you feel about the bake sale ban in New York City schools?

MN: If I thought it would stop the selling of junk foods in schools, I'd be for it. Since it doesn't, it's silly.

GP: When—if ever—do you allow yourself a sweet? Do you have a favorite special treat?

MN: Of course. I am especially fond of Häagen-Dazs vanilla frozen yogurt.

# MUSCOVADO
# FUDGE

*Muscovado is an unrefined dark brown sugar.* But it's not the brown sugar we all know and love. The kind we buy in the grocery store to make Toll House cookies (and then forget in the back of the cupboard until it gets rock hard) is actually just white sugar with molasses added. If someone tells you that brown sugar is healthier than granulated sugar, they've got a screw loose, because that type is just granulated white sugar in disguise. Muscovado, however, is dark because it's *not* refined, and it receives its lovely nutty color and taste from the very sugar-cane juice that's usually sloughed off. It tastes more like molasses than the brown sugar that has molasses added to it. Bottom line: It's a glorious flavor and it makes for splendid fudge.

*Makes approximately 30 squares*

| | | |
|---|---|---|
| muscovado sugar | 2 cups | 400 g |
| granulated sugar | 1 cup | 200 g |
| heavy cream | 1 cup | 240 ml |
| corn syrup | 2 tablespoons | 30 ml |
| salt | ½ teaspoon | 3 g |
| unsalted butter | 2 tablespoons | 28 g |
| vanilla extract or vanilla bean paste | 1 teaspoon | 5 ml |
| pecans, chopped, toasted, and salted | ½ cup | 55 g |

1. In a heavy saucepan over medium heat, stir together the sugars, cream, corn syrup, and salt. Stir until the sugars have melted.

2. Attach a candy thermometer and increase the heat to medium-high. Stop stirring. Continue cooking until the temperature reaches 240°F (116°C).

3. Immediately remove the pan from the heat and add the butter. Allow to sit undisturbed until the mixture is lukewarm and the temperature reads between 110°F and 140°F (43°C and 60°C).

4. Add the vanilla extract or paste and beat with a wooden spoon until the mixture thickens and loses its shine. Fold in the pecans and pour the mixture into an 8-inch (20-cm) square pan.

5. Allow to cool slightly and cover with plastic wrap. Continue to cool until set, a few hours or overnight. Cut into 2-inch (5-cm) squares. Store in an airtight container in a cool, dry place for up to a week.

# NOLA
# PRALINES

*NOLA.* As in New Orleans, Louisiana. Hot jazz, Creole spice, crispy beignets, chicory coffee, and melt-in-your-mouth pralines. There's no other city in the world with as much soul as our one and only New Orleans. Pralines, made with bourbon vanilla and toasted pecans, bring a sweet taste of the Zydeco city to your kitchen. Go one step further: Add the pralines to the New Orleans–inspired bread pudding on page 179 and *laissez les bons temps rouler!*

||||||||||||||||||||||||||||||||||||||||||||||||||||||  *Makes approximately 30*  ||||||||||||||||||||||||||||||||||||||||||||||||||||||

① In a heavy-bottomed saucepan over low heat, combine the sugars, cream, milk, and salt. Cook, stirring constantly, until the sugar has melted.

② Raise the heat to medium, stop stirring, clip on a candy thermometer, and cook to 235°F (113°C).

③ Remove the pan from the heat and add the butter, bourbon vanilla extract, and pecans. Allow to sit undisturbed for 5 minutes, then stir until the mixture is no longer shiny.

| | | |
|---|---|---|
| brown sugar, firmly packed | 1 cup | 220 g |
| granulated sugar | 1 cup | 200 g |
| heavy cream | ½ cup | 120 ml |
| whole milk | ¼ cup | 60 ml |
| salt | ½ teaspoon | 3 g |
| unsalted butter | 2 tablespoons | 28 g |
| bourbon vanilla extract | 1 tablespoon | 15 ml |
| pecan halves, toasted | 30 | |

||||With NOLA Pralines||||
||||Make Île Flotante, page 174||||

④ Transfer the praline mixture into a piping bag fitted with a large open tip. Pipe quarter-sized dollops on a parchment-lined sheet pan and place a pecan half in the middle of each circle. Alternatively, pipe heart-shaped pralines and leave off the pecan halves. Cool until set.

⑤ Store in an airtight container for up to 2 weeks, or turn to page 174 for a NOLA-inspired dessert to end all desserts.

# PERFECT
## *Passion Fruit*
# PARFAIT

*Don't worry, I haven't lost my senses and snuck a Golden Arches–style layered blob into these recipes.* No siree. A genuine parfait is a frozen delicacy made with a hot sugar syrup. *Parfait* means "perfect" in French—and correct me if I'm wrong, but that word applies much better to magnificent, homemade frozen goodness than it does to fast-food mush.

This particular recipe calls for passion fruit, the most tropical of fruits, but you can use any purée that strikes your fancy. I love passion fruit because it reminds me of Germany, where I first experienced it and where it's savored in desserts of all caliber. And I find it most enjoyable as a parfait—neither ice cream nor mousse, just perfect.

|||||||||||||||||||||||||||||||||||||||||||||||| *Makes 6 to 8 servings* ||||||||||||||||||||||||||||||||||||||||||||||||

| | | |
|---|---|---|
| sugar | 1 cup, divided | 200 g, divided |
| water | ½ cup, divided | 120 ml, divided |
| eggs, separated | 10 | |
| passion fruit purée | 1 cup | 240 ml |
| salt | pinch | |
| heavy cream | 2 cups | 480 ml |

① In a small heavy saucepan over medium heat, combine ½ cup (100 g) of the sugar with ¼ cup (60 ml) of the water. With a damp pastry brush, wash down the sides of the pan to prevent stray sugar crystals from forming. Heat until the mixture reaches 235°F (113°C) on a candy thermometer.

② Meanwhile, in the bowl of a stand mixer with a whisk attachment, whisk the egg yolks until they are light and fluffy. When the sugar syrup has reached temperature, with the mixer on medium-high, carefully pour the hot sugar syrup down the side of the mixing bowl and continue beating until the mixture has cooled.

③ Add the purée and mix gently. Scrape the mixture into a metal bowl and set aside in the refrigerator.

④ In a saucepan over medium heat, combine the remaining ½ cup (100 g) sugar and the remaining ¼ cup (60 ml) water and heat until the mixture reaches 235°F (113°C).

⑤ Meanwhile, clean the bowl of your stand mixer and add the egg whites and salt. Whisk until foamy. Slowly add the hot sugar mixture to the egg whites and whip on high until the egg whites are very white and shiny and hold soft peaks.

⑥ Transfer the bowl to the stand mixer fitted with the whisk attachment and beat on high until the mixture forms stiff, white peaks and has cooled.

✪ **A Note from the Sugar Baby:** Did you see what just happened? You used two techniques, one after the other, without batting an eyelash. First you made a pâte à bombe and then you made an Italian meringue! I didn't want to say anything earlier, lest I make you nervous.

⑦ Transfer the egg whites to the purée mixture and gently fold together.

⑧ Clean the bowl of the stand mixer *again* and pour in the heavy cream. Whip the cream until soft peaks form. Gently fold the whipped cream into the egg mixture, making sure no white streaks remain.

⑨ Gently pour the parfait into single-serving glasses, a large serving bowl, or individual rectangular cake molds and freeze until firm, at least 5 hours or overnight. Serve frozen.

⑩ To serve the rectangular cakes, heat the metal mold with a blow-dryer on low heat, then gently remove the mold.

Options!

OPTION 1: **COLORS**
If you'd like a gradation of colors to give the dessert a visual pop, before freezing, add a drop of orange food coloring to half the mixture. Spread the darker parfait in an even layer first, then gently spoon the lighter-colored parfait on top, making sure not to blend the two together and muddy the distinct colors. Freeze as above.

OPTION 2: **CAKE BASE**
If you want to give your parfait a cake base (like I've done in the photo on page 79), use your cake mold to stamp out a layer of cake, then pour parfait into the mold. The coconut cake on page 184 is perfect.

# CARAMEL
# SAUCE

*I pour caramel sauce over ice cream, dish it into sweet pastry shells, and drizzle it over Napoleons. It's a magical treat. Once you get the hang of caramel, you'll see how small changes in temperature can really alter the consistency of the sauce, making it more fluid when brought to a lower temperature and thicker when brought to a higher one. I prefer a thicker caramel, but it's really your preference. And I think we can all agree that no matter its consistency, caramel is always outrageously delicious.*

*Makes approximately 2¼ cups (540 ml)*

① In a medium heavy-bottomed saucepan over medium heat, combine the sugar, water, lemon juice, and salt. Cook until the sugar dissolves. Brush the sides of the pan with a damp pastry brush to get rid of sugar crystals, stop stirring, and boil, undisturbed, until the color changes to a medium-dark copper color.

② Remove the pan from the heat, immediately add the cream, and quickly step back. Adding the cream will cause the hot caramel to bubble vigorously. When the bubbling subsides, clip on a candy thermometer. Add the butter, stir until the cream and butter are perfectly integrated into the caramel, and immediately return the pan to the heat.

③ Boil the caramel until the temperature reaches 240°F (116°C).

④ Set the caramel aside to cool completely before serving. Store in an airtight container in the refrigerator for up to two weeks. To reheat, transfer to a heatproof bowl and set over a saucepan of simmering water.

| sugar | 1½ cups | 300 g |
|---|---|---|
| water | ¼ cup | 60 ml |
| lemon juice | 1 teaspoon | 5 ml |
| salt | 1 teaspoon | 6 g |
| heavy cream | 1 cup | 240 ml |
| unsalted butter | 2 tablespoons | 28 g |

With Caramel Sauce
Make The Jackie, Oh! Cake, page 194

# PARISIAN
# MACARON SHELLS

*Macaron shells are notoriously finicky.* I bet there's been a day when you've just been minding your own business—walking the dog, doing your taxes—and you've heard a gut-wrenching cry pierce the air. What you heard may well have been the plaintive wail of "macaron fail."

Macarons are a beautiful Parisian delicacy consisting of two meringue shells, most often (but not always) made with nuts and filled with a soupçon of sandwiched buttercream. They can also make grown bakers cry.

Now I'll let you in on a secret. Many bakeries use a powdered mix to make macarons. Yup, they cheat. Just add water, and voilà! A no-fuss macaron. To which I say, "Go straight to pastry jail, you lazy varmints!"

Instead of cheating, try my version. It's time-tested for accuracy and minimal frustration—and it's from scratch, not some pitiful powdered mix. It's a little time-intensive, but that's to be expected from such a fussy confection. Read the directions a few times before you embark.

|||||||||||||||||||||||||||||||||||||||| *Makes approximately 200 shells* ||||||||||||||||||||||||||||||||||||||

| almond flour or blanched almond slices | 7 ounces | 210 g |
| confectioners' sugar | 7 ounces | 200 g |
| egg white powder | 2 tablespoons | 14 g |
| egg whites | 3 | |
| salt | ½ teaspoon | 3 g |
| granulated sugar | 7 ounces | 200 g |
| water | ½ cup, divided | 120 ml, divided |
| food coloring | 2 drops | |

If you've seen a Parisian macaron, you've witnessed some crazy hues not necessarily found in nature. Granted, that holds true for many sweets, but macarons are notoriously kaleidoscopic and, therefore, laden with dye. Of course, you can forgo the colorant. You can also rely on the small amount of color a purée can add, although those tones often come out muddy in the end product, and adding them will often ruin the shell. There are dyes created from beta carotene, beets, and other natural sources—I've yet to find them in stores and have to get them online. Just be careful; since they come from natural food sources, too much of the dye can bring a bit of the original flavor along with it. So unless you want borscht macarons, take it easy with any natural dye you add.

① Place the almond flour or almond slices, confectioners' sugar, and egg white powder in the bowl of a food processor. Process until the mixture is very fine. Sift the mixture into a large metal bowl and set aside.

② In the bowl of a stand mixer, add the egg whites and the salt. In the meantime, place the granulated sugar and ¼ cup (60 ml) of the water in a small saucepan over medium heat. Stir until the sugar is completely melted, clip on a candy thermometer, and stop stirring.

✱ **A Note from the Sugar Baby:** Macaron lore dictates that you use "aged egg whites." What, pray tell, are aged egg whites? Are they extra pricey and kept under lock and key in the cooler with the Cristal? No. "Aged" is a euphemism for an old and stale egg white, one that's lost its youthful moisture (lordy, do those words hit home). This means you separate your eggs a day before you bake and leave them out on your kitchen counter overnight. That's right—unrefrigerated! Sin of unholy bacterial sins! Refrigerating the whites will throw your precious albumen into the nest with aerial moisture, which is what we want to avoid, right? So cover your egg whites with plastic wrap, and rest assured that you'll be baking these raw harbingers of *E. coli* at a temperature that will kill 'em dead.

③ When the sugar temperature reaches 210°F (98°C), turn the mixer on high speed and begin beating the egg whites. You want them foamy before you add the sugar syrup but you *do not* want them stiff or chunky and dry.

④ Continue heating the sugar until the mixture reaches 240°F (116°C). Immediately remove the sugar syrup from the heat. Lower the mixer speed to medium-low and carefully pour the sugar syrup down the side of the bowl into the egg whites as they are whipping. Make sure not to pour the syrup directly on top of the egg whites, lest they scramble!

⑤ Return the mixer speed to high and whisk until you achieve soft, white peaks—the tips of the peaks should still fall easily. (There's a reason that the French describe meringue at this stage as holding a *bec d'oiseau*, or "bird's beak," since it should have the gentle curve of a birdie snout.

It should be a soft meringue, still white and airy, not stiff, and certainly not dry.)

⑥ Just before the egg whites are finished whipping, add the remaining ¼ cup (60 ml) water to the almond flour mixture from step 1 and combine to make a paste (don't do this any earlier or the paste will harden). Transfer one-third of the egg white mixture to the almond flour paste and stir well, making sure there are no white streaks remaining. You needn't be overly gentle during this addition—you are mainly loosening and lightening the batter, priming it for the addition of the remaining egg whites.

⑦ Add the remaining egg whites and gently fold them into the batter until there are no white streaks remaining. Now, this is important: You want a loose but not runny consistency. When you eventually start piping the batter, you'll want it to move easily from the piping bag but it shouldn't pour out so quickly that you can't control it; likewise, you don't want your petite dollops to spread into amorphous puddles, nor do you want them to stand rigid, refusing to loosen up and smooth out a little. So if you think that your batter is too stiff, continue stirring until it loosens a bit.

⑧ Transfer the batter to a pastry bag fitted with a large open tip. Pipe round, quarter-sized dollops about ½ inch (12 mm) apart on a nonstick baking mat or parchment-lined sheet pan (if your sheet pans are thin, double them up before you put the macarons in the oven—they burn quite easily on the bottom). Once every last bit is piped, let the macarons sit at room temperature for at least 20 minutes. Meanwhile, preheat the oven to 275°F (135°C).

⑨ Bake the macarons for 20 minutes, rotating the tray once for even baking and to avoid browning. (If you think your oven is too hot, feel free to turn the oven down if you get a hint of browning.) Using a small offset spatula, carefully pull out a shell to test for doneness. (I usually sacrifice the shells at the edges for testing, since they

can get a wee bit brown and that's the last thing you want in a Parisian.) The bottoms of the macarons should be completely flat and crisp and the innards should not look wet or mushy.

❋ **A Note from the Sugar Baby:** After 5 to 10 minutes of baking, you'll notice little ruffles forming along the perimeters of the shells; in French these are called *pieds*, or "feet." This is a very good thing. You also want a shell to have a nice sheen and to be perfectly smooth. You do not want it to crack, and when you bite into it, there should not be a big air bubble between the outer shell and the innards of the macaron. Bad stuff can happen due to overbeating, oven temperature issues, and humidity—this is one of those treats that's going to test your sanity, so be gentle with yourself.

⑩ Remove the shells from the oven and allow to cool completely. Cover them with plastic wrap and let them hang out for a day on your countertop. (Here's another piece of macaron lore: The shells are better when aged—you see, the French are really on to something with this "better with age" stuff.) Only do this if the weather is cool and dry; on a humid day the macarons will get soggy.

⑪ For filling, pipe a dime-size (12-mm) blob of buttercream on one shell and then smoosh it with another shell, just to the point that the filling reaches the edge. Once the shells are filled, serve immediately.

⑫ Macaron shells may be frozen in an airtight container for up to 2 weeks; allow them to thaw for 1 hour before serving.

❋ **A Note from the Sugar Baby:** If you've taken your shells out too early and they are underdone, they may start to buckle and develop strange ridges. They may also start to look damp, as the interior moisture leaches into the dry exterior. If overcooked, the shells will be crunchy throughout and won't have any give. The texture of a perfect macaron should comprise a very slight crispness to the outer shell that immediately gives way to the soft, airy, and delicate chew that's waiting inside.

**Option!**

**FLAVORS**

You can flavor the shell with a touch of extract (but not an oil). My favorites are coffee, lemon, orange, and peppermint. Mix in the extract with the water in step 6. To maintain the balance of your ingredients, if you add 1 teaspoon (5 ml) extract, remove an equal amount of water from the ¼ cup (60 ml). Otherwise, leave the flavor to the filling.

## Soft-Ball and Bake!

Sometimes you have to nudge a confection in just the right way for it to come alive. So while all of the following treats require the soft-ball treatment, they also require a little baking with a shortbread crust to take them the extra mile. Weird, huh? Weird but wonderful.

# FLORENTINER
*à la*
# MAMA

*There's a famous café in Bavaria, Café Reber.* Just thinking of it makes me all verklempt—I went with my mother when I was a kid. It's in a beautiful town, Bad Reichenhall, nestled at the foot of the Alps. It's around the corner from my family in Bergen. It's the home of the famous *Mozartkugel*—that alone would be enough to land this lovely sugar-filled *boîte* on my all-time favorite list. But it's also where you can get bags of *Florentiner-Bruch* (broken pieces of Florentine).

The Florentine cookie is Italian in background but is reimagined spectacularly by Austrian and Bavarian bakers. My mother, strictly healthy though she was, would scarf a bag of *Florentiner-Bruch* faster than you could say bulgur wheat and kale.

|||||||||||||||||||||||||||||||||||||||| *Makes 44 drop cookies or 20 heart cookies* ||||||||||||||||||||||||||||||||||||||||

| | | |
|---|---|---|
| sliced and blanched almonds | 2 cups | 225 g |
| all-purpose flour | ¼ cup | 30 g |
| salt | 1 teaspoon | 6 g |
| sugar | 1 cup | 200 g |
| honey | 2 tablespoons | 42 g |
| heavy cream | 3 tablespoons | 45 ml |
| unsalted butter | ½ cup | 115 g |
| almond extract | 1 teaspoon | 5 ml |
| bittersweet chocolate | 4 ounces | 120 g |

① Preheat the oven to 350°F (175°C).

② In a food processor, grind together 1½ cups (170 g) of the almonds, the flour, and the salt. You want a fine chop but you do not want to pulverize the almonds into a flour or churn it into a paste; there should be some nice bits of almond still visible. Set aside in a bowl along with the remaining ½ cup (55 g) of unchopped almonds.

③ In a saucepan over low heat, combine the sugar, honey, cream, and butter. Stir until the sugar has completely dissolved.

④ Raise the heat to medium-high and clip on a candy thermometer. Heat the mixture to 235°F (113°C).

⑤ Remove the pan from the heat and immediately stir in the almond mixture. Wait a minute for the batter to cool to the touch, and then stir in the almond extract.

⑥ While the batter is still warm and pliable, scoop it in teaspoons onto a parchment-lined sheet pan. I use a teaspoon scoop for 2-inch (5-cm) round cookies. Space the cookies a few inches

(6 to 7 cm) apart because they'll spread. Bake for 10 minutes or until golden brown.

⑦ Alternatively, press the batter into a heart-shaped cake mold sprayed with nonstick cooking spray. Bake for 20 minutes, or until the edges are brown.

⑧ While the cookies cool, place the chocolate in a microwave-safe bowl and microwave in 30-second intervals, stirring between each session and continuing until the chocolate is completely melted.

⑨ Drizzle the chocolate over the cooled Florentiners. Store in an airtight container in a cool, dry place for up to a week.

# Pecan
# BUTTERCRUNCH
## TART

*I'm a sucker for shortbread.* I'm also a sucker for toffee. How about making a shortbread vessel to house some toffee? You game?

|||||||||||||||||||||||||||||||||||||||||||||||||  *Makes 2 (8-inch/20-cm) tarts*  |||||||||||||||||||||||||||||||||||||||||||||||||

PROCEDURE FOR THE **SHORTBREAD**

① Preheat the oven to 325°F (165°C).

② In a large bowl, combine the flour, sugar, and salt. Whisk until combined. Add the butter in small pieces and massage the butter into the flour with your fingers until you have what looks like cornmeal, with no obvious butter chunks. The dough should start holding together when you pinch it.

③ In each of two fluted 8-inch (20-cm) tart pans or pie pans, press and pat half the dough until it forms an even crust in the pan (you can use just about any tart form you like but make sure it has sides to contain the toffee mixture). Chill the crusts in the refrigerator for 20 minutes.

④ Blind bake for 25 minutes (see instructions in Note). Make sure the shortbread doesn't brown. Set aside to cool.

✪ **A Note from the Sugar Baby:** "Blind bake?" Is this some kind of cruel pastry joke? Does it mean you tie a kerchief around your eyes and bake by feel? No. Blind baking a crust simply means that you bake it briefly before filling and baking again. This allows the crust to cook enough that it won't become a soggy mess when you add the filling.

   To blind bake, line the dough-filled tart form with parchment and then fill that with pantry

| FOR THE SHORTBREAD | | |
|---|---|---|
| all-purpose flour | 2 cups | 250 g |
| granulated sugar | ½ cup | 100 g |
| salt | 1 teaspoon | 6 g |
| unsalted butter | 1¼ cups | 285 g |
| FOR THE TOFFEE FILLING | | |
| heavy cream | 2 cups | 480 ml |
| granulated sugar | 2 cups | 400 g |
| brown sugar, firmly packed | ⅔ cup | 150 g |
| vanilla extract | 2 teaspoons | 10 ml |
| corn syrup | 2 tablespoons | 30 ml |
| salt | 1 teaspoon | 6 g |
| pecan pieces, toasted | 1 cup | 110 g |

staples like dry rice or dried beans. (Don't use dry dog food. It's a long story. Don't ask.) There are actually pie weights made for this very purpose that come in cute little ceramic balls or as metal beads strung on a long chain. (I just caution you to make sure none of your beans or beads or balls roll off the parchment into the crust. Again, don't ask.) Bake the crust at 325°F (165°C) for 20 minutes, long enough that the crust starts to lose the sheen of raw dough but not so long that it starts to brown. Remove weights and cool the crust before continuing.

① Preheat the oven to 375°F (190°C).

② In a very large saucepan over medium heat, combine the cream, sugars, vanilla extract, salt, and corn syrup. I'm serious about the large saucepan—this mixture will boil quite angrily.

③ Bring the mixture to a boil, stirring constantly. Attach a candy thermometer and stop stirring. There's a good chance that the cream will start to burn a bit on the bottom of the pan, and you want to keep it there if it does.

④ Heat the mixture to 235°F (113°C). The mixture should thicken and start to caramelize. Remove the pan from the heat and stir in the pecans.

⑤ Pour the filling evenly into the two shortbread shells, making sure not to scrape the bottom of the pan, lest you loosen bits of burnt cream. Bake for about 20 minutes, or until the tops are caramel-brown and the filling is bubbling.

⑥ Allow to cool completely before serving.

## Option!

### CRUNCH VERSUS CHEW
Here's a nifty trick to try if you'd rather your buttercrunch tart have less crunch and more chew. After you've poured the stovetop sugar mixture into the blind-baked tart pan, don't put the tart in the oven immediately but instead allow it to cool completely, about 20 minutes, before baking. Conversely, if you'd like a more solid filling, bake immediately and for 10 minutes longer.

*Clockwise From Upper Right:* **TIRAMISOTTO, CARAMEL-COCONUT SLICES, PECAN BUTTERCRUNCH TART**

# TIRAMISOTTO
## *Coffee Caramel Tart:*
# THE ANTI-TIRAMISU

*This is a riff on the ubiquitous Italian dessert in flavor only.* If you're the least bit Italian, this recipe is going to give you major agita, because it's really a poke in the eye to that light and airy decadence that's aptly named *tiramisu*, or "pull me up." This iteration is made with a slip of cream and a pound of buttery chew. Hence, I have named this delight *tiramisotto*. Translation: "pull me under." The top layer of satiny mascarpone speckled with cocoa powder hints at this dessert's light and airy influence. But cut into it and it's dark and dense, it's chewy and crunchy, and it'll pull you under its lovely spell.

|||||||||||||||||||||||||||||||||||||||||||||||||||| *Makes 2 (8-inch/20-cm) tarts* ||||||||||||||||||||||||||||||||||||||||||||

| FOR THE SHORTBREAD | | |
|---|---|---|
| Shortbread for Pecan Buttercrunch Tart (page 89) | 1 batch | |
| finely ground espresso beans | 2 tablespoons | 6 g |
| **FOR THE FILLING** | | |
| heavy cream | 2 cups | 480 ml |
| sugar | 2½ cups | 500 g |
| coffee | ½ cup | 120 ml |
| vanilla bean paste | 2 teaspoons | 10 ml |
| Marsala wine (optional) | 2 tablespoons | 30 ml |
| corn syrup | 2 tablespoons | 30 ml |
| salt | 1 teaspoon | 6 g |
| **FOR THE TOPPING** | | |
| heavy cream | 2 cups | 480 ml |
| mascarpone cheese | ½ cup | 115 g |
| confectioners' sugar | ¼ cup | 25 g |
| instant espresso powder | 1 tablespoon | 3 g |
| **FOR THE ASSEMBLY** | | |
| cocoa powder, for dusting | to taste | |

PROCEDURE FOR THE **SHORTBREAD**

① Prepare the shortbread for the pecan buttercrunch tart, adding the 2 tablespoons (6 g) ground espresso beans to the flour mixture in step 2 of the instructions. Make sure these are fresh, dry beans ground to a very fine powder. Proceed with the remaining instructions for the shortbread.

PROCEDURE FOR THE **FILLING**

① Preheat the oven to 375°F (190°C).

② In a very large saucepan over medium-high heat, combine the cream, sugar, coffee, vanilla, Marsala, corn syrup, and salt and stir until the mixture reaches a boil. Clip on a candy thermometer and stop stirring. Continue cooking until the mixture has reached 235°F (113°C).

③ Carefully pour the mixture evenly into the two cooled shortbread-lined tart pans.

④ Bake for 20 minutes, or until the filling bubbles.

① Place all the topping ingredients in the bowl of an electric mixer fitted with the whisk attachment and beat until stiff peaks form. I know you know to be careful not to overbeat the cream. But did you know that if your soft and silky cream becomes chunky and buttery, you can turn back time and salvage your topping? Just pour in ¼ cup (60 ml) heavy cream and start whipping again. If you haven't gone completely over the edge, the cream will return to the state just before it starts to peak perfectly. You're welcome!

① Once the tarts have cooled completely, you can just dollop the whipped mascarpone onto the tarts and call it a day. However, I like to get a pastry bag and a large open star pastry tip and pipe lovely, uniform peaks of pillowy cream in very concentric circles over the entire surface of the tarts.

② Using a fine sieve as a dispenser, gently dust the cream-topped tart with cocoa powder. Cut into wedges and serve.

# CARAMEL-COCONUT
# SLICES

*For many years, I resented coconut.* I first got culinary attention for my French *almond* macarons before they became all the rage in the States. These are confections that contain not a shred of the tropical white stuff. But my pastry celebrity opened the door to everyone who didn't know what the hell a macaron was to say to me, "So I hear you make a pretty mean coconut macaroon!" Argh!

And then came a request at my pastry shop: "Please make me a coconut layer cake." I could have said no. But the challenge of making something edible from an ingredient I had long ago disinherited lured me in. And what did I say when I tried the coconut layer cake I created despite my lifelong boycott? "Not bad. Not bad at all."

This led me down the wonderfully slippery slope of meddling in coconut even outside of layer cakes. And what I found is that I secretly loved it, especially toasted and most especially when it's toasted and nestling up against some salty caramel—and a drizzle of chocolate, if you're feeling extra naughty.

|||||||||||||||||||||||||||||||||||||| *Makes approximately 2 dozen generous slices* ||||||||||||||||||||||||||||||||||||||

| FOR THE SHORTBREAD | | |
|---|---|---|
| Shortbread for Pecan Buttercrunch Tart (page 89) | Double batch | |
| toasted shredded sweetened coconut | 1 cup | 70 g |
| FOR THE CARAMEL | | |
| sugar | 1½ cups | 300 g |
| coconut water (or plain water) | ⅓ cup | 75 ml |
| heavy cream | 1 cup | 240 ml |
| unsalted butter | ½ cup | 115 g |
| vanilla bean paste | 1 teaspoon | 5 ml |
| salt | 1 teaspoon | 6 g |
| toasted shredded sweetened coconut | 1 cup | 70 g |

PROCEDURE FOR THE **SHORTBREAD**

① Prepare a double batch of the shortbread for the pecan buttercrunch tart, adding the 1 cup (70 g) toasted shredded sweetened coconut to the mixture in step 2 of the instructions. In step 3, press the shortbread in a flat and even layer into a rimmed half sheet pan (18 x 13 in./46 x 33 cm) with sides that are high enough so the shortbread doesn't reach higher than halfway up—you've got to save room for that caramel. Bake for 30 minutes or until the shortbread just starts to brown.

PROCEDURE FOR THE **CARAMEL**

① Preheat the oven to 375°F (190°C).

2. In a heavy saucepan over medium heat, combine the sugar and coconut water, making sure that the sugar is evenly dampened by the water, and cook, swirling the pan occasionally to avoid clumping, until the sugar has melted completely.

3. Wash down the sides of the pan with a damp pastry brush to remove any rogue crystals, attach a candy thermometer, raise the heat to medium-high, and cook to 235°F (113°C).

4. Remove the pan from the heat, carefully pour in the cream, and quickly step back. The caramel can bubble like an angry volcano. Once the bubbling has subsided, return the caramel to the heat and stir until any bits of hardened caramel have dissolved. Return the caramel to a vigorous boil—it should reach about 218°F (103°C) on the candy thermometer.

5. Remove the pan from the heat and stir in the butter, vanilla paste, coconut, and salt.

6. Immediately pour the caramel evenly over the shortbread crust.

7. Bake for 20 minutes, until the filling is uniformly bubbling.

8. Remove from the oven and allow to cool completely. Cut into wedges and serve.

**Option!**

If you're inclined, gently melt some bittersweet chocolate in the microwave, in 30-second bursts, stirring between sessions so you don't burn it. When the chocolate is completely melted, drizzle it over the caramel once the pan is removed from the oven. Allow the chocolate to harden completely; cut into wedges and serve.

I'm not known to be particularly sweet, aside from my obvious addiction—when someone questioned why they had to use unsalted butter in my recipes, I answered, "Because I said so!" Charming.

But there's a method to my madness.

First, I want control over the seasoning of my food. I don't need an anonymous manufacturer adding a random quantity of sodium to my recipes.

Second, salt is a preservative. Grocery stores keep butter containing salt on the shelves far longer than the unsalted . . . because they can. And that often leads to what we professionals refer to as "extreme butter funk." I jest.

But you'll notice there is a distinct taste and aftertaste to anything made with salted butter. I've found that one stick of salted butter can ruin a perfectly good chocolate chip cookie. That's reason enough to ban the stuff outright.

# SO REMEMBER, NO SALTED BUTTER. UNLESS YOU LIKE THE FUNK.

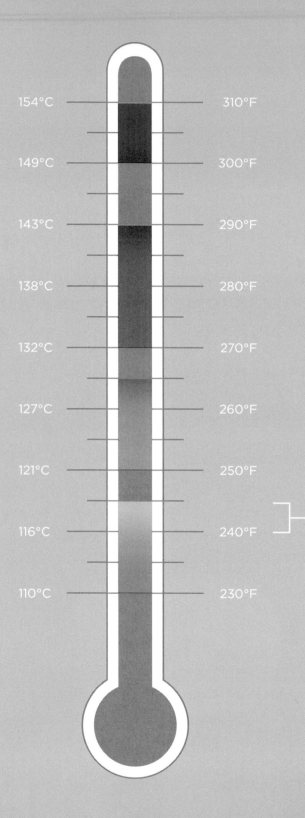

| 154°C | | 310°F |
| 149°C | | 300°F |
| 143°C | | 290°F |
| 138°C | | 280°F |
| 132°C | | 270°F |
| 127°C | | 260°F |
| 121°C | | 250°F |
| 116°C | | 240°F |
| 110°C | | 230°F |

Gesine's Fruit Gummis....98

Coffee Butter Rum Caramels....102

Chocolate–Sea Salt Caramels....104

Chinese Ginger-and-Lime Milk Candy....106

Fruity *Schwester* Taffy....109

Dark Chocolate Taffy....112

Don't Harsh My Mallow: The Guimauve....115

Soft Honey Nougat....120

# FIRM-BALL STAGE

*245°F–250°F (118°C–121°C)    Sugar Concentration: 87%*

Drop sugar in cold water and it will form a firm ball that won't flatten when you take it out but is still malleable.

It's at this temperature that sugar begins to develop a chew and can hold its own as a confectionery component. It's also at this phase that cleanup starts becoming a bear. Loose droplets of hot firm-ball sugar are permanent fixtures on countertops unless you pry them off. Your saucepan will need a good long soak and scrub before you can use it again. But I regard this extra drudgery as a badge of honor. I've gone toe to toe with sugar and I've transformed it from a mere granule into a gloriously gooey treat. That sticky residue on my work table is proof of my sweet powers.

# GESINE'S
# FRUIT GUMMIS

*It's German-made gummi bears that I adore to this day, almost as much as I did as a kid.* Even though I was almost murdered by them. That's how much they mean to me.

One summer when I was eleven, a bunch of families from the southern Bavarian town of Bergen hopped on a plush motorbus and headed to northern Italy for a week-long vacation that the rest of the world knows as Germans on the beach in black socks and sandals. I'd packed *gummi bärchen* for the trip, not trusting the Italians would have anything decent to eat. I slept soundly on the bus, secure in the knowledge of having brought ample foodstuffs for our journey; my head was thrown carelessly back, my mouth hanging temptingly open. I awoke choking, unable to close my mouth. It was full of gummis.

My older sister and my cousin Barbara could very well have killed me. Gummis, when exposed to moisture, increase in volume. I'm known to drool liberally, both when sleeping and when contemplating candy; my oral cavern proved to be a hotbed for gummi expansion. I was well on my way to being exterminated by my most beloved confection. The obituary would have read, "Gesine Vanessa Bullock, beloved daughter and tortured little sister, found asphyxiated by morbidly obese ursine gelatins en route to wearing black socks on the beach." I suppose there are worse ways to go.

This adventure notwithstanding, I still eat gummis. I even make them, but I've grown up (a little) and I now prefer flavors that aren't usually found in a grocery assortment of worms and bears.

These gummis can be made in two ways: (1) with the inclusion of gelatin, which produces a "gummier" gummi, closer to the texture of the store-bought stuff or (2) without the gelatin, which produces a very French sugared fruit candy similar in texture to a very thick jelly.

| | | |
|---|---|---|
| powdered Pomona fruit pectin | 2 tablespoons | 14 g |
| sugar | 3 cups, divided, plus extra for coating | 600 g, divided, plus extra for coating |
| cassis (black currant) or passion fruit purée | 1 ¾ cups | 420 ml |
| water | 2 cups, divided | 480 ml, divided |
| baking soda | ½ teaspoon | 2.5 g |
| salt | pinch | |
| corn syrup | ¼ cup | 60 ml |
| citric acid (optional) | 1 teaspoon, plus extra for coating | 5 ml, plus extra for coating |

**I use frozen purées from Boiron; you can feel free to use other purées, and it's also quite easy to make your own.** For an incredibly quick berry purée, in a heavy saucepan over medium heat, combine ½ cup (100 g) sugar with two 12-ounce bags frozen berries. Warm the ingredients until the berries have defrosted and broken down and the sugar has melted. Transfer the mixture to a food processor fitted with a blade attachment and purée until the mixture is smooth. I pour this all through a fine sieve to get rid of any little seeds.

① Coat a 9-inch (23-cm) square pan lined with parchment or a silicone gelée mold, if you have one, with nonstick spray and set aside.

✸ **A Note from the Sugar Baby:** You'll notice that I use a fancy mold for my gummis. Personally, I love making something really easy and using a piece of equipment to make it look fabulously intricate. The molds I use for gummis are silicone and you can buy all sorts of shapes. Some of them are pricey; that's the only problem. But keep your eyes peeled for silicone molds in the housewares sections of discount stores; you'll be surprised at the bargains you can find.

② In a small bowl, whisk together the pectin and ¼ cup (50 g) of the sugar. (Pectin clumps if you don't cut it with sugar before adding it to liquids.)

③ In a large saucepan over medium-low heat, combine the purée, 1 cup (240 ml) of the water, the pectin mixture, baking soda, and salt and bring to a boil. The mixture will foam from the baking soda, so stir until the foaming subsides. Only let this boil for about 3 minutes. Remove the pan from the heat until the sugar syrup is ready.

④ At the same time, in a second large saucepan over medium heat, combine the remaining 2¾ cups (550 g) sugar, the remaining 1 cup (240 ml) water, and the corn syrup. Cook, stirring occasionally, until the mixture loosens and becomes fluid and the sugar has melted completely.

⑤ Raise the heat to medium-high. When the sugar mixture comes to a boil and registers 250°F (121°C) on a candy thermometer, turn the heat off and allow the sugar mixture's temperature to reduce to 200°F (93°C). Add the purée mixture and bring the mixture back to a boil. Boil for 1 minute.

6. Remove the pan from the heat, pour the mixture into a heatproof pitcher with a spout, and stir in the citric acid, if using.

✴ **A Note from the Sugar Baby:** Pectin is a naturally occurring "setting agent" found in fruits. I add commercial pectin to my gummi candy but it can be a little fussy. Be careful not to heat it much above 225°F (107°C); otherwise it can break down and your gummis will be runny. And don't use liquid pectin; I've found it to be unreliable for getting the gummis to set. I use Pomona brand because it's rather forgiving in terms of the amount of sugar you use, so you can use many types of fruit puree that differ in natural sugar content and still get a consistent gummi.

7. Immediately pour the mixture into your prepared pan or silicone molds. Let stand at room temperature until set, at least 3 hours and preferably overnight. Don't refrigerate.

8. Sprinkle sugar onto a piece of waxed paper the size of your pan or mold; invert the pan or mold onto the sugar. If using a pan, with a knife dipped in warm water, cut the candy into 1-inch (2.5-cm) squares; roll the gummis in additional sugar and citric acid (if using).

9. Place the gummis on a wire rack to cool. Let stand, uncovered, at room temperature overnight. Store in an airtight container in a cool, dry place for up to a week.

With Gesine's Fruit Gummis

Make G's Gelée Shots, page 28

# Coffee
# BUTTER RUM
## CARAMELS

*Rum makes a festive addition to caramel, coffee gives it a little oomph along the way, and turbinado sugar and vanilla bean round out the island influences.*

*Makes approximately 1 pound (455 g) or 60 caramels*

| | | |
|---|---|---|
| turbinado sugar | 1 ¾ cups | 350 g |
| corn syrup | ¼ cup | 60 ml |
| heavy cream | 1 cup | 240 ml |
| unsalted butter | ¼ cup | 55 g |
| salt | ½ teaspoon | 3 g |
| strong coffee | 2 tablespoons | 30 ml |
| dark rum | 2 tablespoons | 30 ml |
| vanilla pod, seeds scraped from the inside | 1 | |

① In a heavy saucepan over low heat, combine all the ingredients, stirring until the sugar has completely dissolved.

② Clip on a candy thermometer, stop stirring, and heat the mixture to 250°F (121°C).

③ Immediately pour the caramel into a parchment-lined quarter sheet pan (9 x 13 in./23 x 33 cm) or a silicone mold coated with nonstick spray. Allow to cool completely in a cool, dry space.

④ If using a mold, invert the mold onto a piece of parchment paper and gently release the caramels. If using a pan, cut the caramels with a very sharp knife sprayed with nonstick spray. Wrap the candies in pieces of wax paper. Store in an airtight container in a cool, dry place for up to a week.

## A Note from the Sugar Baby:

I'm not one to go for normal shapes and sizes when I make individual candies and caramels. I always keep my eyes peeled at the strangest places for possible molds for my confections. To wit, I found five fantastic silicone molds at a stationery store in Hanover, New Hampshire. This particular shop had a host of novelty items, many geared toward cocktail hour. I noticed this and started my hunt, because I knew they'd have some zany silicone ice-cube trays that I would use totally inappropriately for hot sugar work. That day I got my skull mold, my square lolli mold, a swizzle-stick mold, a coffee-bean mold, and some frightening tiki statue molds.

Not all silicone is meant for high heat. For instance, the skull molds started to melt just a bit, giving the skulls a free-form appearance. But hell, a skull isn't meant to be perfect—the more grotesque the better. In general, keep your eyes peeled for thicker-walled silicone if you'd like to follow my lead. Make sure to spray the mold with nonstick baking spray, allow the candy to cool completely, and wrestle the goodies from the mold without getting your

fingerprints all over the shiny confection. If you use a mold for caramel and find that the candy isn't firm enough to extract from the mold without mangling the shape, freeze the caramel in the mold until it firms up.

If you use a sheet pan or a large casserole dish, just be aware that the caramel will probably not fill up the entire pan and will be uneven in places.

Keep your mind open when you're making candy. I use a very traditional nonstick madeleine mold for my chocolate–sea salt caramels because they look like beautiful shells. I use heart-shaped baking molds for fudge. If you want to explore silicone mold options (and other fantastic kitchen supplies), there are wonderful retailers who supply professional chefs but also sell to the public, such as JB Prince (www.jbprince.com) and Pastry Chef Central (www.pastrychef.com). Other fantastic sites are Kerekes (www.bakedeco.com), N.Y. Cake (www.nycake.com), and Fancy Flours (www.fancyflours.com).

# CHOCOLATE—
*Sea Salt*
# CARAMELS

*Caramel. Chocolate. Salt.* Three of my favorite things, and they go so well together. And did I mention they were chewy?!? Personally, I like to make a sheet pan of shortbread, let it cool, and then pour the caramel over it when it's still warm but not *too* warm—because what's better for some buttery, salty caramel than combining it with some buttery, salty shortbread?

||||||||||| *Makes approximately 2 pounds 4 ounces (1 kg) or 26 madeleine-shaped caramels* |||||||||||

| | | |
|---|---|---|
| bittersweet chocolate, finely chopped | 12 ounces | 360 g |
| heavy cream | 2 cups | 480 ml |
| turbinado sugar | 2 cups | 400 g |
| corn syrup | ½ cup | 120 ml |
| unsalted butter | ¼ cup | 55 g |
| coffee | ¼ cup | 60 ml |
| salt | ½ teaspoon | 3 g |
| large flake sea salt, for sprinkling on top | to taste | |

① Place the chocolate in a bowl.

② In a microwave-safe container, preferably with a spout, microwave the cream until it's bubbling. Pour it over the chocolate and allow it to sit undisturbed for 5 minutes.

③ Whisk until the chocolate is completely melted and fully combined with the cream. Set aside.

④ In a large, heavy saucepan over low heat, combine the remaining ingredients and heat, stirring with a wooden spoon, until the sugar is completely dissolved. Add the chocolate mixture—carefully, the cream will make it bubble—and raise the heat to medium-high. Clip on a candy thermometer and stop stirring. Heat to 250°F (121°C).

⑤ Immediately pour the mixture into 26 madeleine cavities sprayed with nonstick cooking spray or into a sheet pan lined with parchment and sprayed with nonstick spray.

⑥ Allow the caramels to cool completely. Cut the caramels with a very sharp knife sprayed with nonstick spray or gently unmold them onto a piece of parchment paper. Wrap individually in wax or parchment paper. Store in an airtight container in a cool, dry place for up to a week.

## *A Note from the Sugar Baby:*

Now that we've gotten through a few caramel recipes, let's discuss the two traditional methods of making the stuff. The first is the wet method. That's what I use almost exclusively. Why? Because the second type, the dry method, was created for the sole purpose of making you cry.

OK, it's got some good things going for it. The dry method is just as it sounds; it requires only sugar and no added water. It also doesn't require an interfering agent—it's the presence of water that leads to that pesky crystallization, because it invites the errant crystals to jump around and seed rebellion. It's also faster, since there's no added moisture to burn away. Here's the problem: It's incredibly fast, and this is where the crying comes in. You'll often see that at the very epicenter of the sugar, the sugar will start to brown rapidly while the perimeter remains unsullied. It's the Eye of Sauron of the sugar world. If you're not all over it, the sugar burns instantaneously and in just one spot. So on low heat you have to shake, shimmy, and stir the sugar (with a wooden spoon) until it is evenly melted; then you stop stirring and let the heat do the rest, until the caramel attains all of its amber splendor. Don't expect to control the hue as you would caramel with the wet method, because it's much harder to get the lighter amber hues from the dry method; the color usually just skips from medium to dark amber and then rapidly to burnt. But hey, if you've got a few minutes to hang around staring at a pot with sugar, why not give it a whirl?

# CHINESE
## *Ginger-and-Lime*
# MILK CANDY

*Milk candy is chewy like a caramel but has a light flavor that is lovely and refreshing.* I add ginger and lime to boost the already happy flavors of milk candy to the next level. Feel free to experiment by adding lively extracts like orange or lemon or lavender—this is a candy made to take on flavor, since it has such a mild, sweet base at its heart.

*Makes approximately 100 pieces*

| | | |
|---|---|---|
| sugar | 2 cups | 400 g |
| corn syrup | 1 cup | 240 ml |
| evaporated milk | 1 cup | 240 ml |
| unsalted butter | 2 tablespoons | 28 g |
| cornstarch | 1 teaspoon | 2.5 g |
| glycerin | ½ teaspoon | 2.5 ml |
| salt | ½ teaspoon | 3 g |
| lime oil | 1 teaspoon | 5 ml |
| zest of 1 lime | | |
| 1 small nub of peeled, fresh ginger, grated | | |

**Milk, evaporated milk, condensed milk.** All three are milk, but they aren't the same. Evaporated milk has had about 60 percent of the moisture removed from whole milk. Condensed milk also has had about 60 percent of the moisture removed but contains added sugar (condensed milk is approximately 45 percent sugar).

① Spray the back of a sheet pan with nonstick spray and set aside—unless you have a marble slab, in which case, spray that instead!

② In a heavy saucepan over low heat, combine the sugar, corn syrup, evaporated milk, butter, cornstarch, glycerin, and salt. Stir until the sugar is completely dissolved.

③ Raise the heat to medium-high, clip on a candy thermometer, and stop stirring! I always mean it when I say stop stirring, but I *really* mean it this time. The milk tends to brown on the bottom and the sides of the pan, and if you stir it up, you'll have bits of burnt milk in your candy. Heat until the temperature reaches 250°F (121°C). The mixture will have a light caramel color.

④ Immediately pour the candy mixture onto the prepared sheet pan, remembering not to scrape the bottom of the saucepan as you pour. With a spatula sprayed with nonstick spray, catch the molten candy as it's about to run off the sheet pan and fold it toward the middle. Keep doing this on all sides until the candy starts to keep its shape but is still very warm (too warm to handle).

(5) When the candy becomes cool enough to handle, pour on the lime oil and place the lime zest and ginger at the center of the candy and continue to fold the ends toward the center so that the oil, lime zest, and ginger become incorporated.

✱ A Note from the Sugar Baby: Be careful not to add flavorings such as zests or extracts when the sugar syrup is too hot; they are likely to burn even if you have already poured the sugar out of the hot pot and onto a cool slab. If the sugar is still molten, flavoring substances aren't very heat stable and will burn.

(6) Spray your hands with nonstick spray. Start pulling the candy and then bring the ends together to fold the candy. Grab both ends again, pull, and bring the ends together, folding the candy rope in half again. Continue pulling and folding, pulling and folding, until the candy is too hard to pull anymore and becomes light and opaque.

(7) On a work surface, stretch the candy into a long rope, about ½ inch (12 mm) in diameter. Spray a pair of scissors with nonstick spray and cut ½-inch (12-mm) pieces from the rope, working quickly before the candy cools completely.

(8) Immediately wrap the candy in pieces of wax paper. Store in an airtight container in a cool, dry place for up to a week.

Option!
The lime zest and ginger will give the candy texture; if you like the idea of the flavors but want to keep your candy smooth, instead add the lime oil and a touch of ginger extract, about ¼ teaspoon (1 ml). Ginger extract is incredibly pungent and you need just a little to impart big flavor.

*Clockwise From Upper Right:* **FRUITY** *SCHWESTER* **TAFFY, COFFEE BUTTER RUM CARAMELS, CHOCOLATE SEA SALT CARAMELS**

# FRUITY
## *Schwester*
# TAFFY

*When I was eleven, we spent the entire summer in Germany.* During those few months, I sharpened my focus on one endeavor: getting my prepubescent paws on as much German confectionery product as humanly possible. I had a few things going for me with regards to my particular mission. First, my grandmother Omi liked to give me treats. Second, my aunt, Tante Christel, wasn't entirely opposed to giving me sweets. Third, both my grandmother and aunt were inclined to giving me gifts in the way of crisp, colorful deutsche marks, which led the way to me purchasing my own stash of candy that no one had to know about. And fourth, my sister and I had a singular passion for Maoam, a fruity taffy confection.

This worked in our mutual favor because we differed in our flavor preferences. She liked raspberry. I preferred lemon. We both tolerated orange. And as the taffy was packaged in multipacks containing one of each of the three flavors, we obligingly pooled our money and split the treats without any hint of the acrimony or stinginess that usually accompanies the parceling of treasured goods.

One day, stuck in my grandmother's third-floor Nürnberg walk-up during a summer rainstorm, we took turns bolting through the rain to the corner market to get more taffy. We kept the relay up all day. Later that evening we were found prone on the living room floor, barely visible under a pile of wax-paper wrappers. There was no difficulty identifying who was who, as Sandy was buried under a mound of pink, while my tomb was primarily yellow, with a scant dusting of orange wrappers on both piles. It's a miracle we didn't go into diabetic shock.

They've since added new and improved flavors to the German taffy lineup, but we're still pretty much wedded to our childhood favorites. So in honor of our mutual admiration for those addictive German chews, I give you lemon and raspberry Fruity *Schwester* Taffy, with orange thrown in for good measure.

| water | ½ cup | 120 ml |
|---|---|---|
| cornstarch | 1 tablespoon | 8 g |
| sugar | 2 cups | 400 g |
| corn syrup | 1 cup | 240 ml |
| glycerin (optional) | 1 teaspoon | 5 ml |
| salt | ½ teaspoon | 3 g |
| unsalted butter | 2 tablespoons | 28 g |
| baking soda | ¼ teaspoon | 1 g |
| lemon, raspberry, or orange extract | 1 teaspoon | 5 ml |
| yellow, pink, or orange food coloring (optional) | 2 drops | |
| citric acid (optional) | 1 teaspoon | 5 ml |

**Some advice for those traveling with purchases from fancy restaurant supply stores: Don't pack glycerin in your carry-on.** The TSA inspectors will take one look at the word "glycerin" and you're screwed. I know this from personal experience. It doesn't matter if you explain to them, in friendly and reassuringly mid-Atlantic tones, that what they've found in your bag is not nitro-glycerin, the bomb-making material, but just plain old glycerin, the stuff you use in sugar work to make things like taffy exceptionally smooth and pliable. Because they've already read "glyc-erin," and who the hell would put glycerin in their carry-on? So if you don't have a fancy restaurant or baking supply store in your area and if you don't feel like ordering it online, don't go out of your way to get glycerin for this recipe. It tastes great without it. And you really don't want glycerin in your carry-on.

① In a bowl, combine the water and cornstarch and stir until the cornstarch has completely dissolved into the water and it resembles milk.

② Pour the mixture into a heavy saucepan along with the sugar, corn syrup, glycerin, salt, and butter. Stir with a wooden spoon over medium heat until the sugar is completely melted.

③ Attach a candy thermometer, stop stirring, and raise the heat to medium-high. Cook until the temperature reads 250°F (121°C).

④ Remove the pan from the heat and immediately stir in the baking soda.

⑤ Pour the sugar mixture onto a prepared surface (the back of a sheet pan, a marble slab, or a silicone baking mat) sprayed with nonstick spray.

⑥ Using a bench scraper or two spatulas, also sprayed with nonstick spray, immediately start folding the outer edges of the sugar syrup into the middle. (The syrup is runny when it's first poured out and you'll naturally want to catch it to stop it from dripping onto the floor.) Keep putting the scraper underneath the outer edges of the syrup and folding it over. It will start to cool and thicken after a few turns.

⑦ When the syrup is no longer runny, add the extract along with the coloring and citric acid (if using) and start the folding process again, occasionally spraying your work surface and your bench scraper with cooking spray to prevent sticking.

⑧ Once the taffy is cool enough to handle, spray your hands with nonstick spray—or put on some latex gloves and spray them, too—and start pulling the taffy. Pull and bring the ends together. Pull and bring the ends back together. Keep pulling until the taffy is almost impossible to pull anymore and it starts to lighten in color. The pulling aerates the candy, making it more pliable and chewy. It's also a phenomenal workout.

⑨ Place the pulled taffy on a sprayed work surface. Pull one end and start to gently twist until the diameter is about ½ inch (12 mm) thick. Using scissors (yes, spray the scissors with nonstick spray), cut the taffy into 1-inch (2.5-cm) pieces, placing them onto a piece of wax paper.

⑩ Wrap your finished pieces in wax paper. Store in an airtight container in a cool, dry place for up to a week. Don't eat them all at once.

# DARK
## *Chocolate*
# TAFFY

*This is the candy I end up shoving into my mouth multiple pieces at a time, ending up with drool pouring liberally out of my mouth and contracting lockjaw when I try to chew all those pieces together.* This particular taffy has the added advantage of having a deliciously dark chocolate base that makes this otherwise childish candy utterly and satisfyingly adult.

IIIIIIIIIIIIIIIIIIIIIIIIIIIIIIIIIIIIIIIIIIIIIIIII *Makes approximately 100 pieces* IIIIIIIIIIIIIIIIIIIIIIIIIIIIIIIIIIIIIIIIIIIIIIIII

| | | |
|---|---|---|
| sugar | 2 cups | 400 g |
| cocoa powder | ½ cup | 40 g |
| corn syrup | 1 cup | 240 ml |
| cornstarch | 1 teaspoon | 2.5 g |
| salt | ½ teaspoon | 3 g |
| unsalted butter | 2 tablespoons | 28 g |
| baking soda | ¼ teaspoon | 1 g |
| espresso powder | 1 teaspoon | 1 g |
| coffee | ½ cup | 120 ml |

① In a heavy saucepan, whisk the sugar and cocoa until they are well combined.

② Add the remaining ingredients and stir over low heat until all the ingredients are combined and the sugar is completely melted.

③ Clip on a candy thermometer, raise the heat to medium-high, and stop stirring! Heat to 250°F (121°C).

④ Immediately pour the hot taffy onto a prepared surface (the back of a sheet pan, a marble slab, or a silicone baking mat) sprayed with nonstick spray.

⑤ Using a bench scraper or two spatulas also sprayed with nonstick spray, catch the ends of the moving hot taffy and fold the ends of the taffy towards the middle. Continue doing this until the taffy is cool enough to handle.

⑥ Spray your hands (or your latex-gloved hands) with nonstick spray and start pulling the taffy, bringing the ends together and folding the taffy in half. Keep pulling and folding until it's impossible to pull the taffy anymore and it starts to lighten in color.

✳ **A Note from the Sugar Baby:** Yes, you have to pull and pull and pull. Why? Pulling aerates the confection, giving it a pliability that you'll really appreciate once you start chewing. So don't think you can get away with no pulling, or just a little pulling. Believe me, I'll know if you've skimped on pulling the taffy because it will call me up the second your back is turned and rat on you. Now get back to pulling.

⑦ On a sprayed work surface, pull the taffy into a long rope about ½ inch (12 mm) in diameter. Using scissors (also sprayed with nonstick spray), cut the taffy into ½-inch (12-mm) pieces. Wrap immediately in pieces of wax paper. Store in an airtight container in a cool, dry place for up to a week.

*"Hey, have you ever had a pot of caramel crystallize on you?"* This is what the nice lady asked as I was standing over a vat of hot sugar. I was waiting for it to turn amber so I could pour in some cream and make a caramel filling. The poor woman was just being gregarious. She'd stopped by my bakery to see how orders were coming in from her gourmet provisions business. And I answered her honestly, "Nope. Never." But I should have taken out the "never," because not two minutes after she left, I looked in my pot and saw not caramel, but what appeared to be Superman's Fortress of Solitude writ small: tiny stalactites of crystal taking shape in my beautiful saucepan. In all my years of working with sugar and hearing about the horrors of crystallization, I'd never witnessed it firsthand. Had I not needed caramel or the pan, I'd have really enjoyed the transformation. I'd have pulled someone in to witness it, like a magic trick: "Hey Bernie, check this out. Ta da!" But when you're working with sugar in earnest, crystallization is a nightmare.

Here's the deal. Sugar is made of crystals. We all know that. When you heat sugar, it breaks down into smaller crystals, and as far as we know it's gone. Melted. Never to be seen again—only to be tasted. But what sugar really wants is to return to its physical form, to be whole again. All it takes is one tiny outside crystal to make this happen. You'll notice while you're heating your sugar that there'll be a rim of granules hanging out on the edge of the pan, just above the melting sugar line. Those are the rogue crystals waiting to jump into the sauce and start a rebellion.

There are a few ways to stop the insurgence. First, have a cup of water and a pastry brush on hand. As you start the heating process, dip the pastry brush in water and brush around the sides of the pan. This sends the errant crystals into the drink so they can melt along with everyone else. Stop brushing once the crystals have melted. You can also put a lid on the pan, trapping the moisture on the underside of the lid and creating an automatic granule eradicator. The problem I find with this common-sense method is that once I put a lid on it, I forget it. And it's difficult to slip on a thermometer *and* put on a lid, so there's no little warning flag protruding out of nowhere, catching your attention when you see it out of the corner of your eye. Which is to say, I also forget sugar that's on the stove *without* a lid, but at some point I'll wonder, "What the hell is poking up out of the pot on the stove? Oh crap! The sugar!"

The other trick is to introduce an "interfering agent." Acids and fats are interfering agents, which is just a fabulous way of saying they impede the re-formation of crystals. When I'm making a clear caramel, for instance, and want a transparent coating to the outside of a cream puff, I use a squirt of lemon juice (an acid) to calm any threat of crystallization. When I'm making a chewy caramel, I boil cream (a fat) with the sugar and turn out luxurious chews without fear of sugar ruin. Yet another way to stop premature crystallization is to add another type of sugar, like fructose or glucose. These sugars get in the way, molecularly speaking. This is why you'll see corn syrup in recipes. It's the hardest-working interfering agent on the block. Give it a break. So if I keep repeating myself in every recipe, "Brush down the sides of the pot with a wet pastry brush, blah blah blah," or if you get your knickers in a twist whenever you read the words "corn" and "syrup," remember I'm just guiding you to a sweeter and happier relationship with sugar work. I speak from experience.

WHEN YOU'RE *working with* SUGAR IN EARNEST, CRYSTALLIZATION IS A NIGHTMARE.

# DON'T HARSH MY MALLOW:
# THE GUIMAUVE

*I don't know what I looked forward to more during our overnight trips to the woodsy Arlington Outdoor Lab in elementary school: the star-gazing in close proximity to my fifth-grade crush, or the chance to lay my grubby paws on some Jet-Puffed goodness.* Chances are the marshmallows edged out the boy by a hair, because while a declaration of love from the blue-eyed, freckled scamp a foot shorter than me would have been very welcome, a close encounter with a pillow of sugary goodness impaled on a stick and set partially ablaze in a bonfire was as close to heaven as a knock-kneed nine-year-old girl could hope to get. Squish that charcoaled cylinder of white mush between a graham cracker and a slab of chocolate and you've just dialed Nirvana.

Marshmallows can be found in the culinary card catalogue filed under "other." It's not candy, it's not cookie, it's not cake. Perhaps the history of this lush little cushion can shed some light. Follow me to Egypt and her marshes where, swaying in the breeze, are—you guessed it—mallows. It's a shrub, really. And to keep it official, her proper name is *Althaea officinalis.* Her roots produce a grotesquely named substance called "mucilage" that, when mixed with water, produces a gel used to soothe sore throats. Modern marshmallows contain neither marsh nor mallow; instead, gelatin is used to produce the soft spongy treat we have come to know and love. And while that medicinal mucilage isn't present in the modern incarnation, I'd argue that soothing is just what the new-fangled concoctions do. They create a delightfully crispy and gooey treat. They transform a raging campfire into a welcoming hearth. They melt in hot chocolate, leaving a sumptuous cloud to accompany each steaming sip. In short, they'll never harsh your mellow.

I prefer to eat marshmallows straight—no roasting, no melting, no chocolate dipping. I also prefer to use their French name, *guimauve.* It takes away any guilt involved in eating fluffy sugar and elevates what could have been an infantile culinary regression into a *moment gastronome.* If you happen upon *guimauve* in France, you may not recognize your fireside friend right away. Often, it's cut into fabulously long strips, wound inside an apothecary jar, and sold by the meter. I also take another cue from the French when I make marshmallows. I use egg whites. Now, most recipes don't call for egg whites and many French recipes leave them out entirely. But I've found they enhance the flavor of this plush sugar bomb immeasurably. If egg whites make you squeamish, by all means leave them out; this recipe will still work. But if you've got the guts of an adventurer, I urge you to add them to the sticky mix.

| | | |
|---|---|---|
| unflavored gelatin | 3 tablespoons | 20 g |
| water | ⅓ cup | 75 ml |
| sugar | 2 cups | 400 g |
| corn syrup | ½ cup | 120 ml |
| hot water | ½ cup | 120 ml |
| egg whites (optional) | 2 | |
| salt | ½ teaspoon | 3 g |
| vanilla bean paste | 1 teaspoon | 5 ml |

① In the bowl of an electric stand mixer fitted with the whisk attachment, add the gelatin and pour the ⅓ cup (75 ml) water over it. Let it rest there on the mixer stand until the sugar syrup is ready. Make sure the gelatin is completely saturated with water before you add your sugar syrup. Also make sure that the whisk attachment is already in place, because once the syrup gets to temperature, you won't have time to do this without burning the hell out of yourself.

② In a heavy saucepan over medium-low heat, combine the sugar, corn syrup, and hot water. Melt the mixture until the sugar has completely dissolved. Raise the heat to medium-high and allow the mixture to boil. With a damp pastry brush, wipe down the sides of the pan to prevent stray sugar crystals from forming. Clip on a candy thermometer and heat to 250°F (121°C).

③ At the same time you're heating the sugar syrup, beat the egg whites with the salt until they hold a stiff peak. I know you've got the gelatin in your mixing bowl. What I do is beat the whites by hand in a copper bowl with a whisk. If you don't have a copper bowl, use a perfectly clean stainless-steel bowl. Make sure it's clean because any trace amount of fat will deflate those puppies so fast you'll be cursing my name. *Never* use a plastic bowl. Plastic will create the same chemical reaction as fat residue. Set the egg whites aside.

④ Bring the hot sugar mixture to the bowl of the stand mixer. Set the mixer speed to medium-low and slowly add the hot sugar mixture, gently pouring it down the side of the bowl to avoid both splashing and scorching the gelatin. (If you heat gelatin at too high a temperature, it loses its efficacy.)

⑤ Raise the mixer speed to high and beat until the mixture has started to stiffen and has doubled in volume. Add the egg whites, if using, the salt, and the vanilla paste. Mix until light, white, and fluffy. At this point, you've got options:

Options!

OPTION 1: **PLAIN JANE**
Cover a sheet pan with aluminum foil and sprinkle the foil with ½ cup (65 g) cornstarch, making sure to cover every centimeter. Spray a plastic spatula with nonstick spray and scoop the entire marshmallow mixture onto the sheet pan. Using an offset spatula, also sprayed with nonstick spray, smooth the marshmallow out into an even layer. Work fast—this stuff tightens up quickly. Let the marshmallow dry for at least 4 hours or overnight. Using a very sharp knife, a pizza cutter, or scissors—each should be sprayed with nonstick spray—cut the marshmallow into bite-sized pieces. Dredge each piece in cornstarch, making sure each cut edge is covered; otherwise the pieces will stick to anything and everything. You can also use a sharp cookie cutter to

make adorable shapes. Just make sure to spray with the nonstick spray and dredge in cornstarch.

Store in an airtight container for up to 2 weeks. (Marshmallows without egg whites can last quite a bit longer. Months. Hell, maybe even years.)

### OPTION 2: CURVY

My preference is to pipe marshmallows into pleasing little mounds using a pastry bag fitted with a large star tip. As in Option 1, cover a sheet pan with aluminum and dust evenly with cornstarch. But instead of just plopping the stuff down willynilly, you can pipe shapely shapes instead. If you're inclined, you can use an extra-small pastry brush to brush a few drops of food coloring along the inside of the pastry bag. For instance, during the holidays I'll paint two red stripes inside the bag to create a squishy candy cane design. Festive! Make sure you dredge the piped pieces thoroughly in cornstarch, as in Option 1.

### OPTION 3: PEEPS

I love Peeps. They are crispy clouds of happiness. Instead of the cornstarch in Option 1, spread 2 cups (400 g) sugar in a nice, even layer over the aluminum foil. Make shapes by piping the marshmallow mixture through a pastry bag fitted with a large, plain, round tip. As you are making the marshmallow recipe, you can add a few drops of food coloring to make your Peeps pink or yellow or blue. And don't limit yourself to the traditional forms. Pipe hearts and snowmen! It's easy, messy, and fun. If you take a look at a professional Peep, you realize that they really aren't that intricately piped anyway. Paint a nose and some eyes with a little brown food coloring, and you've got yourself a happy snack. Make sure you sprinkle sugar on top, before they have set, and over the entire surface of your critter to prevent stickiness.

### OPTION 4: FLAVORS

As you're making the marshmallow recipe, you can always add 1 teaspoon (5 ml) of extract to the mixture without affecting the final product. Almond, lemon, orange, cherry, coconut, peppermint—there are a host of extracts that impart big flavor with just a small amount. But you can work flavor into the marshmallows for even bigger impact by changing up the process. Experiment with flavors and add-ins to make gourmet marshmallows with your personal flavor stamp.

For raspberry marshmallow, replace the initial ⅓ cup (75 ml) water with ¼ cup (60 ml) raspberry purée and ¼ cup (60 ml) water. Also, add 1 extra teaspoon (2.5 g) gelatin. Proceed per the original recipe instructions.

OR

For espresso marshmallow, replace the initial ⅓ cup (75 ml) water with ⅓ cup (75 ml) warm (not hot) coffee and add 1 tablespoon (3 g) instant espresso powder. Proceed per the original recipe instructions.

OR

For chocolate marshmallow, replace the initial ⅓ cup (75 ml) water with ½ cup (120 ml) warm coffee that's been combined with ¼ cup (20 g) of the darkest unsweetened cocoa powder you can find. Add 1 extra teaspoon (2.5 g) gelatin. Chocolate marshmallows are denser due to the cocoa powder content, but they are incredibly delicious. Dredge in cocoa powder instead of the cornstarch in Option 1.

OR

For maple marshmallow, replace the granulated sugar with an equal amount of maple sugar and proceed per the recipe instructions.

OR

Add bits of goodness during the mixing process, immediately after you've added the egg whites. Nuts. Toasted coconut. Chocolate chips. Bits of peppermint. Experiment with add-ins to make gourmet marshmallows.

OR

For peanut butter marshmallow, add 3 tablespoons (45 g) smooth peanut butter with the gelatin and proceed as you would for regular marshmallow. The important thing with this variation is that the mixture may need extra time to set due to the added fat of the peanut butter. My favorite way to use peanut butter marshmallow? As filling for a chocolate whoopie pie (page 170).

After you've added the egg whites to your marshmallow recipe and while the marshmallows are still warm as you're whipping, place a saucepan on a scale and zero it out. Add 12 ounces (340 g) hot marshmallow, then add ¼ cup (55 g) melted unsalted butter. Place over low heat, stirring until the butter and marshmallow are combined.

Pour 6 cups (120 g) Rice Krispies and 2 cups (60 g) corn flakes into a large bowl sprayed with cooking spray. Pour the marshmallow mixture and 1 cup (240 ml) warmed caramel sauce (page 81) over the cereals and stir with a non-stick-sprayed rubber spatula,

Traditionally, you'd spread the treats into a brownie pan sprayed with nonstick spray, let them cool until set (about 2 hours), then cut them into lovely little squares. You can still do this. But my favorite thing to do is to use them as edible sculpting material. I spray a bowl with nonstick spray, transfer the mixture into the bowl, and let it sit for a few hours to stiffen up. (Same theory as letting them sit before you cut them, but this time we want the mixture to be both pliable and sturdy.) Once the mixture has set, you can mold it like Play-Doh.

Once you've created a sculpture worth putting on display, wrap it tightly in plastic wrap to maintain its shape, and refrigerate for at least 1 hour. You've been working the mixture with your hands and that heats it up again, so letting your masterpiece sit in a cool environment is imperative. Once you have your desired edible object, you can move to Option 6 to make it sublime.

OPTION 6: **FONDANT**

Fondant is a covering for cakes. It's basically sugar and a host of alien ingredients suspended together to make a white mass that can be rolled out and used to cover cakes to give them a seamless look. It's a pain to make and it tastes awful—unless you make it with marshmallow. Then it's easy to make and delicious! Use your fondant immediately—it dries out quickly.

Make a batch of marshmallow per the traditional recipe, but add 1 teaspoon (5 ml) glycerin to the sugar and corn syrup mixture and heat the glycerin along with the sugar ingredients.

Once you've made the marshmallow, transfer the sticky goo to a very large saucepan over low heat and add 2 tablespoons (30 ml) water. Heat until the mixture is very fluid. You can also microwave the marshmallow and water together. In this case use a microwave-safe bowl and microwave in 30-second increments, stirring in between blasts.

Transfer the wet mass back to your mixing bowl and add 2 pounds (910 g) confectioners' sugar and ½ cup (120 ml) shortening (I suggest shortening and not butter primarily to keep the color white). If you want to add 1 teaspoon (5 ml) extract, do so at this point. Mix with a paddle attachment until you're afraid that your mixer is going to explode. This usually takes about 2 minutes. Transfer the contents to a work surface dusted with confectioners' sugar.

Coat your hands with a little shortening to keep the fondant moist and to keep it from sticking to you. Knead the fondant like bread dough until it is smooth and elastic. At this point, you can knead in food coloring, dividing the fondant if you want multiple colors. I suggest you wear latex gloves to keep your hands from turning the colors of the rainbow, and be aware that your work surface is going to be colorful as well.

With a rolling pin, roll the fondant out onto a work surface sprinkled with either confectioners' sugar or cornstarch. Also sprinkle confectioners' or cornstarch on your rolling pin to prevent sticking. To cover a cake or a Rice Krispies sculpture, make sure the fondant is rolled out to at least ⅛ inch (3 mm) thick. You can roll it a little thinner if you simply want to cut out shapes to apply to buttercream as decoration, or you can take pieces and form them into shapes (like the decorations on my wedding cake, page 212)—yes, that's an option, too. There are lots of options.

*Once you start down the path of playing with sugar, chances are your output is going to outweigh your appetite.* I get so excited about working with sugar that I tend to create before I have a home for the end result, so the destination for all the treats ends up being my very own piehole. Not smart. Not healthy. Not frugal.

This is where confectionery packaging resources are going to be your best friends. Choose to go hog-wild with your candy thermometer when you know you've got an upcoming gifting event (or make one up).

Stock up on the rest of your packaging materials so you aren't reduced to presenting your gorgeous confections on a paper plate wrapped in mangled foil. As a matter of fact, let's make a pact never to utilize paper plates for gifting. I don't care if angels are stamped all over them—no paper plates!

Instead, go to wonderful sites like Nashville Wraps (www.nashvillewraps.com) and U.S. Box (www.usbox.com) for an unbelievable selection of food and candy boxes, tissue paper, ribbon, and food-safe candy bags. If you're making a high volume of panettone or pound cake, or if you just want to wrap your cupcakes in divine paper, check out Qualita Paper (www.qualitapaper.com), NovaCart (www.novacartusa.com), or Fancy Flours (www.fancyflours.com).

If you plan on giving someone something extraordinary but want to add your own personal culinary touch, visit www.simonpearce.com for a selection of hand-blown glass bowls and platters. Many of the cake platters I use are Simon Pearce beauties and they are made right here in Vermont.

If you need simple personalized labels and mailing boxes (along with gift basket supplies), check out Uline (www.uline.com). If you plan on getting fancier with your labels or gift tags for weddings or holidays, you must spend some time perusing My Own Labels (www.myownlabels.com). Many of these places will give you ideas for the colors and sizes of your confections, so take some time to plan your large-scale confection-making days by choosing your packaging options first.

If you're using your new skills to make larger pastries and cakes, get yourself some professional bakery boxes and ribbon (and even personalized labels). Retailers like Box Depot (www.theboxdepot.com) and Papermart (www.papermart.com) carry bakery boxes in a large array of sizes and colors, along with the cardboard cake circles upon which you'll be wanting to set your cake (instead of—you guessed it—a paper plate).

*Let's make* **A PACT NEVER TO UTILIZE PAPER PLATES** *for* **GIFTING.**

# SOFT HONEY
# NOUGAT

*This soft and luscious stuff is glorious by itself or layered in a cake.* But swirl it into a brownie batter and bake it, and you've got something close to confectionery Valhalla. Just without the Vikings and the Berserkers (unless your kid gets her hands into your batch of nougat, and then we'll talk berserk).

||||||||||||||||||||||||||||||||||||||||||||||||||| *Makes approximately 40 squares* |||||||||||||||||||||||||||||||||||||||||||||||||||

| | | |
|---|---|---|
| sugar | 2 cups | 400 g |
| water | ¼ cup | 60 ml |
| honey | 2 tablespoons | 42 g |
| corn syrup | 1 tablespoon | 15 ml |
| egg whites, at room temperature | 2 | |
| salt | ½ teaspoon | 3 g |
| cornstarch, for dusting | | |

As we begin pouring hotter and hotter sugar syrup into egg whites, it becomes correspondingly important to make sure your egg whites are at room temperature, at the very least. Otherwise you run the risk of the sugar seizing and chunking when it hits cold egg whites, when what you really want is for it to incorporate smoothly and create a fluffy, non-chunky nougat.

① In a heavy saucepan over medium-high heat, combine the sugar, water, honey, and corn syrup. Stir until the sugar has completely melted and wash down the sides of the pan with a damp pastry brush to eradicate those rogue sugar crystals.

② Clip on a candy thermometer, stop stirring, and heat to 245°F (120°C).

③ Meanwhile, when the honey syrup reaches 234°F (112°C), in the bowl of a stand mixer fitted with the whisk attachment, start whipping the egg whites and salt so that they are foamy once the syrup reaches temperature.

✳ **A Note from the Sugar Baby:** As the honey starts to reach high temperatures, it may start to brown. That's OK. What's not OK is letting the temperature rise above 315°F (157°C), because this stuff will burn. No sooner have you turned your back on the honey to turn on the mixer than the temperature will shoot up like crazy. So be on your toes, and work carefully and slowly.

④ Once the honey syrup has reached temperature, transfer it to a heatproof pitcher to make pouring safer and easier. Reduce the mixer speed to medium, and slowly and gently pour the hot syrup down the sides of the bowl and into the egg whites. Return the mixer to high speed and whip until the nougat is light and fluffy and the bowl is cool to the touch.

⑤ Using a rubber spatula sprayed with cooking spray, scrape the nougat out of the bowl and onto a sheet pan lined with parchment and dusted with cornstarch. Use a small offset spatula sprayed with cooking spray to smooth the nougat into an even layer. Allow it to set overnight.

⑥ With a hot knife, cut the nougat into 2-inch (5-cm) squares and coat the sides with a dusting of cornstarch. Wrap each piece in a small square of parchment. Store in an airtight container for up to 2 weeks.

## Options!

### OPTION 1: **VANILLA NOUGAT**

This is outright sacrilege, but my favorite nougat dispenses altogether with honey. I know, I know—just hear me out. I replace the honey with more corn syrup. Wait—keep reading! Then I add 1 tablespoon (15 ml) vanilla bean paste. That's it. I know you don't believe me, but it's delicious. Delicious and an integral part of one of my favorite cakes, which I've gone ahead and named after myself (or the nickname my mother gave me). Take a peek on page 228.

### OPTION 2: **SWIRL**

Dispense with the long whipping. When the nougat looks white and fluffy but is still warm, transfer 1 cup (240 ml) to a pastry bag fitted with a large open tip. Pipe stripes on top of brownie batter. With a toothpick, lightly swirl the nougat into the batter to make a lovely pattern and bake your brownies as usual.

### OPTION 3: **TORRONE**

Torrone is the grandmamma of candies. She's from Italy. Made from honey. Mixed with nuts. Those are all ingredients that scream "The Romans ate this stuff, and how!" to me. Most recipes for torrone are also indicators of its ancient origins and point to the distinct possibility that the indentured made it and only the fancy-pants ate it. Why do I think this, you ask? Well, how does this sound to your modern ears? "Stir honey constantly over a water bath for 1½ hours." (Call me Spartacus—you can't make me stir that long.) My recipe might be calling open rebellion on a time-honored recipe, but it's still mighty fine. So you decide, 1½ hours strapped to a hot stove, or 30 minutes with the help of a stand mixer? I thought so.

Torrone, as I like it, is just a harder version of honey nougat, with added goodies. I heat the syrup to 270°F (132°C) and pour it very carefully into the egg whites. Once the nougat is cool and light and fluffy, I fold in 1 cup (110 g) lightly toasted pistachios. Turn the torrone out onto a parchment-lined sheet pan dusted liberally with cornstarch, and sprinkle cornstarch on top before placing another piece of parchment on top of the torrone. Allow to set overnight and cut into small, bite-size pieces. Store in an airtight container in a cool, dry place for up to a week.

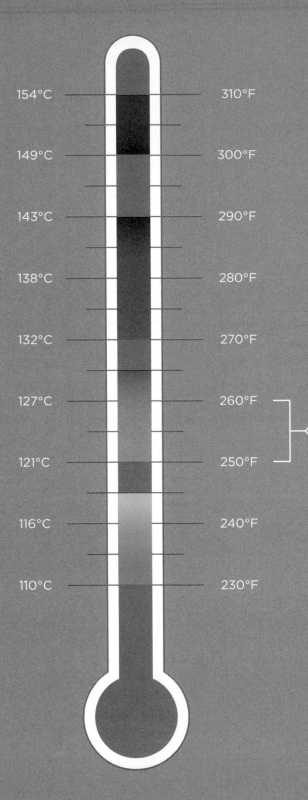

154°C — 310°F

149°C — 300°F

143°C — 290°F

138°C — 280°F

132°C — 270°F

127°C — 260°F

121°C — 250°F

116°C — 240°F

110°C — 230°F

# HARD-BALL STAGE

*250°F–265°F (121°C–129°C)    Sugar Concentration: 92%*

At this stage, the sugar is a thick syrup, clings to a spoon, and forms a hard ball when dropped in cold water. However, the "hard ball" can still be manipulated and won't crack. This is also the stage where everyone laughs when you say, "Heat to hard-ball."

Of all the stages, my favorite is when my thermometer is teetering between 250°F and 265°F (121°C and 129°C) and the boiling bubbles of the hot sugar are getting smaller and starting to pop more slowly. This is the stage when sugar really starts to slow down, when so much moisture has been whisked off into the ether that you know that the stuff can hold its own. Pour it onto a sheet pan and when it cools it won't go anywhere. I enjoy a confection that holds its shape but still has a little give when you bite into it. This, my friends, is when caramel gets good and chewy, your jaw gets a workout, and your salivary gland goes into overdrive.

# SUGAR
*on*
# SNOW

*During the spring maple-sugaring season, we have parties in Vermont to celebrate the end of what was most assuredly a brutal winter.* Of course, there's still snow on the ground at this point, but to a Vermonter, ten degrees above freezing is license to start airing out the winter-white flesh. With the sap running and the sugar shacks going full tilt, there's both sunshine *and* fresh maple syrup to celebrate.

There are only six ingredients for such a party, but each is vitally important. Don't ask me why the last three. After getting wildly different answers, I've stopped asking and have just put it down to the last burst of winter madness before the thaw.

|||| *Makes approximately 10 servings, depending on how generous you are with each drizzle* ||||

| | | |
|---|---|---|
| snow | | |
| unsalted butter | 1 tablespoon | 14 g |
| maple syrup* | 1 cup (or more, to taste) | 240 ml (or more, to taste) |
| sour pickles | 1 jar | |
| doughnuts | 1 box | |
| beer (Vermont brew if you can find it) | | |
| *Grade A fancy is fine, B and below even better. | | |

① Have a large, fresh, and *clean* bowl of snow handy. No yellow snow allowed.

② Run the pat of butter along the rim of a heavy saucepan. This will keep the syrup from boiling over.

③ Pour the maple syrup into the saucepan and clip on a candy thermometer. Boil the maple syrup to 255°F (124°C).

④ Using a large metal spoon, drizzle the hot maple syrup over the snow.

⑤ With a fork, gather the strands of sticky maple from the snow and insert into mouth.

⑥ Take a bite of pickle and/or a bite of doughnut.

⑦ Wash down with beer.

⑧ Repeat.

# FLEUR
## *de Sel*
# CARAMELS

*These salty caramels have a soft chew and melt quite easily in your mouth with very little help from your choppers.* This is the caramel I use when I'm lining the bottom of a tart shell before layering on the bananas and cream for a banana cream tart. It keeps its shape but not stridently so. For a harder chew, try The Sugar, Baby! (page 140). Those are the treats I prefer as straight I'm-sitting-on-my-duff-and-enjoying-a-few-bonbons caramel—I like a tougher chew, as if you couldn't already tell. But this is all a matter of preference, so if you like it a little softer and not so debilitating on the teeth, this is your recipe.

|||||||||||||||||||||||||||||||||||||||||||||||||||||||||||||| *Makes approximately 30* ||||||||||||||||||||||||||||||||||||||||||||||||||||||||||||||

① Prepare an 8-by-8-inch (20-by-20-cm) baking pan by lining it with aluminum foil and spraying the foil with nonstick cooking spray.

② In a heavy saucepan over medium-low heat, combine the cream, sugar, and corn syrup. Heat, stirring occasionally, until the sugar has melted. Raise the heat to medium and continue to stir until the mixture begins to boil.

③ Stop stirring and cook until the caramel reaches 257°F (125°C) on a candy thermometer.

④ Immediately remove the pan from the heat and stir in the butter. Add the vanilla and 2 teaspoons (10 g) of the salt. Stir again until the butter has melted and the vanilla is evenly distributed.

⑤ Pour the mixture into the prepared pan, sprinkle with the remaining 1 teaspoon (5 g) salt and let it set at room temperature until the caramel is firm enough to cut.

⑥ Cut the caramel into small squares or strips with a chef's knife. Wrap individually in wax paper and store in an airtight container in a cool, dry place for up to a week.

| | | |
|---|---|---|
| heavy cream | 1½ cups | 360 ml |
| sugar | 2 cups | 400 g |
| light corn syrup | 1 cup | 240 ml |
| unsalted butter, cut into small pieces | ¼ cup | 55 g |
| vanilla extract | 1 teaspoon | 5 ml |
| sea salt, such as fleur de sel | 3 teaspoons, divided | 15 g, divided |

**A hallmark of caramels is that splendid butter infusion.** This may lead you to believe that more butter is better. And while I'd usually agree with you, in this instance I caution you not to add more than I've specified. Any more and you're courting separation, where the butter refuses to emulsify with the other ingredients and settles all by its lonesome on top of some still very tasty caramel goo. Butter's a snob; if you put too much of it together in one room, it tends to gang up on the rest of the ingredients. So take it easy and know that the flavor you recognize as "buttery" has as much to do with the sugar and cream as it has to do with the butter. Maybe more. Just don't tell the butter.

# DIVINITY

*Divinity is a quintessentially American candy, most identified with the South, where that particularly Southern nut, the pecan, often graces the center of this luscious confection.* (Personally, I like to add salted Virginia peanuts.)

Though it hails from the humid Southeast, the divine divinity is fragile, so it is wise to follow the candy maxim and not even attempt making it when the weather is especially muggy. While you'll be able to reach temperature on the candy thermometer, once you plop those cherubic globs onto the prepared surface, the atmospheric moisture will seep into your precious confections and make them soggy beyond recognition. (Which makes me wonder: When, exactly, is there a good time to make divinity in the South?)

|||||||||||||||||||||||||||||||||||||||||||||||||||||| *Makes approximately 18 dollops* ||||||||||||||||||||||||||||||||||||||||||||||||||||||

| sugar | 2 cups, divided | 400 g, divided |
|---|---|---|
| corn syrup | ¾ cup | 180 ml |
| cornstarch | ½ teaspoon | 1 g |
| water | ½ cup | 120 ml |
| egg whites | 2 | |
| salt | ½ teaspoon | 3 g |
| vanilla bean paste | 1 teaspoon | 5 ml |
| Virginia peanuts, toasted and chopped | ½ cup | 75 g |

① In a heavy saucepan over medium heat, combine 1½ cups of the sugar, the corn syrup, cornstarch, and water. Cook until the sugar is dissolved. With a damp pastry brush, wipe down the sides of the pan to prevent stray sugar crystals from forming. Attach a candy thermometer, stop stirring, and heat the mixture until it reaches 255°F (124°C).

② Meanwhile, place the egg whites and salt in the bowl of a stand mixer and beat with the whisk attachment until foamy. Slowly add the remaining ½ cup (100 g) sugar and continue beating until stiff peaks form.

③ With the mixer running on medium speed, pour the sugar syrup in a thin, slow stream down the side of the bowl.

④ Add the vanilla bean paste and raise the mixer speed to high. Beat until the mixture loses its sheen and holds stiff peaks.

⑤ Remove the bowl from the mixer and gently fold in the peanuts.

⑥ With a large spoon coated with cooking spray, drop spoonfuls of divinity onto a parchment-lined baking sheet, or spread the entirety into a buttered 8-inch (20-cm) square pan and allow to set for a few hours before cutting into squares. Store in an airtight container in a cool, dry place for up to a week.

# MAPLE TAFFY

*Yes.* We like our maple in Vermont. We like it immeasurably. And maple taffy is a way to enjoy it longer than if you simply pour the amber stuff on some pancakes. So chew your way to Green Mountain happiness with this long-lasting treat.

||||||||||||||||||||||||||||||||||||||| *Makes approximately 50 pieces* |||||||||||||||||||||||||||||||||||||||

① In a large saucepan over medium heat, combine the maple syrup, sugar, corn syrup, glycerin, and salt. Stir until the sugar has completely dissolved.

② Stop stirring, clip on a candy thermometer, raise the heat to medium-high, and heat until the temperature reaches 235°F (113°C).

③ Remove the pan from the heat and stir in the cream, butter, and vanilla paste.

④ Once the bubbling has subsided, return the pan to medium-high heat and boil until the temperature reaches 255°F (124°C). Immediately stir in the baking soda.

⑤ Pour the mixture onto a heatproof surface that's been sprayed with nonstick cooking spray.

⑥ Using two bench scrapers sprayed with nonstick spray, fold the ends of the sugar toward the center. Keep folding until it's cool enough to handle.

⑦ Spray your hands (or sugar gloves) with nonstick spray, and pick up the taffy. Pull the taffy into a rope. Pull the ends apart bring them together, folding the rope in half. Pick up the ends of the folded rope; pull and fold the taffy again. Repeat until the taffy begins to cool and is difficult to pull.

⑧ Place the taffy on a nonstick surface and pull it into a rope approximately 20 inches (50 cm) long. Cut the rope in half with scissors sprayed with nonstick spray. Pull each half until the overall diameter is ¼ inch (6 mm).

| | | |
|---|---|---|
| grade B maple syrup | ½ cup | 120 ml |
| sugar | 1 cup | 200 g |
| corn syrup | ½ cup | 120 ml |
| glycerin | 1 teaspoon | 5 ml |
| salt | ½ teaspoon | 3 g |
| heavy cream | ½ cup | 120 ml |
| unsalted butter | 2 tablespoons | 28 g |
| vanilla bean paste | 1 teaspoon | 5 ml |
| baking soda | ¼ teaspoon | 1 g |

⑨ Cut ½-inch (12-mm) pieces with the scissors. Wrap each piece individually in parchment and keep in a very dry and very cool place. (I can't stress enough how important it is to store this properly. If kept in a warm and humid environment, the taffy will harden into something that resembles maple candy. It's actually pretty damn delicious and if this happens to you, simply say you did it on purpose. Otherwise, store in a very cool, dry place.) Store for up to a week!

## Option!

### HONEY TAFFY
Replace the maple sugar with honey and you've got a candy reminiscent of something many of us received in our Halloween bags as kids and then never saw again until Halloween came round again: Bit-O-Honey.

# HOMER'S
# PASTELI

*Herodotus and Homer both wrote of pasteli as a source of life-giving energy.* The combination of sesame and honey is undeniably a brilliant one, imparting both nutritional value and long-burning energy—the world's first Power Bar, if you will.

But when I was a kid, I recognized pasteli as one of the lone sweets available at the health food store. As in a traditional grocery store, the sweet snacks were kept by the checkout counter as a temptation purchase. But unlike in our neighborhood Safeway, here there were no ruby-red Twizzlers, not a single caramel-and-nougat delight smothered in waxy chocolate, no Duds, no Joys, no Jujus. Instead, if there was any smothering, it was done by carob. If there was a hidden center, it was a scantly sweetened nut butter. But there were pasteli, and they were incredibly sweet, a wee bit crunchy, and just-enough chewy. If I was able to badger my mother into buying me some, I considered my day well spent.

|||||||||||||||||||||||||||||||||||||||||||||||||||||| *Makes approximately 30* ||||||||||||||||||||||||||||||||||||||||||||||||||||||

| | | |
|---|---|---|
| honey | 1 cup | 340 g |
| water | ¼ cup | 60 ml |
| salt | ½ teaspoon | 3 g |
| sesame seeds | 2 cups | 300 g |
| almond extract | 1 teaspoon | 5 ml |

① In a heavy saucepan over low heat, heat the honey, water, and salt. Stir until the honey loosens up and becomes fluid.

② Raise the heat, stop stirring, clip on a candy thermometer and heat to 265°F (129°C).

③ Remove the honey from the heat and quickly stir in the sesame seeds and almond extract. Pour the mixture onto a parchment-lined sheet pan. Allow to cool for 10 minutes and score the pasteli into small pieces before it hardens completely.

④ Allow to cool completely. Break apart where you've scored the candy. Wrap the pieces in wax paper. Store in an airtight container for up to 2 weeks.

# BABYSITTING
# POPCORN

*We had very little access to processed sugar when we were growing up.* Our deprivation led to some creative confectionery outlets, the most rudimentary of which was smashing together a stick of butter and a cup of Domino sugar. Disgusting? Yes. Delicious? You bet.

Given a few hours alone in the house, a working flame, and access to my mother's baking supplies, my big sister could intuitively concoct brilliant caramel coatings for popcorn, with the ingredients on hand.

|||||||||||||||||||||||||||||||||||||||||||||||||||||| *Makes approximately 10 cups (2.5 L)* ||||||||||||||||||||||||||||||||||||||||||||||||||||||

① Organize your popcorn-coating area by spraying a large metal bowl and two large spoons liberally with nonstick cooking spray. Pour the popped popcorn and the almonds into the bowl. Stir well to distribute the almonds through the popcorn. Line a sheet pan with parchment paper and set all these things aside, in an easily accessible work area.

② In a large saucepan over medium-high heat, combine the turbinado, butter, water, salt, and vanilla paste. Stir until the turbinado is melted and all granules have dissolved (this may take longer than with traditional granulated sugar since turbinado granules are heartier).

③ Wash down the sides of the pot with a damp pastry brush, stop stirring, clip on a candy thermometer, and raise the heat to high. When the temperature reaches 255°F (124°C), remove the pan from the heat and stir in the baking soda. The baking soda will bubble vigorously, so keep stirring. Keep an eye out for clumps of baking soda that haven't dissolved and smash them with the back of a spoon to break them up.

| microwave popcorn,* popped | 1 bag | |
|---|---|---|
| salted almonds (or any nuts you prefer) | 1 cup | 115 g |
| turbinado sugar** | 1½ cups | 300 g |
| unsalted butter | 2 tablespoons | 28 g |
| water | ⅓ cup | 75 ml |
| salt | 1 teaspoon | 6 g |
| vanilla bean paste | 1 teaspoon | 5 ml |
| baking soda | ½ teaspoon | 2.5 g |

*I use natural/organic popcorn with no added flavoring.

**I use Sugar in the Raw. It's relatively easy to find, and it's exactly the kind of stuff my mother would have had on hand if it had been available when I was a kid.

④ Pour the caramel over the popcorn. Toss the popcorn and almonds with the sprayed spoons as if you were tossing a salad. Continue tossing until the caramel has evenly coated the popcorn and almonds.

⑤ Transfer the popcorn to the parchment in an even layer to cool completely, or gently squeeze handfuls into popcorn balls. Allow to cool. Store in an airtight container for up to 1 week.

# VANILLA
*Cream*
# FONDANT

*Fondant is confectionery waste for many modern Americans.* While fondant is meant to be eaten, more often it's seen. When you lift the lid of a box of chocolates, the ones that have been bitten into and put back in their brown candy wrappers are most likely the fondant-filled. The ones that are gone completely are the caramels.

But homemade fondant is actually quite a lovely taste sensation, especially when coupled with beautifully made caramel or candied nuts. I promise.

|||||||||||||||||||||||||||||||||||||||||||||||||||| *Makes about 1½ cups (360 ml)* ||||||||||||||||||||||||||||||||||||||||||||||||||||

| sugar | 2 cups | 400 g |
|---|---|---|
| water | ½ cup | 120 ml |
| light corn syrup | 2 tablespoons | 30 ml |
| salt | ¼ teaspoon | 1.5 g |
| unsalted butter | ¼ cup | 55 g |
| vanilla bean paste | ½ teaspoon | 2.5 ml |
| cornstarch | 1 tablespoon, plus extra for dusting | 8 g, plus extra for dusting |

① In a heavy saucepan over medium heat, combine the sugar, water, corn syrup, and salt and stir until the sugar dissolves. With a damp pastry brush, wipe down the sides of the pan to prevent stray sugar crystals from forming. Attach a candy thermometer and stop stirring! Continue to cook until the sugar reaches 245°F (118°C).

② Pour the sugar syrup into the bowl of a stand mixer fitted with the paddle attachment. Add the butter and mix on medium speed until the syrup starts to become translucent.

③ Add the vanilla bean paste and turn mixer speed to high. Beat until the mixture starts to thicken and turn white and shiny. Reduce the mixer speed to low and add the cornstarch. Continue beating until the mixture looks as if it's thickening—the fondant will actually start to look like it's drying and will throw off pieces as if it were crumbling. Perfect! Stop!

④ On a work surface lightly dusted with cornstarch, scrape out the fondant and start to knead it with your hands, adding only as much cornstarch to the work surface as you need to stop the fondant from sticking.

⑤ Keep kneading until the fondant is soft and smooth and forms a ball. You can wrap the fondant in a plastic bag and use it as needed. Or you can go to page 219 and get some more ideas!

**Options!**

OPTION 1: **MELTAWAY MINTS**

I love these buttery bits. They are delectable—the perfect after-dinner treat. Which I never eat. Why? Same reason you don't: The only time we see them is in a communal bowl at the hostess station of a restaurant. And while there is usually a minuscule spoon in the bowl, most patrons just use their naked paws to root around willy-nilly among the pastel nuggets, spreading who knows what contagion among the minty pretties.

Here's a way to enjoy meltaways in the confines of your own home without fear of ingesting a school of bacteria as well.

Add 1 teaspoon (5 ml) peppermint extract instead of the vanilla paste, and color with a pastel dye to mimic the restaurant variety, if you so choose. Roll the fondant into a long rope a bit smaller than ½ inch (12 mm) in diameter, and cut small pieces. The cutting action will pinch the sides, mimicking the look of the real stuff. This'll just taste better.

You may also consider dipping the mints in melted bittersweet chocolate.

OPTION 2: **MAPLE CREAM FONDANT**

For a maple-infused fondant, replace ½ cup (100 g) of the granulated sugar with maple sugar. Just remember that the maple can crystallize and impart a granular crunch to the otherwise creamy fondant, but when you combine it with caramelized crunchy nuts, you've got a holiday nut roll that'll blow a Baby Ruth out of the pool.

With Vanilla Cream Fondant
Make Fleur de Sel Spirals, page 226

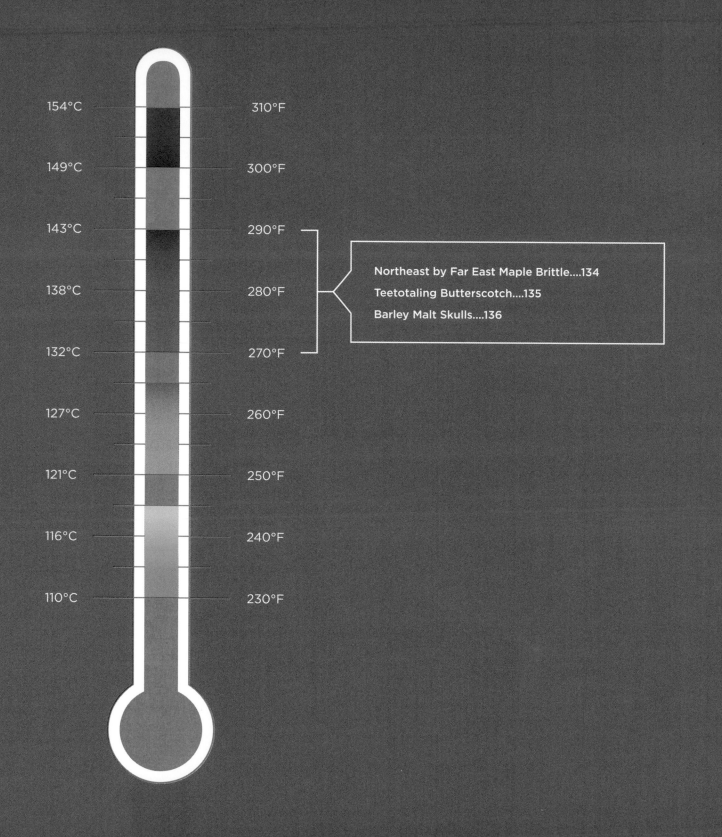

154°C     310°F

149°C     300°F

143°C     290°F

138°C     280°F

132°C     270°F

127°C     260°F

121°C     250°F

116°C     240°F

110°C     230°F

Northeast by Far East Maple Brittle....134

Teetotaling Butterscotch....135

Barley Malt Skulls....136

# SOFT-CRACK STAGE

*270°F–290°F (132°C–143°C)   Sugar Concentration: 95%*

Looking at the boiling sugar syrup, you'll see that the bubbles at this stage are smaller, thicker, and closer together. When you drop the syrup in cold water, it will solidify into hard yet flexible threads that have some give before breaking like too-al-dente pasta.

When the candy completely cools, if you try to bend the stuff it will crack. But as the name foreshadows, that crack is rather soft, and with some mastication, you'll find that the treat starts to develop a hard chew.

# NORTHEAST
## *by Far East*
# MAPLE BRITTLE

*Maple is sweet—almost sweeter than straight sugar—but it's distinctive.* When you add an exotic spice mixture and a touch of butter, the overall flavor of this candy becomes quite sophisticated. I like this as a coating on my Vanilla-Pecan Swirl Tea Cake (page 235) as much as I like it as a straight-ahead candy.

||||||||||||||||||||||||||||||||||||||||||| *Makes approximately 1 pound (455 g)* |||||||||||||||||||||||||||||||||||||||||||

| | | |
|---|---|---|
| baking soda | 1 teaspoon | 5 g |
| ras al-hanout spice mix* | 1 teaspoon | 2 g |
| sugar | 1¼ cups | 250 g |
| grade B maple syrup | ¾ cup | 180 ml |
| corn syrup | ½ cup | 180 ml |
| unsalted butter | 2 tablespoons | 28 g |
| salt | 1 teaspoon | 6 g |
| vanilla bean paste | 1 teaspoon | 5 ml |
| toasted pecan pieces | 1 cup | 110 g |

*\*Ras al-hanout* means "the best of the shop." I use a blend from Afrikya Spices by Marcus Samuelsson that includes cinnamon, turmeric, black pepper, nutmeg, cardamom, cloves, and other spices.

① In a small bowl, combine the baking soda and spice mix. Set aside.

② In a large saucepan over medium-low heat, combine the sugar, maple syrup, corn syrup, butter, salt, and vanilla paste. Stir until the sugar has melted.

③ Clip on a candy thermometer, stop stirring, and raise the heat to medium-high. When the temperature reaches 290°F (143°C), remove the pan from the heat. Add the spice mixture and stir with a wooden spoon until the vigorous bubbling slows down.

④ Immediately stir in the pecans. Pour the brittle onto a half sheet pan lined with parchment and sprayed with nonstick baking spray.

⑤ Tilt the pan so that the brittle forms an even layer. Allow to cool completely before breaking into pieces. Store in an airtight container in a cool, dry place for up to 2 weeks.

# TEETOTALING
# BUTTERSCOTCH

*There is no Scotch in butterscotch.* Believe me. I've tried it. I wish I'd done a little research before diving into my ill-conceived attempt at what I thought would be an authentic turn on the oft-bowdlerized hard candy. Nope, no Scotch involved, either now or in the past. Don't even try it. It's a wasteful disaster waiting to happen (although the fumes of Oban single malt wafting throughout the house took the edge off the catastrophe).

Nor is it likely that the confection even hails from Scotland, because there's only evidence to the contrary; all historic compasses point to the fact that it was actually born in England. Butterscotch most likely took its confusing name from the act of scoring, or "scotching," the sweet before it hardened completely. To whit, a line from Shakespeare's Scottish play, "We have scotch'd the snake, not killed it." And of course there *is* butter involved. That part was never in question.

||||||||||||||||||||||||||||||||||||||||||||| *Makes approximately 88 pieces* |||||||||||||||||||||||||||||||||||||||||||||

① In a large saucepan over medium heat, combine the brown sugar, corn syrup, butter, water, salt, cornstarch, and vanilla paste, stirring constantly until the sugar has melted.

② Increase the heat to medium-high. When the temperature reaches 280°F (138°C), remove the pan from the heat and stir in the baking soda. The mixture will foam.

③ Pour the mixture onto a parchment-lined sheet pan liberally sprayed with nonstick cooking spray, or transfer to a heatproof pitcher (a large glass measuring cup works well) and carefully pour into the individual compartments of a silicone mold sprayed with nonstick spray. If pouring onto a sheet pan, score (or scotch) lines into the still warm candy so that you can break it apart easily after it has cooled.

| brown sugar, firmly packed | 2 cups | 440 g |
|---|---|---|
| corn syrup | ½ cup | 120 ml |
| unsalted butter | ¼ cup | 55 g |
| water | ¼ cup | 60 ml |
| salt | 1 teaspoon | 6 g |
| cornstarch | ½ teaspoon | 1 g |
| vanilla bean paste | 1 teaspoon | 5 ml |
| baking soda | ¼ teaspoon | 1 g |

④ Allow to cool completely. Break into small pieces and store in an airtight container for up to 4 weeks.

# BARLEY MALT
# SKULLS

*Some of my favorite Bavarian candies are called* **Bayrischer Blockmalz.** They've got a few things going for them that I love. One, they taste genuinely of dark malt—not like a malted milk ball but like a dark beer, only sweeter. Two, they are black as pitch. Three, they're shaped like coal. It's pretty much the perfect candy if you want to add coal to your kid's stocking without the outright cruelty.

Being a woman inclined toward things strange and marginally gruesome, I had to take these odd nuggets one step closer to ghoulishness and make them in silicone skull molds. It's the perfect shape to warn people away from touching my candy. And if they do take a bite and find they just don't have what it takes to enjoy such a weird flavor, they can't say they weren't warned.

*Makes approximately 50 scary skulls*

| | | |
|---|---|---|
| muscovado sugar | 2 cups | 400 g |
| corn syrup | ¼ cup | 60 ml |
| barley malt syrup | ¼ cup | 60 ml |
| unsalted butter | ¼ cup | 55 g |
| water | ¼ cup | 60 ml |
| salt | ½ teaspoon | 3 g |
| baking soda | ½ teaspoon | 2.5 g |
| black food coloring (optional) | 2 drops | |

① In a large saucepan over medium heat, combine the sugar, corn syrup, barley malt syrup, butter, water, and salt. Stir until the sugar has completely melted.

② Wash down the sides of the pan with a damp pastry brush, clip on a candy thermometer, and raise the heat to high. Boil until the candy thermometer reads 280°F (138°C).

③ Stir in the baking soda and food coloring (if using). The lovely thing about this candy is that it is naturally very dark, so you can forgo the coloring and still get a very moody effect. Continue stirring until the bubbling subsides.

④ Carefully spoon the candy into silicone molds sprayed with nonstick spray, or spoon round dollops onto a piece of parchment. Allow to cool completely and store for up to 4 weeks in an airtight container.

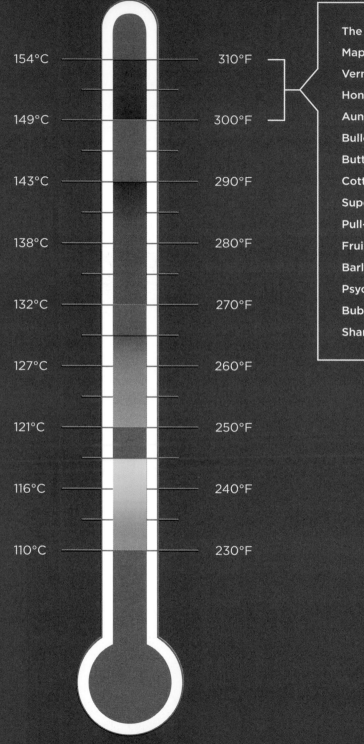

154°C — 310°F

149°C — 300°F

143°C — 290°F

138°C — 280°F

132°C — 270°F

127°C — 260°F

121°C — 250°F

116°C — 240°F

110°C — 230°F

# HARD-CRACK STAGE (AND BEYOND!)

*300°F–310°F (149°C–154°C)    Sugar Concentration: 99%*

This is as hot as you'll want to get, and most recipes won't call for anything hotter. Dropping the syrup into cold water at hard-crack stage will produce rock-hard, crackling threads that break easily. Don't touch this stuff right off the burner. I'll show you my scars if you need more convincing.

My fourth-grade teacher, Mrs. Townsend, kept a shiny red ball the size of a marble next to the chalk on the chalkboard. It looked like candy. It had the hard lacquer sheen of a gumball. It shone red, the crimson hue screaming *cherry flavor*! It was dainty, the exact circumference of a mini gobstopper. It called out to me every single day of that school year. And more than once, when Mrs. Townsend wasn't looking, I'd pop it into my mouth and bite hard. It was wood. It was a wooden, red, lacquered orb. A wooden, red, lacquered orb with bite marks. It's a testament to my deep, abiding love of sugar—and perhaps to a mild case of insanity brought on by addiction—that I kept returning to its radiant glow, praying each time as the stoner prays when he closes his eyes, hoping that while they're shut the Cool Ranch Doritos bag will magically refill.

# THE SUGAR,
# BABY!

*Cross a rock-hard candy with a caramel and you've got the ne plus ultra, in my humble opinion, of candy.* If you need a comparative treat to help you wrap your head around this deliciousness, think of a Sugar Daddy. There's nothing like that chewy sugar lockjaw, that mercury-filling-extracting, unintentionally drool-producing goodness. Don't even think about biting down on this when it's first introduced into your mouth; just let it ride around a bit until it relents just enough for you to get your chew on. The beauty of this treat is that it works just as well as a lollipop as it does as a single-wrap candy. And you can mix it up with an array of delightful infusions to enjoy while your teeth are fused together by that supreme sugar fixative that is The Sugar, Baby!

||||||||||||||||||||||||||||||||||||||||||||||||||||  *Makes 25 lollipops*  ||||||||||||||||||||||||||||||||||||||||||||||||||||

| | | |
|---|---|---|
| sugar | 2 cups | 400 g |
| corn syrup | 1 cup | 240 ml |
| salt | 1 teaspoon | 6 g |
| heavy cream | ½ cup | 120 ml |
| vanilla bean paste | 1 tablespoon | 15 ml |
| unsalted butter | ¾ cup | 170 g |

① In a 4-quart saucepan over low heat, warm the sugar, corn syrup, and salt, stirring until the sugar has melted.

② Raise the heat to medium-high and clip on a candy thermometer. Heat to 310°F (154°C).

③ Meanwhile, in a small saucepan over low heat, combine the cream and the vanilla paste and stir until they just begin to simmer. You can also microwave the two in a microwave-safe bowl for 1 minute. Keep warm.

④ When the sugar syrup reaches temperature, turn off the heat and add the warm cream mixture. The addition of the cream will cause the caramel to bubble vigorously, so step back until the caramel storm has passed. If the temperature of the mixture has dipped below 275°F (135°C), warm the caramel mixture until you reach that temperature.

⑤ Remove the pan from the heat. Add the butter, stirring constantly until it is completely melted and has emulsified.

⑥ Pour the caramel into 25 square silicone molds sprayed with nonstick spray. Let the caramel stand at room temperature for about 20 minutes. While the caramel is still warm and malleable but beginning to firm, insert a lollipop stick in each mold. Allow the caramel to cool completely and then gently coax the lollies out. One trick is to pop the silicone molds in the freezer for a minute; this will help the lollipops come out quite easily. Store in an airtight container in a cool, dry place for up to 2 weeks.

Before we continue into what will be the hottest portion of our adventures in sweetness, I'd like to bring up a very sticky topic: moisture. Even if you've never thought about working with sugar, you've probably heard the candy maker's axiom, "Don't make candy when it's humid." Since sugar work entails the elimination of moisture, boiling down the granulated stuff on a sweltering, thunderstorm-addled summer day isn't the best idea. It's not that you can't get the thermometer to read the right temperature; it's just that the air around you is so damn saturated with $H_2O$ that the second you pour a nougat, a toffee, a brittle, or a honeycomb into its waiting container, the confection that just a moment ago promised to be hard-crack is now taking a nice schvitz in a summer sauna and will probably never set. This is especially true of extremely aerated treats like honeycomb and sponge candy, where all those lovely air pockets that are meant to keep the candy light and crunchy transform into secret passageways for moisture to invade the inner sanctum of crispy deliciousness, leaving you with a soggy blob. Or you'll find that your gummis and nougat never set. Be thoughtful about when you make candy; don't sabotage yourself. Store your finished product in airtight containers and keep them in a dry place—the fridge might seem like a logical candy hideout, but many fridges are havens for excess moisture.

✪ **A Note from the Sugar Baby:** I've got nothing but love for the incessant crop of novelty ice-cube trays crowding the clearance shelves of big-box stores, because they make fantastic lollipop molds. And nothing makes a better lolli than The Sugar, Baby! Have lollipop sticks ready, and once you've poured the mixture into the cavities, wait a few minutes for the mixture to harden just a touch so that the lollipop sticks stay firmly in place without leaning. Allow to cool completely before extracting from the silicone.

### Options!

OPTION 1: **CHOCOLATE**
When you add the butter to the hot caramel in step 5, throw in ¼ cup (30 g) bittersweet chocolate morsels! Proceed as if nothing unusual has happened.

OPTION 2: **LIME-TEQUILA**
Add 1 teaspoon (5 ml) lime oil and 2 tablespoons (30 ml) tequila to the sugar ingredients in step 1, leave out the vanilla in step 3, and proceed with the recipe.

OPTION 3: **CARAMEL APPLES**
Take 8 tart apples, such as Granny Smith, and wash and dry them very well. Remove the stem from each and insert a stick where the sun don't shine. Just after you've added the butter in step 5 and while the caramel is still hot, dip each apple into the caramel and swirl it to cover the flesh completely. Remove the apple and hold it over the pot to allow any excess caramel to drip off. Transfer the apple to a piece of nonstick-sprayed parchment to cool. To add a little oomph to your apple, dip the bottom in chopped dry-roasted peanuts just after you've taken the apple from its caramel bath.

# MAPLE
# PILLOWS

*I created maple pillows while messing around with some old-school nougat recipes.* What I came up with was a fluffy, strikingly maple New England nougat with a slight crunch. The addition of espresso powder rounds out the taste; it keeps the sweetness from being cloying and adds wonderful depth of flavor.

And because a little of this delicacy goes a long way, I often pour half of the finished mixture into an 8-by-8-inch (20-by-20-cm) glass baking dish sprayed with nonstick spray to set. I then cut it into individual pieces. I swirl the other half into bittersweet brownie batter for a gorgeous and delectable dessert.

|||||||||||||||||||||||||||||||||||||||||||||| *Makes approximately 50 squares* ||||||||||||||||||||||||||||||||||||||||||||||||

① In a large saucepan over medium heat, combine the sugar, maple syrup, water, and espresso powder and bring the mixture to a simmer, stirring constantly until the sugar melts. Stop stirring and clip on a candy thermometer.

② Meanwhile, in the bowl of a stand mixer, beat the egg whites and salt on high until foamy, wet peaks form.

③ Once the sugar syrup reaches 300°F (149°C), pour it very slowly and steadily into the egg whites with the motor on medium speed. Continue whisking the hot nougat mixture for 8 to 12 minutes, until it cools slightly and thickens.

④ Stir the vanilla and pecans into the maple pillows and quickly spread the mixture onto a parchment-lined sheet pan liberally sprayed with nonstick cooking spray.

| | | |
|---|---|---|
| sugar | 3 cups | 600 g |
| grade B maple syrup | 1½ cups | 360 ml |
| water | 1 cup | 240 ml |
| espresso powder | ½ teaspoon | 0.5 g |
| egg whites, at room temperature | 6 | |
| salt | ½ teaspoon | 3 g |
| vanilla extract | 2 teaspoons | 10 ml |
| chopped toasted pecans | 1 cup | 110 g |
| pecan halves | 50 | |

⑤ Cover the nougat with plastic wrap and allow it to set for at least 2 hours. Cut into individual pieces (pillows), and garnish each with a pecan half, then wrap the pieces in wax paper. Keeps for up to 1 week in an airtight container.

*Clockwise From Top Right:* **VERMONTER SPONGE CANDY, MAPLE PILLOWS, BULLOCK SISTERS' SPICY BRITTLE, BUTTERY ALMOND TOFFEE**

# VERMONTER
# SPONGE CANDY

*Like honeycomb, Vermonter sponge is a version of that old-fashioned Christmas staple, sea foam.* This is also the wonderful stuff that's at the heart of a Butterfinger candy bar. It's crunchy and chewy and utterly delectable.

IIIIIIIIIIIIIIIIIIIIIIIIIIIIIIIIIIIIIIIIIIIIIII *Makes approximately 20 pieces* IIIIIIIIIIIIIIIIIIIIIIIIIIIIIIIIIIIIIIIIIIIIIII

① In a large saucepan over medium heat, combine all the ingredients except the baking soda. Stir until the sugar has dissolved.

② Clip on a candy thermometer, stop stirring, and raise the heat to medium-high. Boil until the temperature reaches 300°F (149°C).

③ Remove the saucepan from the heat and immediately stir in the baking soda. Make sure you don't dump the baking soda all in one place. Sift or sprinkle it about the surface and then stir well; otherwise you'll be left with clumps that haven't dissolved in the finished product.

④ As soon as the syrup has stopped foaming, pour it onto a parchment-lined sheet pan sprayed with nonstick spray.

⑤ Allow to cool completely and then break into pieces. Store in an airtight container in a cool, dry place for up to a week.

| grade B maple syrup | 1 cup | 240 ml |
| sugar | ½ cup | 100 g |
| distilled white vinegar | 2 teaspoons | 10 ml |
| salt | ½ teaspoon | 3 g |
| baking soda | 2 teaspoons | 10 g |

# HONEYCOMB

*Honeycomb manages to be many things at once: airy, chewy, crunchy, weird, and wonderful.* The large amount of baking soda added at the very end causes the honey syrup to erupt spectacularly. It's a beautiful sight to behold.

|||||||||||||||||||||||||||||||||||||||| *Makes approximately 20 pieces* ||||||||||||||||||||||||||||||||||||||||

| | | |
|---|---|---|
| sugar | 2 cups | 400 g |
| local honey | ½ cup | 170 g |
| unsalted butter | 4 tablespoons | 55 g |
| cream of tartar | ½ teaspoon | 1.5 g |
| water | ½ cup | 120 ml |
| salt | ½ teaspoon | 3 g |
| baking soda | 1 tablespoon | 15 g |

**What's with the baking soda?** Baking soda creates carbon dioxide bubbles that get trapped in the honeycomb and create its airy texture. This is the same concept as adding leavening to a cake; the air bubbles created by the carbon dioxide lead to a steady rise during baking. However, in a sugar syrup, the bubbles get trapped and create a permanent record of their existence— a confectionery Pompeii. Honeycomb is supercharged with baking soda, so you get a texture reminiscent of an English Flake Bar. Smaller amounts are added to peanut brittle and toffee, to keep the hard-crack candy from cracking your tooth enamel.

① Line an 8-by-8-inch (20-by-20-cm) baking dish with parchment and spray with nonstick spray. Place the dish on a parchment-lined sheet pan (in case the syrup boils over the edge of the dish). Set aside.

② In a large, heavy saucepan over medium heat, combine the sugar, honey, butter, cream of tartar, water, and salt. Simmer, stirring occasionally, until the sugar has dissolved.

③ Clip on a candy thermometer and raise the heat to medium-high, stop stirring, and allow to boil until the temperature reads 300°F to 305°F (149°C to 152°C).

④ Remove the syrup from the heat. Immediately sift the baking soda over the syrup and stir. Be careful; this will bubble and rise.

⑤ Immediately pour the honeycomb into the prepared pan. Be *very* careful not to touch the dish or the table before the candy has set. Any agitation after the candy has been poured into the dish will cause the air bubbles to burst and this will ruin the consistency of the candy.

⑥ Allow the candy to cool completely and break into small pieces. Store the honeycomb in an airtight container for up to two weeks. Any hint of moisture will make the candy soggy.

**Options!**

OPTION 1: **MUSKY**
For a muskier flavor, replace the honey with molasses.

OPTION 2: **BUTTERY**
For a lighter, more buttery taste, replace the honey with light corn syrup and add 1 teaspoon of vanilla along with the baking soda.

OPTION 3: **CHOCOLATY**
Dunk the pieces in melted chocolate for a sublime honey-cocoa treat.

# AUNT SIS'S
## *Peanut*
# BRITTLE

*I actually don't have my Aunt Sis's peanut brittle recipe, but this is how I imagine it would be—with a slightly earthy undertone of the molasses that's present in brown sugar and just a hint of salt.* Aunt Sis kept things simple and elegant. After an arduous morning spent lolling in the sun and swimming in the Florida waters, I scampered back to her beach house on stilts at Alligator Point for lunch. She offered me a slender-looking sandwich. My dad was happily chomping on one of his own. He and I both lived under my mother's strict culinary regime of whole grain and tofu back in Virginia and he had never looked this giddy eating lunch in Arlington. So I took Aunt Sis up on her offer and spent a few fleeting minutes savoring three ingredients: white bread, real mayonnaise, and sliced fresh tomatoes. Simple and elegant, like my beautiful Aunt Sis—and just how I imagine her brittle would have been.

|||||||||||||||||||||||||||||||||||||||||||| *Makes approximately 1 pound (455 g)* ||||||||||||||||||||||||||||||||||||||||||||

① In a large saucepan over low heat, combine the brown sugar, corn syrup, water, butter, and salt. Stir until the sugar has completely melted.

② Wash down the sides of the pan with a damp pastry brush to banish those pesky sugar crystals, clip on a candy thermometer, and raise the heat to high. Heat to 290°F (143°C).

③ Remove the brittle from the heat and quickly stir in the baking soda and the peanuts.

④ Immediately pour the brittle onto a parchment-lined sheet pan sprayed with nonstick cooking spray. Spread the brittle as evenly as you can; I find the back of a large spoon sprayed with nonstick cooking spray helpful. Alternatively, put on a pair of dishwashing gloves coated with oil or cooking spray, and pull the candy by hand.

| brown sugar, firmly packed | 1½ cups | 330 g |
|---|---|---|
| corn syrup | ½ cup | 120 ml |
| water | ¼ cup | 60 ml |
| unsalted butter | 2 tablespoons | 28 g |
| salt | ½ teaspoon | 3 g |
| salted dry-roasted peanuts | 1 cup | 150 g |
| baking soda | 1 teaspoon | 5 g |

⑤ Allow the brittle to cool completely and then break into small pieces. Store in an airtight container in a cool, dry place for up to 2 weeks.

# BULLOCK SISTERS'
## *Spicy*
# BRITTLE

*We like it salty, spicy, and crunchy.* And in mass quantities. Enough said.

|||||||||||||||||||||||||||||||||||||||||||||| *Makes approximately 1½ pounds (680 g)* ||||||||||||||||||||||||||||||||||||||||||||||

| | | |
|---|---|---|
| sugar | 2 cups | 400 g |
| corn syrup | ½ cup | 120 ml |
| unsalted butter | ¼ cup | 55 g |
| salt | 1 teaspoon | 6 g |
| cayenne pepper | 1 teaspoon | 2 g |
| baking soda | 1 teaspoon | 5 g |
| salted dry-roasted peanuts | 3 cups | 150 g |

① In a large, heavy stockpot over medium heat, combine the sugar, corn syrup, butter, salt, and cayenne pepper. Stir until the sugar has dissolved.

② Clip on a candy thermometer, stop stirring, and boil until the temperature reaches 300°F (149°C).

③ Immediately remove the pot from the heat. Sprinkle the baking soda over the syrup and stir. The contents will bubble vigorously. Immediately stir in the peanuts.

④ Quickly pour the mixture onto a sheet pan sprayed with nonstick baking spray. Try to pour the brittle evenly; you can use a small offset spatula (also sprayed with nonstick spray) to coax the brittle to spread evenly in the pan while it's still warm.

⑤ Allow to cool completely and break into pieces. Store in an airtight container for up to 2 weeks.

# BUTTERY
## *Almond*
# TOFFEE

*Buttercrunch is really just another name for toffee.* Many recipes for the two are indistinguishable. However, I felt that this particular recipe warranted the title "buttercrunch" more than any other due to the sheer volume of butter. Many people have written me asking if I could find a recipe that rivaled their grandmothers' toffee—they found that the recipes available in most places simply didn't have the buttery quotient their ancestral sweets had. So I wanted to share this old-school way of making toffee that was around before corn syrup invaded our confectionery landscape, and when simple ingredients were the mainstay of delicious treats. The beauty of this recipe is that you can double or triple it with ease; for each cup (200 g) of sugar, you need 1 cup (230 g) of butter.

|||||||||||||||||||||||||||||||||||||||||||||||||| *Makes about 2½ pounds (1.2 kg)* ||||||||||||||||||||||||||||||||||||||||||||||||||

① Preheat the oven to 325° (165°C). Spread the almond flour evenly on a sheet pan, then bake until golden brown, about five minutes. Set aside.

② In a large saucepan over low heat, melt the butter. Add the sugar, salt, and vanilla extract, stirring until the sugar melts. Clip on a candy thermometer, raise the heat to medium-high, and continue stirring until the mixture turns amber and the temperature reads 300°F (149°C).

③ Quickly whisk in the baking soda.

④ Immediately pour the toffee onto a parchment-lined sheet pan sprayed with nonstick cooking spray. Allow to sit, undisturbed, for 5 minutes.

⑤ Sprinkle the chocolate chips evenly over the toffee and leave it to melt for another 5 minutes. Then, using a small offset spatula or the back of a large spoon, spread the chocolate evenly over the toffee and sprinkle with the almond flour.

| unsalted butter | 2 cups | 455 g |
|---|---|---|
| sugar | 2 cups | 400 g |
| salt | 1 teaspoon | 6 g |
| vanilla extract | 1 teaspoon | 5 ml |
| baking soda | ¼ teaspoon | 1 g |
| bittersweet chocolate chips | 1 cup | 130 g |
| almond flour, toasted | 1 cup | 140 g |

⑥ Allow the toffee to cool completely and then break it into small pieces. If you like a thicker toffee, pour the mixture into a parchment-lined and nonstick-sprayed 10-by-13-inch (25-by-33-cm) baking pan or similarly sized high-walled casserole dish. Store in an airtight container in a cool, dry place for up to 2 weeks.

# COTTON
# CANDY

*Or candy floss!* Or fairy floss! Or Papa's beard! Personally, I prefer "candy floss," the British appellation, because it conjures a host of potential nightmares for dental technicians; while I have the utmost respect for those lovely people, there's the evil gnome in me that would love to see "candy floss" in the dental hygiene aisle just to vex them. "Fairy floss" is a perfectly scrumptious name, and it pleases me immeasurably to think of burly, stubbly Aussie blokes ordering up "fairy floss" for their sweet little children. And speaking of stubble, who in the hell thought it was a good idea to call something you wrap on a stick and eat "Papa's beard"?

Regardless of what other people call it, it's heaven on earth. Just not to a dentist.

||||||||||||||||||||||||||||||||||||||||||||||| *Makes 8 cotton candies* |||||||||||||||||||||||||||||||||||||||||||||||

| | | |
|---|---|---|
| sugar | 4 cups | 800 g |
| corn syrup | 1 cup | 240 ml |
| water | 1 cup | 240 ml |
| salt | ¼ teaspoon | 1.5 g |
| raspberry extract (or any flavor you like) | 1 teaspoon | 5 ml |
| pink (or any color) food coloring (optional) | 2 drops | |
| "decapitated" whisk | | |

**We all know you make cotton candy with that big round drum thingy with air shooting through it.** It's a very specialized piece of equipment, made just for cotton candy production. To make cotton candy at home, you also need a very specialized piece of equipment: a decapitated whisk. With a wire cutter, snip the tines at the end of a wire whisk so you have straight metal branches. This will not yield quite as feather-light a result as the carnival iteration, but it's pretty damn close, and you won't have to invest thousands of dollars in eclectic machinery.

① In a large, heavy saucepan over medium heat, combine the sugar, corn syrup, water, and salt. Stir until the sugar is melted. With a damp pastry brush, wipe down the sides of the pan to prevent stray sugar crystals from forming.

② Clip on a candy thermometer, stop stirring, and heat to 320°F (160°C). Pour the molten liquid into a shallow heatproof container. Add the extract and food coloring (if using) and stir well.

③ Line your work table with parchment. I also spread parchment on the floor around the table to catch any stray bits of flying sugar.

④ Dip your decapitated whisk into the sugar syrup and hold it over the pot to let the sugar drip back into container for a second. Holding the whisk a foot (30 cm) above the parchment, swing the whisk back and forth so that thin strands of sugar fall on the paper. Repeat this a few more times until you have a nice nest of spun sugar.

⑤ Immediately wrap the cotton candy around large lollipop sticks (if you wait too long, the

sugar will become brittle and won't bend around the stick). Eat immediately or seal in airtight containers—any moisture will make the cotton candy soggy.

With Cotton Candy
Make Gesine and Ray Get Married, page 213

**Options!**

Now that you've got a handle on spun sugar, you can probably imagine possibilities beyond wrapping these glorious sweet strands around a carnie stick. Instead of swinging the sugar back and forth like a pendulum, spin it into a circle to make a bird's nest or a cloud. Build a mound of cream puffs and spin the sugar round and round to make a gorgeous sugar cage, the glorious French *croquembouche*. See page 206 for all the possibilities.

# SUPER-CRUNCHY
# SALTY NUTS

*One particularly glacial winter, my mother thought it a brilliant idea to attend the public performance of* Jedermann *("Everyman") in Salzburg.* This would have been a splendid idea if the iconic play hadn't been staged outside at the Domplatz, the open square in front of a terrifically baroque cathedral. I spent the entire time wiggling my toes in an effort to regain some feeling and staring longingly at the carts selling steaming hot candied almonds. Making these sweet nuggets always brings back memories of those frigid moments in my favorite city and reminds me that no matter how much I love a place and no matter how iconic a theatrical production is, I'd always rather be at home with my salty, crunchy nuts.

|||||||||||||||||||||||||||||||||||||||||||||| *Makes 3½ cups (750 g)* ||||||||||||||||||||||||||||||||||||||||||||||

① In a large, heavy saucepan over medium heat, combine the sugar, water, salt, and lemon juice. Stir until the sugar has melted.

② Wash down the sides of the saucepan with a damp pastry brush, stop stirring, clip on a candy thermometer, and heat the syrup to 310°F (154°C).

③ Immediately remove the pan from the heat and sprinkle the baking soda into the syrup. Stir briskly to prevent any chunks of baking soda from lingering.

④ Working very quickly, stir in the nuts with a rubber spatula sprayed with nonstick spray. When the nuts are fully coated, pour the mixture onto a parchment-lined sheet pan that's been liberally sprayed with nonstick cooking spray. Use the spatula to spread the nuts out in an even layer.

⑤ Allow to cool completely and break into small pieces. Store in an airtight container in a cool, dry place for up to 2 weeks.

| | | |
|---|---|---|
| sugar | 3 cups | 600 g |
| water | ½ cup | 120 ml |
| salt | 1 teaspoon | 6 g |
| lemon juice | ½ teaspoon | 2.5 ml |
| baking soda | 1 tablespoon | 15 g |
| roasted, salted mixed nuts | 3 cups | 330 g |

**Option!**

**POPCORN MEDLEY**

I'm all for caramel popcorn, but I like to add salted nuts and corn flakes to the mix. Spray a large metal bowl and two large spoons with nonstick spray. Pour your popcorn components into the bowl. When the caramel is ready, immediately pour it over the popcorn. Using the spoons, toss the ingredients until evenly coated. Transfer to a parchment-lined sheet pan and allow to cool completely. You can even add some cayenne as you're making the caramel if you want to give it a little kick. Mix 1 teaspoon (2 g) cayenne with the baking soda and stir them in together in step 3.

# PULL-PARTY
# CANDY

*I've told you about my Nanny and her preternatural skills with hot sugar.* She could boil it without the aid of a thermometer and find her way to hard-crack without courting crystallization or burnt caramelization. I like to think that within my own motley chain of double helixes, I've got some of her skill buried in my DNA. But I still use a candy thermometer, no matter how mad I think my skills are.

You'll notice there's a high ratio of corn syrup to sugar in this recipe. Feel free to substitute honey for the corn syrup. The main reason for the equal amounts is that corn syrup (and honey) are invert sugars and don't crystallize as quickly as granulated sugar, so you can pull them far longer. And the more you pull, the more fun you have. Another perk is that fifteen minutes of pulling sugar will tucker a kid out. Sadly, eating the sugar when it's done will undo all that tuckering.

||||||||||||||||||||||||||||||||||||||| *Makes approximately 2 pounds (910 g)* |||||||||||||||||||||||||||||||||||||||

| sugar | 2 cups | 400 g |
|---|---|---|
| corn syrup | 2 cups | 480 ml |
| salt | 1 teaspoon | 6 g |
| extract of your choice (lemon, raspberry, almond, peppermint) | 1 teaspoon | 5 ml |
| food coloring(s) of your choice | 3 drops | |

① In a large, heavy saucepan over medium heat, combine the sugar, corn syrup, and salt. Stir over medium heat until the sugar has completely dissolved. With a damp pastry brush, wipe down the sides of the pan to prevent stray sugar crystals from forming.

② Clip on a candy thermometer, stop stirring, and raise the heat to high. Boil until the temperature reaches 300°F (149°C).

③ Pour the hot syrup onto a marble slab (or other heatproof and nonstick surface) sprayed with nonstick spray. Using two bench scrapers, fold the edges of the sugar into the middle, making sure to catch it before it goes over the edge of your counter. This helps cool the candy and also keeps the edges from becoming brittle while the middle is still warm and pliable.

④ While the candy is still too hot to handle, add your chosen extract and food coloring. Keep folding the edges of the candy toward the middle to incorporate both. The color probably won't be completely distributed yet, but once you start pulling, it will be fully incorporated.

5. When the candy is just cool enough to handle, spray your hands with nonstick spray (if you're wearing gloves, spray the gloves). Pull it into a rope, pick up an end in each hand, and pull the candy apart—but not so much that the candy thins to the point of snapping. Bring the ends together to fold the rope in two; then keep the joined ends in one hand and grab the new "other" end in your other hand. Pull and join again, and continue to do this for 10 to 15 minutes, or until the candy is opaque, milky, and terribly difficult to pull.

6. Pull the cooling candy into a long rope about ¼ inch (6 mm) in diameter. Using scissors sprayed with nonstick spray, cut the rope into ½-inch (12-mm) pieces.

7. Wrap each piece in a small piece of wax paper. The candy will keep for weeks in a tightly covered container. *Don't refrigerate.*

**Option!**

This is a perfect recipe for candy canes. Add peppermint extract, then divide the warm sugar syrup in half. Keep one half plain and put 2 drops of red food coloring in the other half. Twist the two colors together into a long rope and candy cane away.

If you're an avid Food Network viewer, you've likely watched a sugar sculpture competition, what I've dubbed "the sticky heart attack." The drama! If you've actually been listening and aren't just hypnotized by all the pretty colors and intermittent crashes, you've probably heard the words "isomalt" and "decomalt." These are products used quite often in sugar work due to the fact that they don't caramelize and they don't crystallize. Both are sugar alcohols made from the sugar beet and are actually considered safe for diabetic consumption because they don't affect insulin levels as granulated sugar does. They're also a one-to-one substitute in sugar work recipes calling for granulated sugar, which cuts down on the math. Just be aware that if you consider playing with them, you'll have to boil them to a higher temperature to achieve the same results as granulated hard-crack or soft-ball, So the cold water test really comes in handy. Oh, and they can cause intestinal distress if consumed in large doses. But feel free to experiment if you're game. Just remember, don't eat too much.

# FRUITY
## *Quilt*
# LOLLIPOPS

*One Friday, I had spent a few hours demonstrating a complicated baking technique to some students, knowing from the beginning that the chances of anyone going home and trying it was slim to none.* Sure, it was a super-cool-looking piece of cake decoration, but for a beginner it was a righteous pain in the arse. I had brought something to ease the pain: some multicolored lollipops in myriad shapes—hearts, dragonflies, and apples. When asked where they could be purchased, I said, "Well, I made them myself." There was a collective groan that translated to, "Not another impossible pastry task we'll never master."

I explained that it was not only easy, it was easy peasy. If you can boil sugar, add color to it, and swirl it around in a sprayed cookie cutter, you're golden. And for an added treat, you can use this same technique to adorn your next holiday gingerbread house with actual windows! Since I always eat my gingerbread houses when they're fresh, I make my own colored candy, so I know that all my double-paned windows will be delicious.

||||||||||||||||||||||||||||||||||||||||||||||||||| *Makes 10 large lollipops* |||||||||||||||||||||||||||||||||||||||||||||||||||

| | | |
|---|---|---|
| sugar | 2 cups | 400 g |
| corn syrup | ¾ cup | 180 ml |
| lemon juice | 1 squirt | |
| water | ½ cup | 120 ml |
| food coloring | 2 drops per container | |
| extract of your choice | 1 teaspoon per container | 5 ml per container |

① In a large, heavy saucepan over medium heat, combine the sugar, corn syrup, lemon juice, and water. Stir until the sugar has completely melted.

② Wash down the sides of the pot with a damp pastry brush, clip on a candy thermometer, stop stirring, and increase the heat to high. Heat the sugar syrup to 300°F (149°C).

③ Remove the syrup from the heat and pour the molten candy into multiple heatproof containers with spouts (if you plan on making multiple colors); add 1 to 2 drops food coloring and ½ to 1 teaspoon (5 ml) extract to each container; the amount will vary depending on how many colors you choose to make from one batch. Stir the colorant and extract into the hot sugar. Work quickly—the candy will start to set.

④ For the easy method, spray 10 lollipop molds with nonstick cooking spray. Place the lollipop sticks in the proper nooks on the molds. Pour small amounts of each color of syrup you're using directly into each mold until it is full. Swirl the colors with a toothpick and allow to set until completely cool. Twist the mold to release the lollipops.

⑤ If you'd prefer to try my favorite method, instead of using molds, pour the candy onto a parchment-lined sheet pan sprayed with non-stick cooking spray, giving each color enough room to spread without touching others (but if they do touch, it's really not the end of the world). Allow the candy to cool and harden completely.

⑥ Break the candy into small, dime-size (12-mm) pieces; a rubber mallet works best. (You can also break the sugar up with your hands but I don't recommend it—I've had shards of sugar cut me just as sharply as a knife.)

⑦ Place shaped cookie cutters (hearts, flowers, ducks, the state of Vermont) sprayed with nonstick cooking spray on a parchment-lined sheet pan (also sprayed with nonstick spray). Place the pieces of candy inside the cookie cutters. Don't leave too many gaps in between the pieces of candy, but don't overlap them either.

⑧ Place the sheet pan in a 225°F (110°C) oven for 10 minutes, or until the candy has just melted. Remove from the oven and allow the candy to cool. Remove the cookie cutters and transfer the candy shapes to a parchment-lined work surface to cool.

⑨ Put a few extra broken shards of candy on the sheet pan by themselves. You'll use these as "adhesive." Warm them in the 225°F (110°C) oven for 5 minutes.

⑩ Remove the pan from the oven. Hold a lollipop stick in place on the back side of a candy shape so that about 1 inch (2.5 cm) is on the candy. Using a small offset spatula sprayed with non-stick spray, pick up one of the hot shards you're using as adhesive and place it over the portion of the stick on the candy so that it overlaps like a piece of tape to adhere the stick to the candy. You may need to use more than one piece for each stick, and it takes a little practice to hold the stick and transfer the hot shard, but the good news is that you can reheat the sugar pieces a few times in the event they cool and harden while you're working. Check out www.sugarbabycookbook.com for a picture illustration of how to do this. Store in an airtight container in a cool, dry place for up to 2 weeks.

**Option!**

### WINDOWS

To make lovely windows for your holiday gingerbread house or castle, just cut the window openings as you normally would, lay the gingerbread on the parchment, fill them with hot colored sugar, and let the candy set. If you really want to cheat, you can go to your local five-and-dime and pick up a horrendous bag of super-cheap multicolored hard candies. Unwrap them and stick them in a heavy-duty zip-top bag, then hammer them to pieces. Don't pulverize them, but crack them about the noggin just enough to get multiple pieces from each candy. Before you've baked your gingerbread, arrange candy pieces in the window and door openings, and they'll melt together to form beautiful—and edible—stained glass windows.

# BARLEY
# ROSES

*For such a simple confection, barley candies are a conundrum, historically speaking.* One thing we know is that they have been around for quite a while—they were very popular in the Victorian era, especially during the English Christmas season. It's their etymology that's in question, not their age. There's the obvious conclusion we can draw: barley sugar or barley candies derive their name from their ingredients: barley and sugar. Makes sense.

But then there had been all those pesky wars between the English and the French, making it likely that during breaks in the bloodletting, recipes were exchanged. Of course, it would have been a very one-sided exchange, the French having all the good stuff; one of those good things was *sucre brûlée* (caramelized or burnt sugar). One can imagine that the words *sucre* and *brûlée* might have been transformed over time to become "barley sugar." Today, candies called "barley sugar" contain only sugar. No barley. So the etymological transformation from the French *sucre brûlée* to the English "barley sugar" is possible. But unlike butterscotch, where there is nary a recipe to be found containing Scotch, there are recipes for barley sugar that *do* contain barley, and that work—like mine. To evoke a Victorian candy feel, I pour the hot barley sugar into miniature decorative baking molds. My favorite is a rose.

|||||||||||||||||||||||||||||||||||||||||||||||||||  *Makes 24 barley roses*  |||||||||||||||||||||||||||||||||||||||||||||||||||

| barley | 1 cup | 225 g |
|---|---|---|
| water | 1 gallon | 3.8 L |
| sugar | 4 ½ cups | 900 g |
| salt | ½ teaspoon | 3 g |
| lemon juice | 1 squirt | |
| food coloring | 2 drops | |
| extract of your choice* | 1 teaspoon | 5 ml |
| *My favorites are raspberry and orange. | | |

① Liberally spray a nonstick rose mini Bundt pan with nonstick cooking spray. (I use a Nordic Ware Sweetheart Rose Mini Bundt with twelve cavities.) Set aside.

② Place the barley and water in a large stockpot over low heat and simmer for 3 hours. Keep the temperature low enough that all of the water does not evaporate—it's the barley water we're going to use in the recipe, not the barley itself.

③ Strain the barley through a sieve over a large measuring cup to catch the barley water. You should have between 1 and 2 cups (240 and 480 ml) of gelatinous barley water.

✱ **A Note from the Sugar Baby:** If you're like me, the leftover barley will not go to waste. Unfortunately, it's going to be overdone to the point where it's useless in many cooking applications. But I add this extra-mushy barley directly to finished soups. Or if it's summer and a heavy soup isn't on the agenda, I feed the barley to my chickens. No creature likes mushy barley more than a hen. Just don't give her any candy.

④ In a large saucepan over medium heat, combine the sugar, 1 cup (240 ml) barley water, the salt, and lemon juice. (You can save any leftover barley water in the fridge for the next time you make candy.) Stir with a wooden spoon until the sugar dissolves.

⑤ Raise the heat to medium-high, clip on a candy thermometer, stop stirring, and heat to 300°F (149°C).

⑥ Pour the sugar into a heatproof container with a spout. Quickly stir in the food coloring and extract. Pour the sugar syrup into the cavities of the rose Bundt so they are a little less than one-quarter full. Allow to cool for about 10 minutes.

⑦ With a small offset spatula sprayed with nonstick cooking spray, gently pry each rose from the form. If the candy has cooled and hardened too much, the prying will cause it to crack at the edges. If this happens, put the baking mold in a 225°F (110°C) oven for about 5 minutes and try again. You'll find that the roses come out best when the sugar is firm but still malleable.

⑧ You can individually package the roses as-is, or you can melt dime-size pieces of hard sugar in the oven for a few minutes until they are hot but still hold their shape, then use a hot piece of sugar to adhere a lollipop stick to the back of each rose as I did on page 220. Store in an airtight container in a cool, dry place for up to 2 weeks.

**Option!**

### SWIZZLES

If you're feeling adventurous, you can hand-pull the barley sugar into long ropes and twist them into swizzle sticks. You can even split the syrup among different slabs, vary the colors, pull two ropes of different hues, hold them side by side, and twist them together.

Pour the sugar syrup onto a prepared surface (a marble slab or the back of a sheet pan) sprayed with nonstick spray. Using two offset spatulas, also nonstick-sprayed, fold the edges of the hot candy toward the middle to ensure that the candy cools evenly. After the candy has thickened considerably but is still too hot to handle, add a few drops of food coloring and 1 teaspoon (5 ml) of the extract of your choice (if you choose to doctor the candy at all). If you're using a white marble slab, you run the risk of staining your marble with the food coloring, so be careful. Continue to fold the ends toward the middle to incorporate the coloring and the extract.

When the candy is cool enough to handle, yet still warm and malleable, start pulling it into a long rope. Fold the rope in half and pull again, as you would taffy, but only do this for 2 or 3 turns. This is to simply incorporate the coloring and the extract and *not* to aerate the candy. The candy should be relatively clear and too much pulling will cause it to turn opaque.

This is a lot to pull at once, so you can cut the candy into thirds, put two of those pieces onto a parchment-lined sheet pan, and keep the pan in a 200°F (90°C) oven to keep it soft. Pull the candy into a long rope, a little less than ½ inch (12 mm) in diameter, and cut the rope into pieces 4 inches (10 cm) long. Twist the pieces on either end so that they look like long pieces of candy fusilli. Store in an airtight container in a cool, dry place for up to 2 weeks.

# PSYCHEDELIC
## *(Yet Patriotic)*
# SUGAR BOWL

*This free-form bowl is the perfect centerpiece for a sweet-centric party.* Let it stand on its own or fill it with treats; either way you can eat it when you're done.

|||||||||||||||||||||||||||||||||||||||||||||||||||| *Makes 1 large bowl* ||||||||||||||||||||||||||||||||||||||||||||||||||||||

① Place a 10-inch (25-cm) cake ring on a parchment-lined sheet pan. Liberally spray the inside of the ring and the parchment with nonstick cooking spray. Set aside. Have toothpicks and a small mixing bowl turned upside down next to the sheet pan.

✱ **A Note from the Sugar Baby:** The size of the bowl is important. Though it doesn't have to be exact, it does have to be larger than a cereal bowl but not so large that the sugar circle you'll drape over the upside-down bowl barely covers it. Ideally, when you drape the sugar over the bowl, the sugar bowl sides should reach at least halfway down the sides of the mixing bowl.

② In a large, heavy saucepan over medium heat, combine the sugar, corn syrup, lemon juice, and water. Stir until the sugar has completely melted.

③ Brush down the sides of the pan with a damp pastry brush to eradicate rebellious crystals, stop stirring, and clip on a candy thermometer. Heat the sugar to 310°F (154°C).

④ Immediately pour the sugar into the prepared cake ring. Mentally divide the circle of sugar into three zones, like a peace sign. Each zone will contain one color: One will be blue, one will be red, and the third will be left clear for white. Squeeze a drop of blue food coloring into the

| sugar | 2 cups | 400 g |
|---|---|---|
| corn syrup | ¾ cup | 180 ml |
| lemon juice | 1 squirt | |
| water | ½ cup | 120 ml |
| red food coloring | 1 drop | |
| blue food coloring | 1 drop | |

middle of one zone and, with a toothpick, swirl the color around the zone. Do the same in the next zone with the red food coloring, overlapping with the blue just at the edges to make a little purple where they meet (after all, it's not psychedelic if it doesn't have a hint of purple). Since this is psychedelic, you can stray into another zone and let the colors mix at the edges, and you can swirl very light streaks into the area you leave "white" so that it shares in the color fun.

⑤ If you find that the sugar is setting too quickly for you to successfully pull the toothpick through, place the sheet pan in a 225°F (110°C) oven for 5 minutes to loosen it up a bit.

⑥ When you've finished swirling the colors, gently touch the sugar to make sure it's cool enough to hold its shape when you remove the ring but still warm enough to bend. Carefully remove the ring; check the malleability of the sugar by lifting an edge of the sugar circle. It should bend easily but the shape of the circle should remain set. If it has hardened too much to bend safely without cracking, place the ring back around the sugar and warm in a 225°F (110°C) oven for 5 minutes.

⑦ Immediately transfer the parchment with the sugar circle to the top of the inverted bowl, the parchment side down and touching the bowl. Cover the top of the sugar with another sheet of parchment sprayed with nonstick cooking spray. With your hands, gently shape the sugar so that it bends to the shape of the bowl. It doesn't need to be perfect—as a matter of fact, the sugar bowl has more character and life if there are bends and folds in it. The main objective is to create a vessel that clearly resembles a bowl. Allow the sugar bowl to cool completely and remove the parchment pieces from both sides of it.

⑧ If you don't use the sugar bowl immediately, store it in an airtight container in dry and cool conditions. It will last for up to 1 month. Don't place moisture-laden things (like fresh cut fruit) in the bowl unless you want the bowl to melt!

# BUBBLE
# SUGAR

*I'm not a woman prone to sharing recipes for novelty food.* And by novelty food, I mean food that is not to be eaten. And by food to be eaten, I mean food that is not just edible, but delightful. Bubble sugar is my one culinary exemption, because I believe it's OK to share a recipe that's so damn fun it doesn't matter whether it's delicious . . . or even edible.

The uses for bubble sugar are finite. Left clear or tinted blue, it makes for a lovely water feature on a cake. Tinted fiery orange or red, it's the magma to your volcano. That's a pretty limited spectrum of uses, but damn it's fun—so fun that you'll invent excuses to make it.

|||||||||||||||||||||||||||||||||||||||||||| *Makes approximately 8 ounces (225 g)* ||||||||||||||||||||||||||||||||||||||||||||

① Pour the alcohol into a small bowl.

② Line a sheet pan with parchment. With a pastry brush, "paint" the alcohol onto the parchment. If you want more "movement" in your bubble sugar wave, first crinkle the parchment and then smooth it out on the sheet pan before painting it. Set aside.

| clear grain alcohol | 2 tablespoons | 30 ml |
|---|---|---|
| sugar | 1 cup | 200 g |
| corn syrup | 3 tablespoons | 45 ml |
| water | ⅓ cup | 75 ml |
| food coloring (I like blue) | 2 drops | |

③ In a large, heavy saucepan over medium-high heat, combine the sugar, corn syrup, and water. Stir until the sugar dissolves.

④ Wipe down the sides of the saucepan with a damp pastry brush, stop stirring, clip on a candy thermometer, and raise the heat to high. Heat the sugar to 315°F (157°C).

⑤ Quickly stir in the food coloring.

⑥ Holding the sheet pan at a slight angle, pour the sugar from the top and let it run down the expanse of the pan. The alcohol will cause the sugar to bubble.

⑦ Allow the sugar to cool completely and then break into pieces large enough to serve as ersatz water features or volcanic spray. Store in an airtight container in a cool, dry place for up to 2 weeks.

# SHANGHAI
## *Caramel*
# APPLES

*What's better than a gooey caramel apple on a crisp Halloween evening?* How about a deep-fried bite of tart Granny Smith smothered in crackling sugar glaze? Meet the mother of caramel apple recipes, a delight for all the senses and a combination that will kick that sticky apple on a stick to the curb.

||||||||||||||||||||||||||||||||||||||||||||||||||||||||| *Makes 16 slices* |||||||||||||||||||||||||||||||||||||||||||||||||||

| | | |
|---|---|---|
| all-purpose flour | ¾ cup, divided | 90 g, divided |
| cornstarch | ½ cup | 65 g |
| salt | ½ teaspoon | 3 g |
| baking powder | 1 teaspoon | 5 g |
| water | 1 cup, divided | 240 ml, divided |
| medium apples, cored, quartered, each quarter cut into 2 slices | 2 | |
| cinnamon | 1 teaspoon | 2 g |
| canola oil, for frying | 4 cups | 960 ml |
| sugar | 2 cups | 400 g |
| lemon juice | 1 squirt | |
| baking soda | 1 teaspoon | 5 g |
| black sesame seeds (optional) | 2 tablespoons | 20 g |

① Stir together ½ cup (60 g) of the flour, the cornstarch, salt, baking powder, and ½ cup (120 ml) of the water until the mixture comes together into a smooth batter.

② Place the apple slices, the remaining ¼ cup (30 g) flour, and the cinnamon in a large zip-top bag. Seal the bag and shake until the pieces of apple are evenly coated with the flour mixture.

③ In a large saucepan or a wok, heat the oil. Attach a candy thermometer and allow the oil to reach 350°F (177°C).

④ Coat the individual pieces of apple in the batter just before frying. Using a large slotted spoon or a large wire-mesh spider skimmer, gently lower the apple pieces into the oil, being careful to avoid hot oil splattering in your general direction. Fry until golden brown, 3 to 4 minutes. With a clean wire skimmer or a slotted spoon, carefully remove the apple pieces. Transfer the pieces to a sheet pan lined with paper towels. Set aside.

5. Clean the wok or saucepan (remember to dispose of the oil in an environmentally friendly manner, assuming your car doesn't take biofuel) and spray with nonstick cooking spray. Add the sugar, the remaining ½ cup (120 ml) water, and the lemon juice. Cook over medium-low heat, stirring until the sugar has completely melted. Wipe down the sides of the wok or saucepan with a damp pastry brush, stop stirring, clip on your cleaned candy thermometer, and raise the heat to high. Heat the sugar until it reaches 300°F (149°C).

6. Reduce the heat to low, add the baking soda, stir quickly, then immediately add all the apples, stirring to coat them completely.

7. Transfer the apples to a serving platter sprayed with nonstick cooking spray and sprinkle with the sesame seeds (if using). Serve immediately, along with a bowl of ice water and a cup full of chopsticks. Instruct your guests to grab a piece of apple with the chop sticks and dunk it quickly into the ice water to harden the caramel before shoving it into their mouths.

You've probably heard the term "mouthfeel." You may have even used it. (If you have, chances are you've also managed to finesse "tablescape" and "soupçon" into a sentence. Well done.) I think a lot about mouthfeel. For instance, I've given hours of contemplation to my aversion to slippery slivers of canned beets versus the great pleasure I find in slurping slimy oysters. I have a definite viewpoint on how food should feel in my mouth, and it's no surprise that my staunchest opinions have to do with candy.

I'm not a fan of mushy, easily masticated nubs of sugar. I like the sweet stuff to put up a fight, and how I achieve this has everything to do with temperature. When you see the ranges within a temperature zone, you'll start to realize that you can use temperature to customize candies to suit your own mouthfeel preferences. This holds true primarily in confections within the higher ranges—the "balls" and the "cracks"—and not so much in the lower ranges, where you are often combining ingredients with the heated sugar to achieve a very specific (and not-to-be-tampered-with) result. But when it comes to caramels, hard candies, and brittles, one person's pleasantly crunchy may be another person's dental Waterloo. Some people like to suck on a lemon drop until it melts into oblivion (show-offs); others (such as me) attempt to savor slowly and end up employing their molars to pulverize that tart little nub so they can grab another to start on. If you lean toward the long savor, you land pretty solidly in Hardcrackville, but if you're among the impatient, you might consider moving to Softcrackistan, if only to give your tooth enamel a rest.

Additions like baking soda and physical processes like pulling sugar also go a long way in achieving mouthfeel by aerating the dense sugar helixes, so take some time in your sugar travels to divine what it is that you crave when you slip a gum drop onto your tongue. You now have the tools to modify your favorites and achieve the perfect mouthfeel for you.

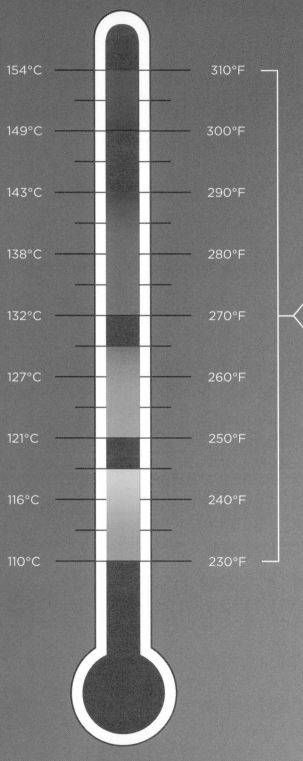

| | |
|---|---|
| 154°C | 310°F |
| 149°C | 300°F |
| 143°C | 290°F |
| 138°C | 280°F |
| 132°C | 270°F |
| 127°C | 260°F |
| 121°C | 250°F |
| 116°C | 240°F |
| 110°C | 230°F |

# PUT IT ALL TOGETHER

Every good recipe deserves to be manhandled, to be introduced to a world outside its comfortable and predictable confines. I find this especially true in confectionery work and baking, where the party line has always been that following the rules to the micron is an order, not a suggestion. I think that's malarkey. It also makes for boring baking and sugar work.

There's no reason you can't play with your food and your recipes. Why not use jerry-rigged Rice Krispie treats as a cake layer? Why not schmear a cake with nougat baked into a crisp and luscious topping? Why not add caramel to anything and everything? The worst that could happen is that your experiment will fall flat—and the best that could happen is dessert transcendence.

*I started my career as a pastry professional years ago, peddling French macarons.* I started with a mail-order business and eventually opened a little shop in Montpelier, Vermont. I made both the sandwiched, colorful Parisian and the more rustic versions of the French macaron, which isn't sandwiched and is much more dense. In those early days, I spent as much time explaining macarons as I did making them. People would ask, "So, what's in these besides coconut?" To which I'd respond, for the gazillionth time, that yes, this is a "macaroon," but the French iteration—therefore, no coconut, just almonds. "Well, that's certainly a new kind of macaroon!" To which I'd respond, with clenched teeth and hyperbole, "No, indeed. The French macaron predates the coconut version by centuries."

These days, the macaron is all the fashion. You can't swing a cat in any American metropolis without hitting a shop that peddles macarons. They still aren't as ubiquitous as those damn cupcake shops (you can't swing a mouse in any American metropolis without hitting three cupcake stands), but they certainly are the parvenu of American pastry, even though they've been around in France since the Stone Age and are just as delicious as ever.

|||||||||||||||||||||||||||||||||||||||||||||||| *Makes approximately 100 macarons* ||||||||||||||||||||||||||||||||||||||||||||||||

| | |
|---|---|
| Italian Buttercream (page 63) | 1 batch |
| Parisian Macaron Shells (page 82) | 1 batch |

① Fit a pastry bag with a large, plain, open pastry tip (I use an Ateco #7 tip) and fill the pastry bag with the buttercream.

② Dollop a nickel-size (15-mm) round of buttercream onto the flat side of a macaron (the part that's been sitting on the parchment) and sandwich with the flat side of another macaron shell of similar size. (Even a seasoned pastry chef— ahem—can have trouble keeping the sizes of shells consistent so before you start assembling,

I'd place like-size shells together so you can quickly burn through this process.) Gently press the shells together until the buttercream just peeks out at the *pieds*.

③ Keep filling until you've run out of shells. Eat immediately! Otherwise, place the filled macarons on a sheet pan and cover tightly with plastic wrap. (Don't refrigerate them or the moisture of the fridge will make the shells soggy.)

④ You'll likely have some buttercream left, which you can transfer to an airtight container and freeze. If you aren't serving all of your macarons immediately, they can be frozen, tightly covered, for 2 weeks.

# WHOOPIE PIES!

## *The Chocolate-and-Peanut-Butter*
## EDITION

*Every Sunday night during my fourth year at the University of Virginia, my roommates and I hosted a night of sci-fi decadence.* The combination of *Star Trek: The Next Generation* and Colt 45 was potentially lethal. So we added a fittingly lunar treat to the mix: MoonPies. They helped sop up the cheap malt beer—but did little else. While MoonPies look tantalizing, their singularly cardboard flavor did nothing to satisfy my perennial sweet tooth.

Enter the whoopie pie. It has all the characteristics of a MoonPie—the cakelike rounds sandwiching marshmallowy filling—with none of the sandlike texture. Instead, it's lush and moist. The filling is pillowy and delicious. Bring on the Starship *Enterprise* and you've got a real party.

|||||||||||||||||||||||||||||||||||||||||||||||||||||||||||||||| *Makes 1 dozen* |||||||||||||||||||||||||||||||||||||||||||||||||||||||||||

**Ingredients, I'm sure you know, are key.** I only use unsalted butter, and preferably the style that's labeled "European," which means it contains a high percentage of butterfat (and less moisture) than your run-of-the-mill American butter. I only use King Arthur flour because they guarantee the gluten content in every batch, something most large mills find impossible to do.

And I am particularly persnickety about the chocolate products I use. When I list a chocolate or cocoa powder, you can feel free to use your favorite high-quality brand. However, when I make a recipe that calls for chocolate, I always use Callebaut 60/40 bittersweet callets. The 60 refers to the percentage of cocoa present in that particular chocolate, and a callet is really just a chip. The cocoa I use is Callebaut Extra Brute. It's dark as pitch, robust, and all-around glorious. My personal preference is a very robust and straightforward cocoa flavor with heavy chocolate notes. Ooh la la! I'm talking so fancy! But it's true. You get to eating enough chocolate and it starts to tell its origin story. I have another favorite, Valrhona. If you like your chocolate with a fruity flavor and subtle acid undertones, Valrhona is queen. Those are my choices. I'm sure you have your own.

1. Preheat the oven to 350°F (175°C).

2. Pour the chocolate chips into the hot coffee. Set aside.

3. In a mixing bowl, whisk together the flour, cocoa powder, salt, and baking powder. Set aside.

4. In the bowl of a stand mixer fitted with the paddle attachment, cream the butter and sugar on high speed until light and fluffy. Scrape down the sides of the bowl.

5. Add the eggs, one at a time, mixing for 1 minute between each incorporation. Scrape down the sides of the bowl.

6. Add the vanilla and the coffee mixture and mix until completely incorporated.

7. With the mixer running at medium-low speed, add one-third of the buttermilk and one-third of the flour mixture. Continue alternating one-third portions of the two until everything is added. Scrape down the sides of the bowl one last time and mix for 30 seconds on high.

8. Spray a large cookie scoop with nonstick cooking spray and scoop the whoopie batter onto a parchment-lined sheet pan, spacing the scoops about 2 inches (5 cm) apart to allow for spreading.

9. Bake the whoopies for 20 to 25 minutes, checking for doneness by gently poking a whoopie to see if it springs back.

| | | |
|---|---|---|
| bittersweet chocolate chips | 2 ounces | 60 g |
| hot coffee | ¾ cup | 180 ml |
| all-purpose flour | 3 cups | 375 g |
| cocoa powder | 1 cup | 85 g |
| salt | 1 teaspoon | 6 g |
| baking powder | 1 tablespoon | 15 g |
| unsalted butter | 1 cup | 230 g |
| sugar | 2 cups | 400 g |
| eggs | 2 | |
| vanilla extract | 1 tablespoon | 15 ml |
| buttermilk | 1 cup | 240 ml |
| Peanut Butter Marshmallow (page 117) | 1 batch | |

10. Allow the whoopies to cool completely.

11. Fill a pastry bag fitted with a large open tip with the marshmallow. Pipe an egg-size mound on the flat side of one of the whoopies and sandwich with the flat side of another whoopie half. Since peanut butter marshmallow does not set as readily as plain due to its higher fat content, you don't want to add an excessive amount in between the whoopies or it will ooze out the sides. You want to pipe just enough so that when you add the second half and gently press down, the filling just reaches the edges of the whoopie.

# TORRONE
# TRUFFLES

*No trip to Europe is complete without schlepping a dinosaur-size Toblerone you bought at the duty-free shop through airport customs.* Despite its novelty shape and size, in reality it's a damn fine candy: high-quality chocolate studded with almond-honey nougat.

This simple truffle is a tip of the tricornered hat to that wonderful Swiss confection.

||||||||||||||||||||||||||||||||||||||||||||||||||||||||||||||| *Makes approximately 60* |||||||||||||||||||||||||||||||||||||||||||||||||||||||||

| FOR THE GANACHE | | |
| --- | --- | --- |
| bittersweet chocolate, finely chopped | 1½ pounds (approximately 4 cups chips) | 720 g |
| heavy cream | 1 cup | 240 ml |
| coffee | ⅓ cup | 75 ml |
| unsalted butter | ¼ cup | 55 g |
| salt | pinch | |
| egg yolks | 2 | |
| FOR THE ASSEMBLY | | |
| Torrone (page 121) | ¼ batch | |
| cornstarch | 1 tablespoon | 8 g |
| cocoa powder | ¼ cup | 20 g |

## PROCEDURE FOR THE GANACHE

1. Place the chocolate in a large metal bowl. Set aside.

2. In a large saucepan over low heat, combine the cream, coffee, butter, and salt. Heat to a simmer. Remove from the heat.

3. Place the egg yolks in a small bowl and whisk until the yolks break apart. Take ¼ cup (60 ml) of the hot cream mixture from the saucepan and slowly pour it into the yolks, whisking constantly to temper the yolks.

✳ **A Note From the Sugar Baby:** "Tempering" an egg simply means you add a small portion of hot liquid to the cool eggs to stabilize the eggs' temperature before you add the eggs to the rest of the hot ingredients. This allows the eggs to gently acclimate to the warmer clime so they won't suddenly scramble.

4. Add the tempered eggs to the saucepan with the cream and return to the stove over medium heat. Attach a candy thermometer and heat the mixture to 160°F (71°C), whisking *constantly*. The cream should begin to gently simmer.

5. Pour the simmering cream over the chocolate. Allow to sit, undisturbed, for 5 minutes, to allow the chocolate to melt.

6. Whisk the cream and chocolate until the chocolate has completely melted and the mixture has emulsified. If you find that there are unmelted bits of chocolate, place the bowl over a gently simmering pot of water and stir until the last bits are melted.

7. Use immediately as a filling or glaze for cake, or proceed as instructed below for truffles.

So many recipes, not enough pictures! I'm a visual baker and need a photo cue now and again to aid my understanding of a recipe. That's why I've launched a website as a sisterly companion to this sweet tome. Pictures and tutorials bring it all home on www.sugarbabycookbook.com, your resource for all things Sugar Baby.

If you want to see how to make puff pastry and the lamination process in action, or if you want a detailed how-to of piping and assembling a *croquembouche*, or a step-by-colorful-step of assembling a lemon-coconut cake, come visit!

## NEVER FEAR—I'M ALWAYS HERE TO GUIDE YOU IN THE WAYS OF HOT SUGAR, BABY.

PROCEDURE FOR THE **ASSEMBLY**

1. Place the torrone in the freezer to make it rock hard, at least a few hours.

2. Place the torrone on a cutting board sprinkled with cornstarch; coat the top of the torrone with cornstarch as well. Using a very sharp chef's knife, cut the torrone into very small shards and bits about the size of lemon seeds until you have at least ¼ cup (50 g).

3. Test the temperature of the ganache; it should be cool to the touch (otherwise the torrone will start to melt in the mixture), but you should be able to stir it. (If it's become too firm, warm it gently over simmering water to loosen it.) Stir the small torrone bits into the ganache, cover, and refrigerate until the ganache is firm.

4. Use a teaspoon-sized cookie scoop to create perfect balls of chocolate. Sprinkle the cocoa powder on a parchment-lined work surface and roll the chocolate balls in the powder, coating evenly.

5. Serve immediately, or store in an airtight container in a cool, dry place for up to 1 week.

# ÎLE
# FLOTTANTE

*Floating island—this is a dessert I love like no other.* It can stop a room dead in its tracks. When my Raymo took me to Paris for the birthday that shall remain nameless, we went to the famous bistro Fontaine de Mars on Rue Saint-Dominique. All discourse in the restaurant stopped when my dessert made its grand entrance into the dining room: islands of meringue floating in a sea of crème anglaise. It was quiet, until our lovely waiter placed that divine soup in front of me and I exclaimed "Hot damn!"

|||||||||||||||||||||||||||||||||||||||||||||||||| *Makes 2 servings* ||||||||||||||||||||||||||||||||||||||||||||||||||

| | | |
|---|---|---|
| whole milk | 2 cups | 480 ml |
| sugar | ¼ cup | 50 g |
| water | 3 tablespoons | 75 ml |
| egg whites | 4 | |
| salt | ½ teaspoon | 3 g |
| Crème Anglaise (page 31) | 1 batch | |
| NOLA Pralines (page 77) | 4 pieces | |

① In a large skillet (10 inch/25 cm should do) over low heat, bring the milk to a simmer. Do not boil.

② In a small saucepan over low heat, combine the sugar and water. Heat until the sugar has dissolved.

③ Raise the heat to medium-high, clip on a candy thermometer, and stop stirring. Heat until the temperature reaches 234°F (112°C).

④ In the bowl of a stand mixer, whip the egg whites and salt until foamy.

⑤ With the speed on medium, carefully pour the sugar syrup down the side of the bowl and into the whipping egg whites. Turn speed to high and whip until the egg whites are white and shiny and hold stiff peaks.

⑥ With a large soup spoon, scoop out a mound of egg white and transfer it to another soup spoon, smoothing the sides of the egg white as you transfer it back and forth so that the mound starts to take on the shape of a goose egg. Carefully transfer the "egg" into the simmering milk. Poach for 1 minute. With a heatproof spatula, flip the egg over to poach for 1 minute on the other side. Transfer the egg to a paper towel. Repeat the process to make 3 more eggs.

⑦ Pour a layer of crème anglaise into each of two shallow soup bowls, about 1 cup (240 ml) per bowl. Place 2 meringues on top of the crème in each bowl, then place a piece of praline on top of each meringue. Voilà!

# I HEART
# MOUSSE CAKE

*If you have a few pieces of equipment, you can make rather ordinary things appear extraordinary—to wit, chocolate mousse.* Yes, it's rather spectacular to see it just standing in a glorious column in all its grand chocolate-mousse simplicity—no adornment, no fuss. But add a few extras and you'll elevate a palate-pleasing mousse to a work of art. This technique works with any combination of mousses. The trick is preparing the raspberry heart mousse a day ahead so that it's frozen for assembly. The next day, make the flourless chocolate bottom and allow it to cool completely before you move on to making the chocolate mousse. There are steps involved, but the results will make you say, "I heart mousse cakes!"

|||||||||||||||||||||||| *Makes 1 (10-inch/25-cm) cake with 4 raspberry heart centers* ||||||||||||||||||||||||

| | | |
|---|---|---|
| **FOR THE RASPBERRY MOUSSE**<br>Fruit Mousse (page 51), made with raspberry purée | ½ recipe | |
| **FOR THE FLOURLESS CHOCOLATE CAKE**<br>bittersweet chocolate, finely chopped | 8 ounces | 240 g |
| unsalted butter | 1 cup | 225 g |
| very strong coffee | 2 tablepoons | 30 ml |
| espresso powder | 1 tablespoon | 3 g |
| sugar | 1¼ cups | 250 g |
| cocoa powder | 1 cup | 85 g |
| eggs | 3 | |
| salt | 1 teaspoon | 6 g |
| vanilla bean paste | 1 teaspoon | 5 ml |
| **FOR THE ASSEMBLY**<br>Dark Chocolate Mousse (page 49) | 1 batch | |
| **SPECIAL EQUIPMENT**<br>heart-shaped pastry rings (3¾-by-3¼-by-1¼ inches/9-by-8-by-3 cm) | 4 | |
| cake ring (10-inch/25-cm) | 1 | |
| heat gun or blow dryer | | |

PROCEDURE FOR THE **RASPBERRY MOUSSE**

① Place heart-shaped pastry rings on a parchment-lined sheet pan. Spoon the raspberry mousse into the forms and level off the tops with a small offset spatula. Place in the freezer overnight.

PROCEDURE FOR THE **FLOURLESS CHOCOLATE CAKE**

① Preheat the oven to 350°F (175°C).

② Over a double boiler, gently melt the chocolate and butter, stirring occasionally. Set aside.

③ Stir together the coffee and espresso powder until the powder has completely dissolved.

④ In the bowl of a stand mixer fitted with the whisk attachment, whip together the sugar, cocoa, eggs, coffee-espresso mixture, salt, and vanilla paste on high until just combined.

⑤ Reduce the mixer speed to medium. Pour in the melted chocolate mixture, using a plastic spatula to get every last bit of chocolate into the batter.

⑥ Increase the mixer speed to high and beat the ingredients until well combined.

⑦ Pour the batter into a 10-inch (25-cm) cake ring, generously sprayed with nonstick spray and placed on a parchment-lined sheet pan. The batter should be more than ½ inch (12 mm) thick.

⑧ Bake for 20 minutes, or until the cake pulls from the sides of the ring and a toothpick inserted in the center of the cake comes out clean. Allow to cool completely. Don't remove the ring from the cake, and keep everything on the sheet pan.

PROCEDURE FOR THE **ASSEMBLY**

① Pour enough of the chocolate mousse into the cake ring to fill it halfway. Freeze for 1 hour, or until very firm. Set the remaining chocolate mousse aside.

② Release the raspberry mousse from the molds by setting each heart on a small piece of parchment set atop a small container, like a jar of cinnamon. Heat the sides of the metal ring with a heat gun or a blow dryer, and gently pull the ring down so it falls onto the table.

③ Gently place each raspberry mousse on top of the chocolate mousse in a symmetrical pattern, with the fat end of the heart touching the ring and the heart tips pointing toward the middle.

④ Carefully pour the remaining chocolate mousse around the hearts until it is just level with them. If there are hard nooks to reach, place the mousse in a piping bag with a medium open tip and gently squirt the mousse into the hard to reach areas.

⑤ Gently tap and shimmy the sheet pan holding the cake to gently distribute and even the mousse. Freeze overnight.

⑥ Place the frozen mousse on a cardboard cake round or cake pedestal. Heat the sides of the cake ring with a heat gun or a blow dryer and gently lift the ring from the cake.

⑦ Thaw the cake for at least 2 hours in the refrigerator. Serve immediately.

# BREAD PUDDING

*That's NOLA—as in New Orleans, Louisiana.* This aptly-named recipe is a jazz riff on delectable flavors and isn't afraid to play with strong ones. This rich bread pudding incorporates some of the loveliest ingredients on the planet: pralines, pastry cream, and bourbon. The pastry cream acts as a sweet binding custard, the pralines add a lovely texture when sprinkled on top, and the bourbon . . . well, it's bourbon. And there's nothing wrong with that.

*Makes approximately 10 servings*

| | | |
|---|---|---|
| French baguettes, preferably day-old | 2 | |
| golden raisins | 1 cup | 150 g |
| bourbon | ½ cup | 120 ml |
| vanilla extract | 1 tablespoon | 15 ml |
| cinnamon | 1 teaspoon | 2 g |
| Crème Anglaise (page 31) | 1 batch | |
| Vanilla Pastry Cream (page 38) | 1 cup | 240 ml |
| Italian Meringue (page 62) | 1 batch | |
| NOLA Pralines (page 77) | 1 batch | |

1. Preheat the oven to 350°F (175°C).

2. Cut the baguettes into 1-inch (2.5-cm) cubes. You should have about 10 cups (550 g). Set aside.

3. Soak the raisins in the bourbon for 1 hour, until they plump.

4. Spray a large casserole dish with nonstick cooking spray.

5. In a bowl, whisk the vanilla, cinnamon, and raisins (including all the bourbon) into the crème anglaise.

6. Place the bread cubes in a large mixing bowl and pour the crème anglaise mixture over them. Toss until every piece of bread is coated. Allow to sit until the bread has soaked up the sauce, stirring occasionally to distribute the sauce, about 15 minutes.

7. Give the pastry cream a quick stir to make sure it's loose, and stir it into the bread mixture.

8. Transfer half of the mixture to the casserole dish.

9. Fold the meringue into the remaining half of the mixture and spread this on top of the first layer. Cover the top layer with pralines, reserving some to garnish the finished cake.

10. Cover with foil and bake for 45 minutes. Remove the foil and bake until the meringue top is golden-brown and puffy, the pralines are melted, and a cake tester inserted in the center comes out clean.

11. Serve immediately, with a few pralines on top of each serving.

# MANGO
## *Mousse*
# CAKE

*One of our favorite customers at Gesine Confectionary, Alison Nielsen, once brought me a beautiful present.* It was a painting of mango mousse cakes. So inspired was she by their delightful presence in my pastry case that she painted them. The mango mousses now hang over my new main workspace in my commercial bakery, reminding me that the things that I love to make can inspire others as well. And this mango mousse is definitely inspirational.

*Makes 18 petite cakes*

① Preheat the oven to 350°F (175°C).

② In the bowl of a stand mixer, whisk the egg whites with the cream of tartar on medium until just foamy. With the mixer running, slowly add ½ cup (100 g) of the sugar. Increase the speed to high once the sugar is completely incorporated. Beat until the egg whites are glossy and hold firm peaks.

③ Transfer the egg whites to a clean metal bowl and set aside.

④ In a separate small bowl, whisk together the flour, salt, and baking powder. Set aside.

⑤ In the same stand mixer bowl you just used for the egg whites (you don't have to clean it, just proceed as if nothing happened), using the paddle attachment, beat together the remaining ½ cup (100 g) sugar and the butter until light and fluffy, about 3 minutes. Scrape the bowl and beat for a few more minutes.

⑥ With the mixer on medium speed, add about one-third of the flour mixture and then one-third of the buttermilk, alternating this way between the two until both are incorporated

| | | |
|---|---|---|
| egg whites | 6 | |
| cream of tartar | ½ teaspoon | 1.5 g |
| sugar | 1 cup, divided | 200 g, divided |
| cake flour | 1 cup | 140 g |
| salt | ½ teaspoon | 3 g |
| baking powder | 1 teaspoon | 5 g |
| unsalted butter, at room temperature | 1 cup | 230 g |
| buttermilk | ½ cup | 120 ml |
| orange extract | 1 tablespoon | 15 ml |
| Fruit Mousse (page 51), made with mango purée | 1 batch | |
| Gesine's Fruit Gummis (page 98) | 18 | |
| SPECIAL EQUIPMENT small cake rings | 18 | |

into the batter. Add the orange extract and mix until incorporated. Scrape down the bowl.

⑦ Take a large scoop of the egg whites and add them to the batter. Mix on high for a moment to lighten the batter.

8. Remove the bowl from the mixer. With a rubber spatula, fold in one-third of the remaining egg whites. Once you no longer see any white streaks, very gently fold in the remaining egg whites, mixing until they are completely incorporated. Spread the batter evenly with an offset spatula onto a parchment-lined sheet pan sprayed with nonstick cooking spray.

9. Bake for 15 to 20 minutes, until the top is golden brown, the sides start to pull from the edges of the sheet pan, and the cake springs back when you give it a gentle poke. Cool completely.

10. Press cake rings into the cake, as if you were stamping out cookie dough with a cookie cutter. However, leave the rings in place. Insert the rings as close together as you can so you don't waste any cake.

11. Ladle the mousse into the rings, filling to the tops. Freeze until set, at least 3 hours or overnight.

12. Remove the rings by placing each individual cake on a tall object that's slightly smaller in diameter than the cake itself. For instance, I often use a tall jar of cinnamon. Using a heat gun or a blow dryer, warm the sides of the ring and then gently tug on it so it falls to the table.

✦ **A Note From the Sugar Baby:** So this recipe makes quite a few little cakes—too many for some. But here's what I like to do: I make all the cakes and only unmold as many as I need, leaving the rest in the freezer, snug in their little metal rings. I wrap them in plastic wrap to prevent freezer burn. If I have an unexpected need for a fancy dessert, I can just unmold as many small cakes as I'll need.

13. You can serve the cakes frozen or thaw them in the refrigerator for a few hours. Serve thawed cakes immediately, topped off with one of Gesine's Fruit Gummis (page 98).

# GINGERED
## *Drop*
# SCONES

*Drop scones were the hands-down morning pastry favorite at Gesine Confectionary.* The beauty of this scone doesn't lie in its outward appearance—frankly, the drop scone is unsightly. It's called a drop scone for a reason: You just grab a handful of dough and drop it on a sheet pan. That simple act of grab-and-drop is one of the factors that keeps this pastry very supple, since you don't manhandle the dough by rolling and shaping and patting; overmanipulation of scone dough is what contributes to tough eats.

I rotated the scone flavors daily, but ginger was a standout.

*Makes 1 dozen*

① Preheat the oven to 350°F (175°C).

② In a medium bowl (preferably with a spout), whisk together the buttermilk and egg. Set aside.

③ In a large bowl, combine the flour, salt, ground ginger, butter, and baking powder in a large mixing bowl. Work the mixture with your finger-tips, massaging the butter into the flour, until the mixture resembles pebbly cornmeal. Stir in the candied ginger.

④ Make a well in the center of the flour mixture. Pour the buttermilk mixture into the well. Work the mixture with your hands (it's going to get sticky) until the dough is uniformly wet and there are no clumps of flour remaining.

⑤ Grab fistfuls of dough about the size of tennis balls and mound them on a sheet pan lined with parchment, spacing the scones a few inches (7 to 8 cm) apart. Sprinkle the tops of the scones with the sanding sugar.

| | | |
|---|---|---|
| nonfat buttermilk, at room temperature | 1½ cups | 360 ml |
| egg | 1 | |
| all-purpose flour | 5 cups | 625 g |
| salt | 1 teaspoon | 6 g |
| ground ginger | 1 tablespoon | 6 g |
| unsalted butter, diced | 1½ cups | 345 g |
| baking powder | 1½ tablespoons | 23 g |
| chopped candied ginger | 1 cup | 140 g |
| sugar | 1½ cups | 300 g |
| sanding sugar, for sprinkling | 1 cup | 200 g |

⑥ Bake for 35 minutes, or until the scones brown slightly and spring back when gently poked. (I usually make one particularly scrappy-looking scone as a tester to take apart in the event I'm not sure if the scones are cooked through).

# COCONUT CAKE
## *with*
## LEMON CURD FILLING

*I don't love coconut.* There. I said it. That doesn't mean I don't work with it now and again. Through the years, customers have requested coconut cake and I've done my best to project nothing but positive coconut vibes when, in reality, there's a ghastly grimace just waiting to surface. Who am I to judge someone's love of that noxious, tropical cannonball?

Yet, over time I found a way to dampen my aversion by developing recipes that merely hint at the presence of the nut (or is it a fruit?). I now find myself not so much dreading the shredded stuff but looking for ways of making it palatable. At least to me.

|||||||||||||||||||||||||| *Makes one 5-by-12-inch (12-by-30-cm) rectangular 3-layer cake* ||||||||||||||||||||||||||

| | | |
|---|---|---|
| egg whites | 12 | |
| cream of tartar | 1 teaspoon | 3 g |
| sugar | 2 cups, divided | 400 g, divided |
| cake flour | 2 cups | 280 g |
| salt | 1 teaspoon | 6 g |
| baking powder | 2 teaspoons | 10 g |
| unsalted butter | 1 cup | 225 g |
| cream of coconut (Coco Lopez or Goya) | 1 cup | 240 ml |
| vanilla extract | 1 tablespoon | 15 ml |
| Lemon Curd (page 42) | 1 batch | |
| Italian Buttercream (page 63), made with 1 teaspoon (5 ml) lemon extract | 1 batch | |
| large coconut flakes | 2 cups | 140 g |

SPECIAL EQUIPMENT
Pullman loaf pan

**You have to use your noggin—and some creativity—when you're building cakes.** Often I'll have some preconceived idea of how a cake should look. For instance, this coconut-lemon cake just had to be a perfect rectangle. But I didn't have a cake ring in which to build this perfect cake. I did, however, have a Pullman loaf pan, which is a long, rectangular bread form with straight sides and a lid. I measured and cut the cake layers so they would fit exactly in the Pullman and then built the cake inside the loaf pan. With cakes that have fillings (like lemon curd) that need to set before serving, this kind of vessel is a godsend. So before you go about making the components of this cake, look around your kitchen for a suitable form. A large coffee can would make a great cylindrical cake mold. Hell, look around the tool shed. Use your imagination. Just make sure what you're using is food-safe.

① Preheat the oven to 350°F (175°C).

② In the bowl of a stand mixer, whisk the egg whites with the cream of tartar on medium until just foamy. With the mixer running, slowly add 1 cup (200 g) of the sugar. Increase the speed to high once the sugar is completely incorporated. Beat until the egg whites are glossy and hold firm peaks. Transfer the egg whites to a clean metal bowl and set aside.

③ In a separate small bowl, whisk together the flour, salt, and baking powder. Set aside.

④ In the same stand mixer bowl you just used for the egg whites (you don't have to clean it, just proceed as if nothing happened), using the paddle attachment, beat together the remaining 1 cup (200 g) sugar and the butter until light and fluffy, about 3 minutes. Scrape the bowl and beat for a few more minutes.

⑤ With the mixer on low, add about one-third of the flour mixture and then one-third of the coconut cream, alternating this way between the two until both are incorporated into the batter. Scrape down the bowl. Take a large scoop of the egg whites and stir into the batter.

⑥ With a rubber spatula, fold in one-third of the remaining egg whites. Once you no longer see any white streaks, very gently fold in the remaining egg whites, mixing until they are completely incorporated. Spread the batter onto a parchment-lined half sheet pan (18 x 13 in./46 x 33 cm) sprayed with nonstick cooking spray. Spread the batter evenly with an offset spatula.

⑦ Bake for 20 to 25 minutes, until the top is golden brown, the sides start to pull from the edges of the sheet pan, and the cake springs back when you give it a gentle poke. Cool completely.

⑧ Lay a piece of parchment on an upside-down sheet pan. Place the parchment-covered side of this sheet pan gently on top of the cake. Carefully flip the sheet pans over and release the cake onto the parchment of the bottom pan.

⑨ Turn the cake so that the longer side faces you. Trim the edges of the cake. Measure the width of the cake and divide by three. I use a standard measuring tape and make notches on the cake where I'm going to be making a cut. Using a straight-edge ruler aligned with these notches, cut three even slices. Each layer should measure roughly 5 by 12 inches (12 by 30 cm).

⑩ If you don't have a form in which to build this cake, pipe a thick ribbon of buttercream along the inside edge of the cake to form a dam to keep in the lemon curd. Layer half of the lemon curd over the first layer and top with a second layer of cake. Top that with the remaining lemon curd and then the last layer of cake. Don't press on the layers. Freeze for at least 2 hours or overnight.

⑪ Using a small offset spatula, spread the buttercream evenly over all sides of the cake. The beauty of this particular cake is that you're going to adhere coconut to the buttercream, so it doesn't have to be perfectly spread. But one warning: Work rapidly. The cold cake will quickly start to harden the buttercream.

⑫ Cover the cake with the coconut flakes: First, firmly press handfuls onto the sides; then create a layer on top. If you prefer, toast the coconut at 275°F (135°C) for 5 minutes—just keep a close watch, as coconut browns very quickly.

⑬ Refrigerate the cake for at least 2 hours to allow the interior to thaw before serving.

# STRAWBERRY-BASIL
# NAPOLEON
## with Olive Oil Ice Cream

*That's a lot of strangeness in one dessert—I bet that's what you're thinking.* But before you dismiss this endeavor entirely, I ask you to have a little forbearance in the imagination department. I could have added a balsamic drizzle to the party, after all.

Consider this: Basil is a happy herb that imparts an exuberant freshness to anything it touches, strawberries included. By macerating it with the strawberries, you cut through some of that outrageous butter bomb of puff pastry and add a hint of sunshine to the flaky layers. I also wanted a foil for the olive oil ice cream, since it's rather headstrong in the flavor department. With the addition of bright notes and textural variety, this combination manages to be sophisticated and delicious without eliciting every cook's nightmare reaction: "Gee, that's . . . interesting."

|||||||||||||||||||||||||||||||||||||||||||||||||||  *Makes 8 servings*  |||||||||||||||||||||||||||||||||||||||||||||||||||

**You can buy puff pastry—well-made and delicious puff pastry—at high-quality supermarkets.** One brand in particular is extraordinary: Dufours. Look for it in the freezer section and thaw it in the refrigerator before rolling out and baking. However, I highly recommend entering the world of laminated-dough preparation yourself. Puff pastry, croissants, and Danish all are part of the same family, and once you learn the technique of laminating puff pastry, you'll feel confident trying your hand at the others. If you need more detailed, pictorial instruction, go to the *Sugar Baby* companion website: www.sugarbabycookbook.com.

| FOR THE DOUGH | | |
| --- | --- | --- |
| unsalted butter, at room temperature | ¼ cup | 55 g |
| all-purpose flour | 3 cups | 375 g |
| salt | 1 teaspoon | 6 g |
| cold water | 1¼ cups | 300 ml |
| lemon juice | 1 teaspoon | 5 ml |

| FOR THE FOLD-IN BUTTER | | |
| --- | --- | --- |
| unsalted butter, slightly cooler than room temperature | 2 cups | 455 g |
| all-purpose flour | ½ cup | 60 g |
| salt | pinch | |

| FOR THE ASSEMBLY | | |
|---|---|---|
| strawberries, hulled and halved | 1 pound | 455 g |
| minced fresh basil | 2 tablespoons | 12 g |
| zest of ½ lemon | | |
| juice of ½ lemon | | |
| sugar | 2 tablespoons | 25 g |
| Olive Oil Creemee (page 34), thawed just enough to be spreadable | 1 batch | |

### PROCEDURE FOR THE DOUGH

① In the bowl of a stand mixer fitted with the dough hook, mix the butter, flour, and salt together until the butter breaks up and the mixture resembles cornmeal. Add the water and lemon juice and mix for a few minutes, until the dough is smooth. It will be very sticky. This is normal.

② Transfer the dough to a large piece of plastic wrap. Form the dough into a rough rectangle. Refrigerate for 30 minutes.

### PROCEDURE FOR THE FOLD-IN BUTTER

① In the same bowl of the stand mixer fitted with the paddle attachment, beat together the butter, flour, and salt until there are no butter lumps remaining. Using a bowl scraper, transfer the butter mixture to a large piece of plastic wrap and pat into a 10-by-7-inch (25-by-17-cm) rectangle. Refrigerate the butter until it is cool and slightly firm but still malleable.

### PROCEDURE FOR LAMINATING THE DOUGH (SEE NOTE)

① Flour a work surface. Remove the dough from the refrigerator and roll it out into a 12-by-16-inch (30-by-40-cm) rectangle, taking care to roll the dough evenly and keep the corners very square.

② Remove the fold-in butter block from the refrigerator. Place it on one half of the dough and fold the other half over the butter, sealing it in. Press along the edges to make a tight seal.

**✱ A Note From the Sugar Baby:** This type of dough is called "laminated dough." A "lock-in" refers to the process of securing the butter in the dough package. If you imagine the process of laminating paper—sandwiching paper between two layers of plastic sheeting—you get the idea of laminated dough and the process of "locking in" the butter.

In order to make the pastry "puff," you need to complete a series of "turns," which simply means you roll the dough into a rectangle, fold the sides to meet in the middle (for a double turn) as if you were folding a T-shirt, and then fold the dough again as if you were shutting a book. The "turn" refers to the fact that each time you roll, you turn the dough by ninety degrees, so that the long side of the dough now faces you. When you've finished the turn and have folded the sides, the narrow end of the dough faces you. For puff, you make four double turns. Phew! Sounds complicated. It's not. It comes with practice.

To keep track of each turn, mark the dough by *gently* poking it with your finger to make an indentation: one indentation to indicate you've already made one turn, and so on.

③ Turn the dough 90 degrees and roll it again into a 12-by-16-inch (30-by-40-cm) rectangle, making sure to keep the sides even, the corners square, and the depth of the dough and butter even throughout the rectangle.

④ Make a "book fold" by folding each end to meet in the middle and then folding in half again, like closing a book. Repeat this 3 more times (for a total of 4 turns).

⑤ Once you've finished your last turn, cover the dough in plastic wrap and place in the refrigerator to "rest" for at least 2 hours before using. (Laminated dough keeps for a few days in the fridge and freezes beautifully for up to 1 month—just thaw in the refrigerator before using.)

① Roll the rested puff pastry into a 12-by-16-inch (30-by-40-cm) rectangle and transfer to a parchment-lined sheet pan. (The rectangle should be slightly smaller than the area of the sheet pan. A professional half-sheet pan is perfect for this measurement but many noncommercial sheet pans are slightly smaller. Do a quick measurement of your sheet pan before you roll out the dough and adjust the measurement of the finished rectangle to take into account the smaller area.

② Cover the dough and sheet pan with plastic wrap and refrigerate for 30 minutes. Meanwhile, preheat the oven to 375°F (190°C).

③ Remove the dough from the refrigerator and remove the plastic wrap. Cover the dough with a large piece of parchment. Place a second sheet pan on top of the parchment-covered dough, so the bottom of the sheet pan rests directly on the parchment and acts as a weight to keep the pastry from puffing too dramatically in the oven.

✱ **A Note From the Sugar Baby:** Even dough needs a rest now and again. When you've kneaded and rolled a dough, you've worked up quite a bit of gluten in it, and this causes the dough to become rubbery and hard to work with. Think of it as you would your own body. You work up a sweat as you exercise, you slow down, and eventually you need a rest before you can play again. So it is with dough. We rest laminated dough between turns for this reason, and we rest it before baking it. If you were to stick the dough straight into the oven after rolling it, it would shrink terribly. (I think of this as dough cramping.) So refrigerate, rest, and relax—then you and your dough can go play.

④ Bake the puff pastry for 30 to 45 minutes, or until the surface of the pastry is uniformly golden brown. Remove from oven and allow to cool.

⑤ Cut the pastry in half, lengthwise so you're left with 2 long strips. Trim the sides and ends so the 2 strips are clean and even.

⑥ Spread the ice cream over the first layer of puff pastry and top with the second layer. Freeze overnight.

⑦ Place the strawberries in a large bowl. Stir in the basil, lemon zest, and lemon juice. Sprinkle the mixture with the sugar and toss so that the sugar coats each element evenly. Allow to sit until the juices of the strawberries start to run, about 15 minutes.

⑧ Dip a very sharp serrated knife in scalding-hot water and dry it off. Trim the ends of the Napoleon. Dip and clean the knife often.

⑨ Cut the Napoleon into 2-inch (5-cm) slices and top with the macerated strawberries. Serve immediately.

# BANANAS FOSTER
# CREAM PIE

*My relationship with cream pies evolved from an innocent question someone asked Ray: "What's your favorite dessert?"* The questioner was intrigued by his close proximity to all the things that came from my ovens and hoped to get some insight into the gullet of a man who was surrounded with the best and the freshest sweet treats.

"Banana cream pie."

"Geez. Gesine must make a killer cream pie."

"She's never made me one."

DOH!

It's true. I didn't make cream pies. The very idea evoked week-old, Cool Whip–drowned, artificially flavored diner dreck or the punch line of a lame vaudeville prank. Cream pies offended my tender culinary sensibilities.

This wouldn't be the first time my unfounded food prejudices kept me from enjoying the delights of a perfectly good dessert. I'm happy to have rectified the problem, and I now enjoy a slab of fluffy banana cream pie as much as Ray. Of course, I had to jazz it up a bit . . . .

|||||||||||||||||||||||||||||||||||||||||||||||||||||||| *Makes 1 large pie* ||||||||||||||||||||||||||||||||||||||||||||||||||||||||

| | | |
|---|---|---|
| all-purpose flour | 2 cups | 250 g |
| unsalted butter, chilled and cut into small pieces | 1¼ cups | 285 g |
| salt | ½ teaspoon | 3 g |
| very cold water | 6 tablespoons | 90 ml |
| Caramel Sauce (page 81), made with 2 tablespoons rum | 1 batch | |
| ripe bananas, sliced | 3 | |
| Vanilla Pastry Cream, flavored with banana syrup (page 38) | 1 batch | |
| very cold whipped heavy cream | 1 cup | 200 g |

① Place the flour in a large bowl and add the butter and salt. Work the butter into the flour by rubbing with your fingers until it starts to look like cornmeal, but with discernable chunks of butter still left.

② Pour the water into the flour. Stir the mixture first with a wooden spoon, then using your hands, until it just comes together. Shape the dough into a rough square in the bowl and cover with plastic wrap. Let it rest for 10 minutes.

③ Dust a work surface with flour and turn the rested dough out onto the surface. It will probably fall apart a bit. This is normal.

④ Gently roll the dough into a small rectangle ½ inch (12 mm) thick. Give the dough four single turns by folding one narrow side of the dough to the middle and then folding the other half over, as if you were folding a business letter. Turn the dough 90 degrees and do this three more times.

⑤ Cover the dough with plastic wrap and allow to rest in the refrigerator for 30 minutes.

⑥ Preheat the oven to 350°F (175°C).

⑦ Roll the dough out into a loose circle, 1 inch larger in diameter than the pie plate you'll be using. Transfer the dough into the pie plate and gently smooth it with your hands so that it forms to the contours of the plate—be careful to not pinch the sides of the dough. Dock the dough with a fork. Refrigerate for 20 minutes.

⑧ Using clean scissors, cut any excess dough that's hanging over the side of the pie plate so the edges look clean. (I don't pinch the dough in any fancy way, since the pastry will defy all of your work and just expand any which way it pleases. But if you cut a clean perimeter and don't pinch down the dough, the sides of the pie dough will puff and fan out beautifully. Better than a decorative pinched edge any day). Freeze the dough for 30 minutes more.

⑨ Place a piece of parchment on top of the dough and fill the cavity with unbaked beans, uncooked rice, or pie weights. Bake for 20 minutes. Take the crust from the oven; carefully remove the parchment and weights and return the crust to the oven and bake until it's golden brown and cooked through, about 20 minutes more. The middle of the pie crust may bubble. No worries. That just means it's extra buttery and tasty.

⑩ Cool the crust completely. Pour a layer of caramel sauce on the bottom of the crust. Only use enough to create an even layer, no more than ⅛ inch (3 mm) thick. Reserve a small amount of the sauce to drizzle over the finished pie.

⑪ Arrange the banana slices in even layers over the caramel. Spread half of the pastry cream over the bananas. If the pastry cream has been refrigerated and is hard, whip it in your stand mixer fitted with the paddle attachment until it loosens up and becomes smooth before spreading.

⑫ Fold the whipped cream into the remaining pastry cream until no white streaks are visible. With a pastry bag fitted with a large star tip, pipe the lightened pastry cream in lovely peaks or roses over the first layer of pastry cream. Drizzle caramel sauce over the top of the pie. Refrigerate for 1 hour and then serve immediately. Refrigerate any leftovers.

# MAPLE WHITE CAKE

*with*

## MAPLE FROSTING

*I'm notorious for killing angel food cakes.* Someone slams the door right next to the oven (Agnes), a dog finds the resting cake at dog-face height and has a snack (Tallulah), some idiot oversprays the angel food pan and the cake slides gleefully out the moment it's turned upside down to cool on an empty wine bottle (me—I also emptied the wine bottle). But I love that airy, sweet perfection of a cake so damn much that I had to jerry-rig a recipe to work against my inherent angel food jinx. This recipe is light and airy but can handle kitchen catastrophe with aplomb. It's also sturdy enough to bake as a layer cake, as long as you choose a filling and/or topping that is on the lighter side, like Seven-Minute Frosting (page 60). The addition of maple sugar gives the entire cake a depth of flavor usually missing in such a simple confection, but feel free to substitute regular granulated sugar for the maple sugar if you have a tough time finding the stuff. Just don't use maple syrup.

|||||||||||||||||||||||||||||||||||||||||||||| *Makes 2 large Bundt cakes* ||||||||||||||||||||||||||||||||||||||||||||||

| | | |
|---|---|---|
| egg whites | 12 | |
| cream of tartar | 1 teaspoon | 3 g |
| granulated sugar | 1 cup | 200 g |
| cake flour | 2 cups | 280 g |
| salt | 1 teaspoon | 6 g |
| baking powder | 2 teaspoons | 10 g |
| maple sugar | 1 cup | 220 g |
| unsalted butter, at room temperature | 1 cup | 225 g |
| buttermilk | 1 cup | 240 ml |
| vanilla extract | 1 tablespoon | 15 ml |
| Seven-Minute Maple Frosting (page 60) | 1 batch | |

① Preheat the oven to 350°F (175°C).

② In the bowl of a stand mixer, whisk the egg whites with the cream of tartar on medium until just foamy. With the mixer running, slowly add the granulated sugar. Increase the mixer speed to high once the sugar is completely incorporated. Beat until the egg whites are glossy and hold firm peaks. Transfer the egg whites to a clean metal bowl and set aside.

③ In a separate small bowl, whisk together the flour, salt, and baking powder. Set aside.

④ In the same mixing bowl that you used to whisk the egg whites (you don't have to clean it, just proceed as if nothing happened), using the paddle attachment, beat together the maple sugar and butter until light and fluffy, about 3 minutes. Scrape the bowl and beat for a few more minutes.

⑤ With the mixer on medium speed, add about one-third of the flour mixture and then one-third of the buttermilk, alternating this way between the two until both are incorporated into the batter. Add the vanilla extract. Scrape down the bowl.

⑥ Remove the bowl from the mixer, and, with a large rubber spatula, take a large scoop of egg whites and stir into the batter to lighten.

⑦ Fold in one-third of the remaining egg whites. Once you no longer see white streaks in the batter, very gently fold in the remaining egg whites until completely incorporated.

⑧ Divide the batter between two Bundt pans sprayed liberally with nonstick spray. Bake for 40 minutes, or until the tops of the cakes are golden brown, the sides pull away from the pan, and the cakes spring back when gently poked. Allow the cakes to cool completely.

⑨ With a small offset spatula, apply the frosting liberally over the two cooled cakes, creating swirls with the spatula. Serve immediately.

# The
# JACKIE, OH!
# CAKE

*I have a natural aversion to cupcakes.* I'm just a contrarian by nature, I suppose, and I was also raised with my mother's mantra, "Don't be normal!" Helga Mathilde Bullock née Meyer despised even a whiff of conformity emanating from her children. So my inclination to shun the horrifyingly ubiquitous and cloying cupcake is perhaps an inherited trait.

I'd cave in now and again at my pastry shop, but the vast majority of my confections were and are individual pastries. If it was a small cake, it wasn't a cake in a cup, but a unique, stand-alone creation, like my Jackie, Oh! Cake. The neat row of Jackie, Oh!s were just minding their own business in the pastry case one fine day when someone happened upon them and remarked, "Goodness! That could be an edible Jackie O pillbox hat!"

|||||||||||||||||||||||||||||||| *Makes 1 (10-inch/25-cm) three-layer cake* ||||||||||||||||||||||||||||||||

## FOR THE DARK CHOCOLATE FUDGE CAKE

| | | |
|---|---|---|
| bittersweet chocolate, finely chopped | 3 ounces | 90 g |
| freshly brewed hot coffee | 1½ cups | 360 ml |
| all-purpose flour | 2½ cups | 310 g |
| unsweetened dark chocolate cocoa powder | 1½ cups | 125 g |
| baking soda | 2 teaspoons | 10 g |
| baking powder | 1 teaspoon | 5 g |
| salt | 1 teaspoon | 6 g |
| sugar | 3 cups | 600 g |
| eggs | 3 | |
| vegetable oil | ¾ cup | 180 ml |
| vanilla extract | 1 teaspoon | 5 ml |
| nonfat buttermilk | 1½ cups | 360 ml |

## PROCEDURE FOR THE **DARK CHOCOLATE FUDGE CAKE**

① Preheat the oven to 350°F (175°C).

② In a bowl, add the chocolate to the coffee. Stir slightly until the chocolate has melted. Set aside.

③ In a large bowl, combine the flour, cocoa powder, baking soda, baking powder, and salt. Whisk together well. Set aside.

④ In the bowl of a stand mixer fitted with the paddle attachment, beat the sugar, eggs, oil, and vanilla until fluffy.

⑤ In a separate bowl, combine the buttermilk and coffee mixture and stir. With the mixer on low speed, slowly add one-third of the flour mixture and then one-third of the buttermilk mixture, alternating between the two until both mixtures are incorporated into the batter.

⑥ Divide the batter evenly among three 10-inch (25-cm) cake pans sprayed with nonstick cooking spray. Bake for 30 minutes, or until the cakes start to pull away from the sides of the pans and a toothpick inserted into the middle of each cake comes out clean.

⑦ Remove from the oven and allow to cool completely.

FOR THE ASSEMBLY

| | | |
|---|---|---|
| Caramel Sauce (page 81) | 1 cup | 240 ml |
| Italian Buttercream (page 63) | 1 batch | |

#### PROCEDURE FOR THE **ASSEMBLY**

① In the clean bowl of your stand mixer, slowly pour the caramel sauce into the buttercream and whisk on medium speed until the caramel is incorporated.

② Place a layer of cake on a cardboard cake round or a cake pedestal. Spread 1 to 2 cups (200 to 400 g) buttercream evenly over the layer. (I have a heavy hand with filling, but you know what you prefer, so proceed to your taste. I'm always conscious of how much buttercream I've got for the entire cake and split it up accordingly.) I like to build layer cakes inside cake rings. So if you have them, use them. Place your first layer of cake within a ring and spread the buttercream evenly; then place the second layer of cake on top, frost, and repeat with the third layer. As you get higher, you can stack the rings one on top of the other to keep the cake contained and very even. I like to build the cakes

to the exact height of the top of the last ring so that I can use the ring to guide my finishing top layer so it's perfectly smooth. If you don't have cake rings, follow the same procedure for assembling and frosting the three layers on the cardboard cake round or pedestal, taking care to build the layers as evenly as possible.

③ Refrigerate the cake for 2 hours, until the buttercream feels cool and set to the touch.

④ Finish the sides of the cake with the remaining buttercream. (If you're using cake rings, remove the rings with the help of a heat gun or blow dryer before finishing the sides.)

⑤ If you'd like to coat the sides with cake crumbs (see Note), place parchment under the cake on a work surface. Take hearty handfuls of the crumbs (you'll need about a cup) and gently smoosh them onto the sides of the frosted cake. Don't press too aggressively—just enough to get an even layer. Collect the stray bits from the parchment to finish the cake.

✱ **A Note from the Sugar Baby:** I keep extra pieces of cake to use as a coating for the sides of cakes. For instance, these three layers may rise in the middle and this might offend my sense of symmetry. So I'd be inclined to level the layers, which would leave me with errant bits of cake. I'd then pulse these in the food processor until the pieces are very fine. When you finish a cake with buttercream, you only need to apply a very thin scratch coat to the sides of the cake, enough to act as an adhesive for the crumbs.

# PANETTONE

*When I was a kid panettone was pretty exclusive.* These days, you can't hit the motley gift-basket aisle at T.J. Maxx without running into a hoard of off-season panettoni. This might lead you to believe that the stuff tastes of stale biscuit and rancid olives. Not so. It's light, it's sweet, and it's delicious. But do take a cue from the discount stores: Panetonne is delicious any time of year.

|||||||||||||||||||||||||||||||||||||||||||||||||||| *Makes 1 panettone* ||||||||||||||||||||||||||||||||||||||||||||||||||||||||

PROCEDURE FOR THE **SPONGE**

① In a small bowl, sprinkle the dry yeast over the milk and stir in the flour and sugar. Cover and allow to bloom for 30 minutes.

PROCEDURE FOR THE **DOUGH**

① In a small bowl, soak the raisins in the rum until they are plump.

② Add the additional teaspoon (4 g) dry *instant* yeast to the sponge. Whisk together the milk and egg and add this to the bowl of the stand mixer fitted with a paddle attachment. Turn the mixer to low.

③ In a large bowl, whisk together the flour, sugar, and salt and slowly add this to the mixer bowl. Add the butter in small pieces. Drain the rum from the raisins and add them to the mixture. Add the lemon and orange peels. Mix on low for 10 minutes, until the dough is very smooth, shiny, and elastic.

④ Cover the dough with a damp towel and place the bowl in a warm part of your kitchen. Allow the dough to double in volume, about 1 hour.

⑤ Shape the dough into a round loaf and allow to rest for about 20 minutes. Transfer the dough to a large paper panettone mold with the seam side down. Brush the top of the dough with the egg wash. Allow to proof for 1 to 1½ hours.

| FOR THE SPONGE | | |
| --- | --- | --- |
| dry yeast | 1 tablespoon | 12 g |
| whole milk, at room temperature | ¼ cup | 60 ml |
| bread flour | ½ cup | 70 g |
| sugar | 1 teaspoon | 4 g |
| FOR THE DOUGH | | |
| golden raisins | 1 cup | 150 g |
| rum | ½ cup | 120 ml |
| dry instant yeast | 1 teaspoon | 4 g |
| milk | 3 tablespoons | 75 ml |
| egg | 1 | |
| bread flour | 1½ cups | 210 g |
| sugar | ⅓ cup | 65 g |
| salt | 1 teaspoon | 6 g |
| unsalted butter, very soft | 2 tablespoons | 42 g |
| lemon peel, chopped into small pieces | ¼ cup | 35 g |
| orange peel, chopped into small pieces | ¼ cup | 35 g |
| egg wash (1 egg whisked with 1 tablespoon/15 ml water) | | |

⑥ While the bread is proofing, preheat the oven to 400°F (205°C). Bake for 45 minutes to 1 hour. Gently poke the sides of the panettone through the wrapper. If they spring back, the panettone is done. Cool and serve.

# NANNY'S
# TORTE

*Bless my grandmother.* She did all right by me. She traveled all the way from Birmingham to D.C. just after I was born. She cooed at me, as any good grandma might. She got extra points for expounding on my adorableness—with a straight face—when in fact I emerged with a cranium both resolutely square and beset by plumes of inky hair. I was indeed a baby with a noggin only a mother and the family Frankenstein could love.

But Nanny, she had no complaints about her new granddaughter—aside from one. It's widely reported that Nanny was overheard leaving my mother's hospital room muttering, "Why the hell did they name her that?" If I could see my Nanny again today, I'd say, "Why indeed?"

And then I imagine she'd make some fudge and I'd make some cake and we'd slap them together and wash it all down with bottle of Coke and come up with a nickname for me that we could both live with, because she never could pronounce my name.

|||||||||||||||||||||||||||||||||||||||||||||| *Makes 1 (10-inch/25-cm) torte* ||||||||||||||||||||||||||||||||||||||||||||||

① Preheat the oven to 325°F (165°C). Spray three 10-inch (25-cm) round cake pans with nonstick spray and line them with parchment. Set aside.

② In the bowl of a stand mixer fixed with the whisk attachment, cream together the sugar and butter until light and fluffy. Add the eggs, one at a time, and beat between each addition.

③ Slowly add the cocoa powder and salt. Mix briefly, then scrape down the sides of the bowl. Mix again until the cocoa is completely integrated into the batter.

④ Simultaneously, melt the chocolate in a metal bowl over a pot of simmering water, stirring often.

⑤ With the mixer running on low speed, scrape the melted chocolate into the batter. When all

| | | |
|---|---|---|
| sugar | 2½ cups | 500 g |
| unsalted butter, at room temperature | 2 cups | 455 g |
| large eggs | 6 | |
| cocoa powder | 2 cups | 170 g |
| salt | 1 teaspoon | 6 g |
| bittersweet chocolate, chopped | 1 pound | 455 g |
| Nanny's Peanut Butter Fudge (page 70) or Gesine's Damn Good Peanut Butter Fudge (page 71) | 1 batch | |
| Sachertorte Glaze (page 56) | 1 batch | |
| roasted peanuts | 1 cup | 150 g |
| peanuts, finely ground in a food processor | 1 cup | 200 g |

the chocolate is added, raise the speed to high and beat briefly. Scrape down the sides and bottom of the bowl and stir in any lingering cocoa.

⑥ Divide the batter evenly between two of the prepared cake pans. Bake for 40 to 45 minutes, until the cakes pull away from the sides of the pans and a toothpick inserted into the center of each cake comes out clean. Allow to cool completely on racks.

⑦ Immediately pour the fudge into the third cake pan and allow to set.

⑧ Turn the fudge out onto a layer of the cake and top with the second cake layer. Press gently to adhere the fudge to the cake.

⑨ Place the layered cake on a cooling rack that's set over a parchment-lined sheet pan. Pour the glaze smoothly and evenly over the cake. Do not use a spatula or other implement to spread the glaze over the cake. Instead, pour the glaze strategically to cover any naked spots. Manipulating the glaze with any utensils will ruin the sheen.

⑩ Using a set of tweezers dedicated to pastry work, arrange the roasted peanuts on top of the cake in flower patterns while the glaze is still warm enough for them to adhere.

⑪ Gently press the ground peanuts onto the sides of the cake.

# RED SOX NATION
# TORTES

*The year we moved to Vermont from Los Angeles, 2004, I watched baseball in earnest for the first time in my life, for the entire American League Championship.* I cursed the Yankees, and conversely, I cheered for the Red Sox vociferously, sending Ortiz, Martinez, and baseball's McDreamy—Johnny Damon—copious amounts of "can do!" and "kick some a**!" vibes.

It worked. I continued with my Uri Geller tactics through every game of the World Series against the Cardinals, complete with my satellite stink-eyes and can-do vibes. The Sox won, for the first time in 86 years, since they traded Babe Ruth in 1918. I got a *little* help from Martinez, Schilling, Damon, Ramirez, Ortiz, Millar…okay, I had nothing to do with it. But I was officially inducted into the Red Sox Nation. In honor of all those New England states that gather around the big red "B," I give you the Red Sox Nation Torte: a McDreamy vanilla cake, American buttercream, and a kick-a** dollop of toasty meringue.

|||||||||||||||||||||||||||||||||||||| *Makes 12 small "baseball" cakes* ||||||||||||||||||||||||||||||||||||||

① Preheat the oven to 350°F (175°C).

② In the bowl of a stand mixer fitted with the paddle attachment, beat together the sugar and butter until light and fluffy, about 5 minutes.

③ Add the egg yolks and whole eggs, one at a time. Beat well between additions. Scrape down the sides of the bowl. Add the vanilla and beat to combine.

④ In a large bowl, whisk together the flour, baking powder, and salt. With the mixer on low speed, add about one-third of the flour mixture to the bowl, then one-third of the buttermilk. Continue alternating additions in this way until both are incorporated.

| | | |
|---|---|---|
| sugar | 2 cups | 400 g |
| unsalted butter, at room temperature | 1½ cups | 345 g |
| egg yolks | 4 | |
| eggs | 2 | |
| vanilla bean paste or extract | 1 tablespoon | 15 ml |
| all-purpose flour | 3 cups | 375 g |
| baking powder | 1 tablespoon | 15 g |
| salt | 1 teaspoon | 6 g |
| buttermilk | 1 cup | 240 ml |
| French/American Buttercream (page 33) | 1 batch | |
| ganache (optional) (page 172) | ½ cup | 115 g |
| Italian Meringue (page 62) | 1 batch | |

SEE SPECIAL EQUIPMENT ON FOLLOWING PAGE

⑤ Spray your baking mold with nonstick cooking spray. Using a large cookie scoop, fill each of the twelve cavities about three-quarters full. Bake for 25 minutes, until the cake springs back when poked.

⑥ While the cakes are still warm, release them from the molds. I divide the cakes evenly into "tops" and "bottoms." I reserve the cleaner-looking cakes for the tops. I immediately flip the bottoms, round side facing down, while they are still hot so that they are in position to receive the filling. Press gently on each bottom to keep it from being wobbly (if the bottom half stayed genuinely round, all the cakes would tip over). Allow the cakes to cool completely.

⑦ I like to mix it up a little and fill some of the cakes with French/American buttercream and some with a ganache-buttercream combo. If you'd like to try this, divide the buttercream evenly between two bowls. Stir the ganache into one bowl and leave the other plain. If you'd rather stick with straight vanilla, proceed to step 8. Otherwise, transfer the plain buttercream to a pastry bag fitted with a large, open pastry tip, and transfer the ganache buttercream to another. Pipe dollops of approximately ¼ cup (100 g) each onto the bottoms and gently press the tops on to sandwich the buttercream.

⑧ If you're sticking with vanilla, transfer the buttercream to a pastry bag fitted with a large, open pastry tip and pipe dollops as described above.

⑨ Transfer the meringue into a pastry bag fitted with a large star tip. Pipe a dollop of meringue onto the top of each cake. Brown each dollop of meringue gently with a kitchen torch. (Don't use a broiler for the browning—you'll melt the buttercream.) Serve immediately.

# PUMPKIN
# ÉCLAIRS

*For me, 4:30 a.m. means one thing and one thing only: choux paste and pastry cream.* For it was at this very hour, when I started to crank the ovens in my little bakery on Elm Street, that I would always preheat one oven to 400 degrees in preparation for making the daily batch of éclairs. I'd have made the pastry cream the night before, so that it could chill overnight in the fridge and be perky and cool in the morning. When I was feeling particularly frisky, I'd add a touch of pumpkin purée and some lovely spices to the mix and top the crunchy choux with a gleaming layer of hard-crack caramel. Heavenly gourd, it took everything in my being not to scarf down every last sweet morsel as I delicately placed those shiny pastries on their trays by 7:00 A.M. But who's to say I didn't sneak a few for breakfast?

|||||||||||||||||||||||||||||||||||||||||| *Makes approximately 2 dozen* ||||||||||||||||||||||||||||||||||||||||||

| FOR THE CHOUX SHELLS | | |
|---|---|---|
| all-purpose flour | 1 cup | 125 g |
| sugar | 1 teaspoon | 5 g |
| salt | ½ teaspoon | 3 g |
| water | 1 cup | 240 ml |
| whole milk | 1 cup | 240 ml |
| unsalted butter | ¾ cup | 170 g |
| eggs | 10 | |
| FOR THE FILLING | | |
| Vanilla Pastry Cream (page 38), chilled | 1 batch | |
| pumpkin purée | 1 cup | 240 ml |
| cinnamon | 1 teaspoon | 2 g |
| nutmeg | ½ teaspoon | 1 g |
| ground cloves | ¼ teaspoon | 1 g |
| heavy cream, whipped to stiff peaks | 1 cup | 240 ml |

PROCEDURE FOR THE **CHOUX SHELLS**

① Preheat the oven to 425°F (220°C). If you have a convection oven option, leave it off. Don't use convection for choux; otherwise it will rise in an ungainly fashion and not uniformly.

② In a large bowl, whisk together the flour and salt. Set aside.

③ In a very large saucepan over medium heat, bring the milk, water, and butter to a rolling boil.

④ Reduce the heat to medium-low and add the flour carefully but all at once. Start stirring with a wooden spoon immediately. Continue stirring until the mixture pulls together into a very thick paste. The ball should pull away completely from the sides of the pan, should be relatively smooth, and should not contain any flour clumps. This takes just a few minutes.

⑤ Transfer the ball to the bowl of a stand mixer fitted with a paddle attachment. Beat on medium speed to cool the paste a bit.

⑥ Add the eggs, one at a time, beating after each addition to make sure it's fully incorporated. There is a chance, depending on the humidity or dryness of the day, that 10 eggs will not be enough. The mixture should be a nice paste that will hold its shape when piped. Add an extra egg if you feel the dough is too thick.

⑦ Transfer the dough into a large pastry bag fitted with a large open tip.

⑧ On a sheet pan lined with parchment, pipe even strips 4 inches (10 cm) long, spacing the shells 2 inches (5 cm) apart.

⑨ Bake for 10 minutes. Reduce the heat to 350°F (175°C) and bake for 30 minutes more.

⑩ Allow the shells to cool completely before filling.

### PROCEDURE FOR THE FILLING

① In the clean bowl of your stand mixer fitted with the paddle attachment, beat together the pastry cream, pumpkin purée, and spices until the mixture is smooth and creamy.

② Remove the bowl from the mixer and add the whipped cream. Using a large rubber spatula, gently fold the whipped heavy cream into the pastry cream. The mixture should be slightly stiff and hold its shape easily when piped. Refrigerate the pastry cream until you're ready to fill the shells.

### PROCEDURE FOR THE CARAMEL

① Have a large metal bowl filled with ice ready on your countertop before you start.

② In a large saucepan over medium heat, combine the sugar, water, and lemon juice. Stir until the sugar has completely melted. Brush down the sides of the pan with a damp pastry brush to get rid of any rogue sugar crystals.

③ Increase the heat to high, clip on a candy thermometer, and stop stirring. Heat to 300°F (149°C); the sugar should just begin to caramelize to a light amber.

| FOR THE CARAMEL | | |
|---|---|---|
| sugar | 1 cup | 200 g |
| water | ⅓ cup | 75 ml |
| lemon juice | 1 squirt | |

④ Remove the pan from the heat and immediately place it into the bowl of ice to stop the caramel from browning any further. The bottom of the pan should touch the ice but you don't want any ice to actually plop into the pan with the caramel.

### PROCEDURE FOR THE ASSEMBLY

① Cut each choux shell in half.

✱ **A Note From the Sugar Baby:** If the shells feel soft or soggy and the innards are a little undone when you slice them, simply continue slicing all of the shells in half and then pop them in a 350°F (175°C) oven for 10 minutes to let them crisp up a bit. It's much easier to slice a not-quite-finished choux shell in half than to try cutting a too-done shell. A too-brittle shell will shatter and be useless. Make sure to keep the correct bottoms and tops together when reheating.

② One at a time, carefully dip the top half of each shell into the caramel. (I keep a long pair of tweezers on hand just for pastry work so that I can pluck the shell out of the caramel without burning my fingers.) Place each covered half-shell on a second parchment-lined sheet pan and allow the caramel to cool and harden.

③ Meanwhile, transfer the pastry cream to a pastry bag fitted with a large, open tip.

④ Pipe the filling in an even layer onto the bottom half of each choux shell. Gently place the caramel-covered half of each shell on top of the filling to make a lovely pumpkin éclair sandwich. Fill each éclair enough that you can see a nice layer of pastry cream when you top it with the caramel choux layer, but not so much that the éclair topples over. Continue filling the éclairs until you run out of ingredients.

# CROQUEMBOUCHE
# PYRAMID

*You've no doubt seen the traditional* croquembouche, *that singularly French treat composed of caramel-drenched choux puffs built into a pyramid of goodness.* You can make the process much easier than the traditional method (single cream puffs stacked to create the pyramid) and instead make rings that stack upon each other. You have the option of filling the rings with lightened pastry cream (page 38) once they are stacked by poking several small holes along the inside of each ring. Fill a pastry bag fitted with a medium open tip with lightened pastry cream, insert the tip into the hole, and squirt the cream into the ring.

|||||||||||||||||||||||||||||||||||||||||||||||||||||||||| *Makes 1 pyramid* |||||||||||||||||||||||||||||||||||||||||||||||||||||||||||

| FOR THE CHOUX | | |
|---|---|---|
| all-purpose flour | 1 cup | 125 g |
| salt | ½ teaspoon | 3 g |
| whole milk | 1 cup | 240 ml |
| water | 1 cup | 240 ml |
| unsalted butter | ¾ cup | 170 g |
| eggs | 10 | |
| egg wash (1 egg beaten with 1 tablespoon/15 ml water) | | |
| **FOR THE CARAMEL** | | |
| sugar | 1 cup | 200 g |
| water | ⅓ cup | 75 ml |
| lemon juice | 1 squirt | |
| **SPECIAL EQUIPMENT** | | |
| cake pans, for drawing circles | in diameters from 4 to 10 inches | in diameters from 10 to 25 cm |
| large cardboard cake round | | |
| sugar whisk* | | |
| *This is a balloon whisk with the tines snipped with a wire cutter to straight, even lengths (see page 208). | | |

PROCEDURE FOR THE **CHOUX**

① Preheat the oven to 425°F (220°C). If you have a convection oven option, leave it off. Don't use convection for choux; otherwise it will rise in an ungainly fashion and not uniformly.

② In a large bowl, whisk together the flour and salt. Set aside.

③ In a very large saucepan over medium heat, bring the milk, water, and butter to a rolling boil.

④ Reduce the heat to medium-low and add the flour carefully but all at once. Start stirring with a wooden spoon immediately. Continue stirring until the mixture pulls together into a very thick paste. The ball should pull away completely from the sides of the pan, should be relatively smooth, and should not contain any flour clumps. This takes just a few minutes.

⑤ Transfer the ball to the bowl of a stand mixer fitted with a paddle attachment. Beat on medium speed to cool the paste a bit.

⑥ Add the eggs, one at a time, beating after each addition to make sure it's fully incorporated.

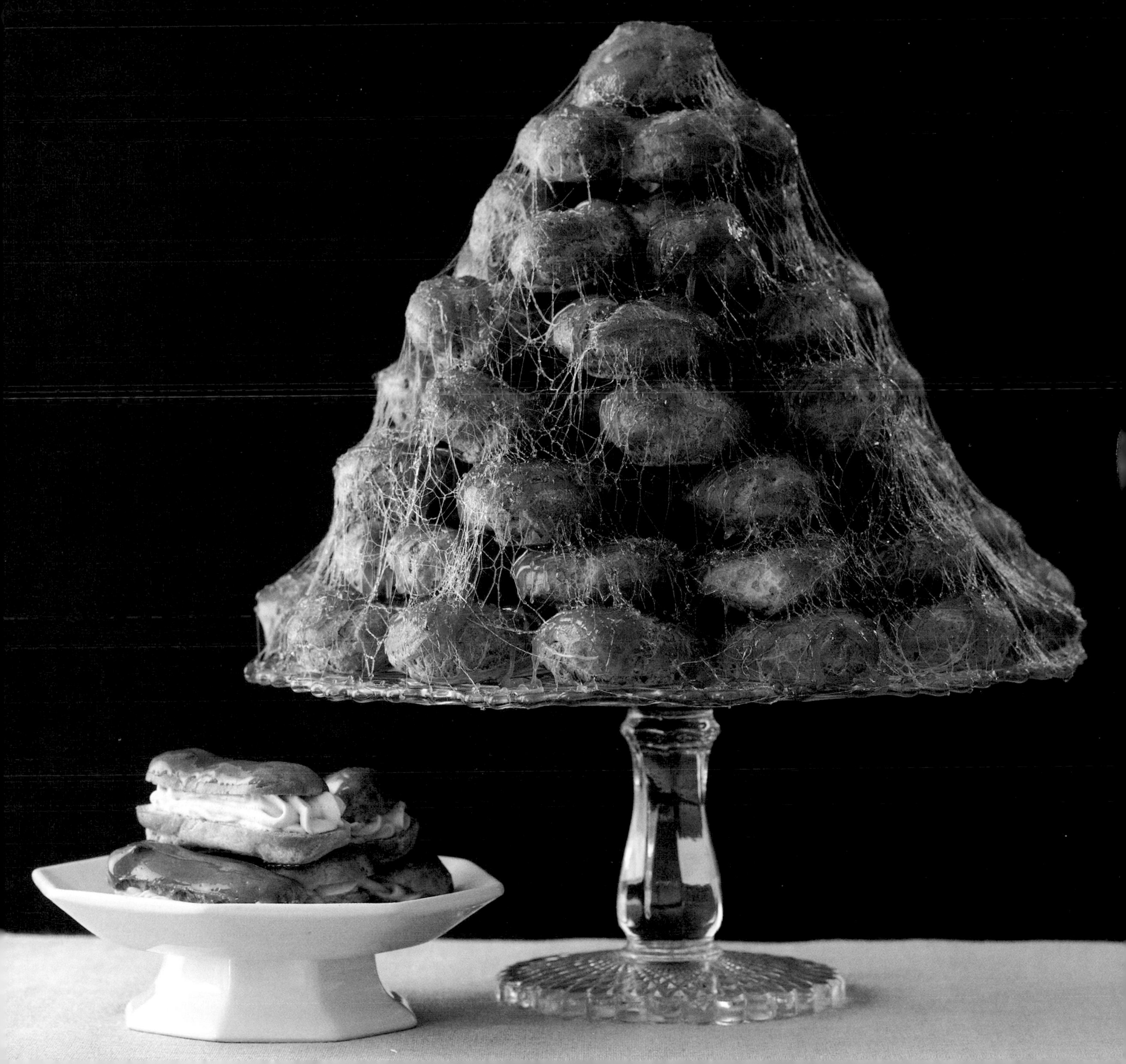

*Top:* **CROQUEMBOUCHE PYRAMID**
*Bottom:* **PUMPKIN ÉCLAIRS**

There is a chance, depending on the humidity or dryness of the day, that 10 eggs will not be enough. The mixture should be a nice paste that will hold its shape when piped. Add an extra egg if you feel the dough is too thick.

⑦ Transfer the dough into a large pastry bag fitted with a large open tip.

⑧ Using cake rings as guides, draw circles on parchment of decreasing diameter: a 10-inch (25-cm), 9-inch (23-cm), 8-inch (20-cm), and so on, all the way down to 4 inches (10 cm). You'll clearly need more than a few sheet pans to get all your circles done and you may have to do the baking in a few batches.

⑨ Flip the parchment over on pans so that the ink can be seen through it. Pipe the choux into the circles, either in a ring, or creating a loop pattern (remember spyrographs?) so that the ring looks like a flower. (Go to www.sugarbabycookbook.com for an example.) Also pipe a single cream-puff-size dollop to sit at the very top of the pyramid.

⑩ Bake the rings for 10 minutes; then reduce the temperature to 350°F (175°C) and bake for 30 minutes longer.

PROCEDURE FOR THE **CARAMEL**

① Have a large metal bowl filled with ice ready on your countertop before you start.

② In a large saucepan over medium heat, combine the sugar, water, and lemon juice. Stir until the sugar has completely melted. Brush the sides of the pan down with a damp pastry brush to get rid of any rogue sugar crystals.

③ Raise the heat to high, clip on a candy thermometer, and stop stirring. Heat to 300°F (150°C); the sugar should just begin to caramelize to a light amber.

④ Remove the pan from the heat and immediately place it into the bowl of ice to stop the caramel from browning any further. The bottom of the pan should touch the ice but you don't want any ice to actually plop into the pan with the caramel.

PROCEDURE FOR THE **ASSEMBLY**

① Place the largest cake ring on a large cardboard round or cake plate. For greater stability, you can attach the ring to the cardboard by placing small dollops of caramel underneath the ring.

② Take a hearty spoonful of hot caramel and pour it in a circle on top of the ring. You want the ring to be coated so that you can see the glistening caramel on the periphery; you also want the caramel to act as the adhesive for the next ring.

③ Immediately place the next smaller ring on top, making sure it is placed on the hot caramel. If the ring doesn't adhere easily, feel free to add more caramel. Continue in this manner with the rest of the rings, and finally with the single cream puff. Allow the caramel to cool and harden.

④ Make sure the remaining caramel is still viscous. If it is not, place it over low heat until it falls easily from a spoon.

⑤ Line a work space and the floor area immediately around the work space with parchment. Dip the sugar whisk into the caramel. Hold the whisk about 1 foot (30 cm) above the pot and let the large clumps fall until the sugar starts to fall from each tine in thin, even strands. Circle the whisk around the *croquembouche*, about 1 foot (30 cm) away from the pastry, so that the sugar strands wrap around the pyramid. Keep dipping and circling until you have an even layer of caramel strands around the entirety of the *croquembouche* (they will look like sugar cobwebs—Miss Havisham, anyone?). You may need a stepping stool to get the best vantage point.

⑥ Display the *croquembouche* in a cool, dry place. Remember, heat and moisture are not your friends.

# DRESDENER
# STOLLEN

*Stollen is a traditional German Christmas cake that dates back to the fourteenth century.* I doubt that I have to tell you this, but Germans take their cake seriously. So seriously, in fact, that through the ages the princes of Germany petitioned five different popes to lift the Lenten ban on butter in baking so that their stollen would be perfect. All the princes were denied, and stollen remained butterless and bland. But the noblemen would not be denied. It took Pope Innocent VIII and his "Butter Letter" of 1490 to lift the ban on the use of the good stuff; bakers and noble persons of Saxony rejoiced and, presumably, ate their fill of fruitcake that year.

Fast-forward centuries later to find a German woman named Helga contemplating Christmas stollen. It goes without saying that hers would have butter. But Helga took her requirements further; her stollen had to contain marzipan at its core. Nothing and no one could stop her from including it, not even the pope. Helga passed along her devotion to what she felt was a superior stollen to her daughter, and I'm happy to pass the recipe along to you in my mother's honor.

*Makes 1 stollen*

| FOR THE SPONGE | | |
|---|---|---|
| sugar | 1 tablespoon | 12 g |
| lukewarm milk | ½ cup | 120 ml |
| all-purpose flour | ½ cup | 60 g |
| dry yeast | 2 tablespoons | 25 g |
| FOR THE DOUGH | | |
| golden raisins | 1 cup | 150 g |
| rum | ¼ cup | 60 ml |
| egg | 1 | |
| milk | ½ cup | 120 ml |
| zest of 1 lemon | | |
| slivered blanched almonds, toasted | ½ cup | 55 g |
| all-purpose flour | 2½ cups | 310 g |

PROCEDURE FOR THE **SPONGE**

① In a small bowl, stir together the sugar, milk, flour, and yeast. Cover and allow to bloom for about 30 minutes.

PROCEDURE FOR THE **DOUGH**

① Soak the raisins in the rum until they are plump.

② Pour the sponge into the bowl of a stand mixer fitted with the dough hook.

③ In the small bowl you used for the sponge, whisk together the egg and milk until the egg is well beaten. Pour into the bowl with the sponge. Mix on low speed.

4. Slowly add the zest, almonds, flour, sugar, cinnamon, nutmeg, and cardamom. Mix until the dough just comes together. Add the butter, a small piece at a time. Add the citrus peel. Add the raisins and any remaining rum to the mixture. Continue to mix for 5 minutes, until the dough is very smooth and elastic.

5. Cover the dough with a damp towel and place the bowl in a warm, moist area of your kitchen. Allow the dough to double in volume, about 2 hours.

PROCEDURE FOR THE **ASSEMBLY**

1. In a clean bowl of your stand mixer fitted with the paddle attachment, beat the marzipan until it's smooth. If you find it's dry, add a few tablespoons (about 40 g) of softened butter and mix until smooth.

2. Roll the marzipan into a 9-inch (23-cm) log.

3. Turn the dough out onto a lightly floured work surface and knead gently for a few seconds. Roll the dough into a rough 10-inch (25-cm) square and place the marzipan log in the middle. Fold each side of the dough over the marzipan so it overlaps in the middle. This fold is meant to be asymmetrical, mimicking a baby's swaddling (guess which baby).

4. Preheat the oven to 375°F (190°C).

5. Transfer the stollen to a parchment-lined sheet pan and cover it with a damp towel. Allow it to rise until doubled in volume, about 1 hour.

| | | |
|---|---|---|
| sugar | ¼ cup | 50 g |
| cinnamon | 1 teaspoon | 2 g |
| nutmeg | ½ teaspoon | 1 g |
| ground cardamom | ½ teaspoon | 1 g |
| unsalted butter, very soft | ½ cup, plus extra if needed for assembly | 115 g, plus extra if needed for assembly |
| Candied Citrus Peel (page 54), orange and lemon, diced | ¼ cup | 35 g |
| FOR THE ASSEMBLY | | |
| Odense marzipan | 7 oz | |
| unsalted butter, melted and cooled | ½ cup | 115 g |
| confectioners' sugar | ½ cup | 50 g |

6. Remove the towel from the stollen and bake for 45 minutes. While the stollen is still hot, brush it with the melted butter and immediately sift half of the confectioners' sugar over it to coat it completely. (The butter will help the sugar to adhere.) Once the stollen cools, you can sift a fresh layer of confectioners' sugar over it before serving.

7. Wrap the stollen in plastic wrap and store in a cool, dry place for up to 2 weeks.

# GESINE AND RAY
### Get
# MARRIED

*My mother had an expertly calibrated palate.* She could give you the ingredient list, down to the quarter-teaspoon, of the recipe for any culinary concoction that graced her taste buds. We'd quake in fear for the wait staff of any restaurant, waiting for my mother to take the inaugural bite of her entrée and declare, "It's clean." If she didn't give the all-clear—or all-clean, as it were—there'd be hell to pay in the kitchen. And we'd be mortally embarrassed for the rest of the evening.

And so it was when it came time to taste wedding cakes. Mom found the traditional brouhaha surrounding wedding planning tedious. Helga, unlike most mothers of the bride, wanted only two things for the nuptials of her youngest: a daughter happy with her marriage partner, and a wedding cake suitable to her discerning European gustation.

And then I made the rookie mistake of taking her to a cake tasting at a renowned L.A. bakery.

Stupid. Stupid. Stupid. It hadn't occurred to me that I'd never be able to show my face in the little shop again if I brought along my mother. Petite portions of cakes of infinite variety, all festooned with their coordinating dollops of icing, arrived for our tasting pleasure. And, like clockwork: "This is *not* real buttercream. This is *not* clean." I can't be certain that my mother even made the effort to chew; a nanosecond in the vicinity of my mother's golden buds divined the truth in the cake. It was not clean. This shop would not make the cake.

We proceeded, Mom and I, to bake—clearly something we should have done from the start. Our plan was simple. We'd find a recipe we loved, and when it was perfected, we'd deliver said recipe to the caterer and warn them not to stray from our instruction. Neither of us cared if the wedding cake was a sculptural masterpiece. The requirement was that it didn't collapse and that it was delicious. Ray and I cut the cake. We fed each other pieces of cake. And then I proceeded to feed my family cake. And to the great relief of the lingering caterers, my mother gave the all clear: "It's clean!"

I hereby share with you our very clean—but scrumptious—almond cake featuring ganache, almond toffee, and a cotton-candy bird's nest.

| FOR THE ALMOND CAKE | | |
|---|---|---|
| egg whites | 12 | |
| cream of tartar | 1 teaspoon | 3 g |
| sugar | 2 cups, divided | 400 g, divided |
| cake flour | 2 cups | 280 g |
| salt | 1 teaspoon | 6 g |
| baking powder | 2 teaspoons | 10 g |
| unsalted butter, at room temperature | 1 cup | 225 g |
| buttermilk | 1 cup | 240 ml |
| almond extract | 1 tablespoon | 15 ml |
| FOR THE ASSEMBLY | | |
| Buttery Almond Toffee (page 149) | 1 batch | |
| ganache (page 172) | 1 batch | |
| Italian Buttercream (page 63) | 1 batch | |
| Cotton Candy (page 150), formed into a bird's nest | ¼ batch | |
| Marshmallow Fondant (page 118; optional) | 1 batch | |
| SPECIAL EQUIPMENT | | |
| square cake pans (10-inch/25-cm) | 3 | |
| square cake board | 1 | |
| square cake rings | 3 | |
| heat gun or blow dryer | | |

### PROCEDURE FOR THE **ALMOND CAKE**

① Preheat the oven to 350°F (175°C).

② In the clean mixing bowl of a stand mixer, whisk the egg whites with the cream of tartar on medium speed until just foamy. With the mixer on medium, slowly add 1 cup (200 g) of the sugar, then increase the speed to high once the sugar is completely incorporated. Beat until the egg whites are glossy and hold firm peaks. Transfer the mixture to a clean metal bowl and set aside.

③ In a small bowl, whisk together the flour, salt, and baking powder. Set aside.

④ In the same mixing bowl you used to whisk the egg whites (you don't have to clean it, just proceed as if nothing happened), using the paddle attachment, beat together the remaining sugar and the butter until light and fluffy, about 3 minutes. Scrape down the sides of the bowl and beat for a few more minutes.

⑤ With the mixer on medium speed, add about one-third of the flour mixture and then one-third of the buttermilk, alternating this way between the two until both are incorporated into the batter. Scrape down the sides of the bowl. Add the almond extract and mix briefly.

⑥ Take a large scoop of the egg whites and add it to the batter. Mix on high for a moment to lighten the batter.

⑦ Remove the bowl from the mixer. With a rubber spatula, fold in one-third of the remaining egg whites. Once you no longer see any white streaks, very gently fold in the remaining egg whites, mixing until the egg whites are completely incorporated.

⑧ Divide the batter evenly among the three square cake pans, sprayed with nonstick spray. Bake for 30 minutes, or until the cake springs back when you gently poke it.

### PROCEDURE FOR THE **ASSEMBLY**

① Break the toffee into small bits and place about 1 cup (140 g) in a food processor fitted with the metal blade attachment. Pulse a few times until at least ½ cup (70 g) of the toffee is broken into small pieces but not pulverized; the pieces should be no larger than a corn kernel. Set aside.

② Place the first layer of almond cake on a cake board, inside a square cake ring. Smooth 2 cups (480 ml) of the ganache evenly over the cake layer and sprinkle ¼ cup (35 g) of the toffee evenly on top of the ganache. Gently press the toffee into the ganache so that it sticks. Continue with the next layer of cake, stacking another cake ring for each layer, and top again with 2 cups (480 ml) ganache and ¼ cup (35 g) of toffee. Place the final layer of cake on top of the toffee and refrigerate overnight.

✱ **A Note From the Sugar Baby:** One important trick for a successful layer cake assembly is the use of professional cake rings. Don't let the name fool you—cake rings come in all manner of shapes, including square. Cake rings are bottomless, and I use them as the forms in which I both bake cakes and build cakes. I buy most of my rings at a professional culinary vendor called JB Prince (www.jbprince.com). Luckily for you, they sell their wares to everyone, not just professionals.

To bake with a cake ring, simply place the ring on a parchment-lined sheet pan and spray the parchment as well as the sides of the ring with nonstick spray. Pour the batter into the ring and bake as you would in a regular cake pan. One warning: If your cake batter is particularly runny, it will leak from underneath the bottomless ring. The batters in this book are all rather fluffy and sturdy and shouldn't present this problem, but if you do encounter it, refrigerate your batter for an hour to firm it up enough so that it will stay within the confines of the ring.

To assemble a cake in a cake ring, simply place the ring over the first layer and continue to ice and layer the cake inside the ring. You can stack rings on top of each other for very high cakes. Refrigerate or freeze the cake for an hour and use a heat gun or blow dryer to heat the rings so they slide off. Frost the cake as you normally would. But just notice how straight those sides are now—you'll be accused of buying the cake in a fancy shop at this rate.

③ Unmold the cake layers by heating the cake rings with a blow dryer or heat gun.

④ Using a small offset spatula, spread a very thin and even layer of buttercream over the entire cake. Use a bench scraper to smooth out the tops and sides of the cake so that there are no peaks or valleys. At this stage, it's okay if a small amount of cake and filling are still peeking through the buttercream—this is a "crumb coat" that will seal in crumbs, obviously, but also provide a smooth base for the finishing layer. Refrigerate the cake until the crumb coat is firm to the touch.

⑤ At this point you can go over the cake with a heavier layer of buttercream, or you can roll out the fondant and cover. For instructions on covering cakes in rolled fondant and adding fondant cutouts, see page 118.

⑥ Top the cake with the cotton-candy bird's nest.

# SALTED
## *Dulce de Leche*
# CUPCAKES

*I'm not big on most cupcakes, with their dry cake and shortening-laden icing.* Sometimes, however, they can be surprisingly delicious, and they are at their most scrumptious when they are filled with a lusciously hidden flavor bomb. In this case, fudgy dark chocolate cake is strategically injected with silky milk caramel and topped with a thin layer of fudge. Nothing dry or shortening-laden here.

||||||||||||||||||||||||||||||||||||||||||||||||||||||||||||| *Makes 2 dozen* |||||||||||||||||||||||||||||||||||||||||||||||||||||||||

| FOR THE DARK CHOCOLATE FUDGE CAKE | | |
|---|---|---|
| bittersweet chocolate, finely chopped | 3 ounces | 90 g |
| freshly brewed hot coffee | 1½ cups | 360 ml |
| all-purpose flour | 2½ cups | 310 g |
| unsweetened dark chocolate cocoa powder | 1½ cups | 125 g |
| baking soda | 2 teaspoons | 10 g |
| baking powder | 1 teaspoon | 5 g |
| salt | 1 teaspoon | 6 g |
| sugar | 3 cups | 600 g |
| eggs | 3 | |
| vegetable oil | ¾ cup | 180 ml |
| vanilla extract | 1 teaspoon | 5 ml |
| nonfat buttermilk | 1½ cups | 360 ml |
| FOR THE ASSEMBLY | | |
| Dulce de Leche (page 27) | 1 batch | |
| Dark Chocolate Fudgy Frosting (page 53) | 1 batch | |
| coarse sea salt, for sprinkling | | |

PROCEDURE FOR THE **DARK CHOCOLATE FUDGE CAKE**

① Preheat the oven to 350°F (175°C).

② In a medium bowl, mix the chocolate into the hot coffee and allow to melt. Set aside.

③ In a large bowl, whisk together the flour, cocoa powder, baking soda, baking powder, and salt. Set aside.

④ In the bowl of a stand mixer fitted with the paddle attachment, beat the sugar, eggs, oil, and vanilla until fluffy. Pour the buttermilk into the chocolate mixture and stir. With the mixer on low speed, slowly add one-third of the chocolate mixture, followed by one-third of the flour mixture. Continue alternating between the two until both mixtures are incorporated into the batter.

⑤ Line 24 muffin-tin cups with muffin papers of your choice.

⑥ Using a large cookie scoop, add one scoop of batter to each muffin paper, filling each about three-quarters full. Bake for 20 minutes, or until a toothpick inserted in the middle of the cake comes out clean. Remove the cakes from the tins and allow to cool completely on racks.

PROCEDURE FOR THE **ASSEMBLY**

① Once the cupcakes have cooled, poke a hole halfway into the center of each cupcake with your index finger.

② Fill a pastry bag fitted with a large open tip with dulce de leche. Insert the tip into each cupcake hole and squeeze the caramel into the cupcake until you see the cupcake expand a bit.

③ Roll a golf ball–size portion of cooled fudge frosting in your hand and flatten it into a neat circle approximately the size of a cupcake top. Place the fudge disk on top of a cupcake and sprinkle with sea salt. Repeat with remaining cupcakes.

④ Serve immediately.

# FONDANT WITH THE SUGAR BABY

Fondant makes for a lovely, smooth finish to any cake, if it doesn't tear or dry or bubble. To make your coverage successful, follow a few simple rules:

① You need to provide a "glue" surface, or a "crumb coat," for the fondant to adhere to the sides of the cake. This means you'll have to scrape a thin base layer of buttercream (or whatever you choose to use) onto the top and sides of the cake. Make sure that you've applied this layer smoothly, as any divots or bulges will show through the fondant. However, apply as thin a layer as possible. Make sure that you chill the cake with the crumb coat well prior to covering with the fondant.

② Sprinkle a work surface lightly with cornstarch and dust your rolling pin with cornstarch as well. Only use enough to keep the fondant from sticking because too much will make it dry.

③ Roll out the fondant at least ⅛ inch (3 mm) thick; measure the overall surface of your cake and roll the fondant out slightly larger than this area, so you have some room to work with when you start to drape and smooth. If you roll out too much fondant and it drapes far below the bottom edge of the cake, the weight of the fondant will cause the beautiful smooth surface to tear. So only roll out just a bit more than you'll need to cover the entire surface.

④ Invest in a fondant smoother. Smoothers are cheap and very helpful, especially when you've been working with coloring agents and other ingredients that may not leave your hands pristine. The surface area of the smoother is also very slick and won't stick to the fondant.

⑤ Place the cake to be covered on a cardboard round that you've cut to the exact size of the cake. Anything larger will prevent you from keeping a clean edge.

⑥ Before you cover the cake, place it on a cake pedestal—this will give it some height so you don't have to bend over and give yourself a backache while smoothing the fondant.

⑦ Place the dull side (the side that's been face-down on the cornstarch) face-down on the crumb layer, so the dull side sticks to the cake while the polished side faces up. Work quickly, as fondant dries in minutes. Gently pick up the fondant piece by sliding your hands underneath it, sweaty palms down, and drape it over the cake. Smooth the cake with a fondant smoother or your cornstarch-dusted palms. Begin at the top of the cake, working in circular motions from the middle toward the edge to get rid of any air bubbles. Move down the cake, smoothing along the edges in a circular motion, all along the perimeter first and then down the actual sides of the cake. Trim any pieces that are too long with a sharp knife; do not stretch the fondant. Work in circles all along the sides until the fondant is adhered and smooth.

⑧ Do not use water to smooth fondant; this will only make it tacky and even potentially melt it. However, if you are adhering fondant decorations onto a fondant base, moistening the back of the fondant decoration will act as a glue.

# THE
## *Birthday-That-Shall-Remain-Nameless*
# CAKE

*OK, fine.* I'm no longer a spring chicken. But that doesn't mean I like my birthday cakes stodgy and boring. As a matter of fact, when I get to baking my own birthday cake, you'd be surprised to find that it is composed of no less than two layers of Rice Krispie treats à la Sugar Baby. I like to wrangle the sticky mass and stomp it into a cake ring, forming a crispy and chewy layer that I wedge between layers of devil's food cake. This recipe is simply for the middle tier of the cake shown in the photo at left. Bake one cake, or go nuts and bake multiple batches in pans of varying shape.

|||||||||||||||||||||||||||||||||||| *Makes 1 (10-inch/25-cm) tier of a three-layer cake* ||||||||||||||||||||||||||||||||||||

PROCEDURE FOR THE **DEVIL'S FOOD CAKE**

① Preheat the oven to 350°F (175°C).

② In a large bowl, whisk together the flour, cocoa powder, salt, and baking soda. Set aside.

③ In the bowl of a stand mixer, whisk the egg whites and cream of tartar on medium-high speed until they become foamy. Slowly add ⅓ cup (65 g) of the sugar. Raise the mixer speed to high and beat until the egg whites are white and shiny and hold stiff peaks. Transfer the egg whites to a clean metal bowl and set aside.

④ Fit the stand mixer with the paddle attachment. In the same bowl you just beat the egg whites in (you do not need to clean it), cream together the butter and the remaining 1 cup (200 g) sugar until light and fluffy, about 3 minutes. Add the whole eggs, one at a time, and mix until incorporated.

| FOR THE DEVIL'S FOOD CAKE | | |
| --- | --- | --- |
| cake flour | 2 cups | 280 g |
| dark cocoa powder, such as Callebaut Extra Brute | ¾ cup | 60 g |
| salt | 1 teaspoon | 6 g |
| baking soda | 1 teaspoon | 5 g |
| egg whites | 5 | |
| cream of tartar | 1 teaspoon | 3 g |
| sugar | 1⅓ cups, divided | 265 g, divided |
| unsalted butter, at room temperature | 1½ cups | 345 g |
| whole eggs | 2 | |
| buttermilk | 1 cup | 240 ml |
| coffee | 1 cup | 240 ml |
| vanilla extract | 1 tablespoon | 15 ml |

**A Note From the Sugar Baby:** Here's a secret weapon I use to avoid spilling flour everywhere when I'm adding large amounts to a tiny mixing bowl with a moving object whirling around inside: parchment paper. I dump a portion of the flour mixture—in this case about one-quarter of the devil's food dry ingredient mixture—onto a piece of parchment for each incorporation and then fold it into a funnel. You see, when I try to add dry ingredients straight from a bowl, or even a mixing cup with a spout, half of the intended ingredients end up on my countertop. With the parchment, I just dump it onto the paper and use the parchment to deliver the ingredients straight into the bowl, mess-free.

⑤ With the mixer on medium speed, slowly add ½ cup (120 ml) of the buttermilk followed by one-third of the flour mixture. Add the remaining buttermilk and then one-third more of the flour mixture. Then, add the remaining coffee and flour mixture.

⑥ Remove the bowl from the mixer, and, using a large rubber spatula, take a large spoonful of the beaten egg whites and add to the batter, stirring vigorously to lighten.

| FOR THE GANACHE | | |
|---|---|---|
| bittersweet chocolate, finely chopped | 1½ pounds (approximately 4 cups chips) | 720 g |
| heavy cream | 1 cup | 240 ml |
| coffee | ⅓ cup | 75 ml |
| unsalted butter | ¼ cup | 55 g |
| salt | pinch | |
| egg yolks | 2 | |
| FOR THE ASSEMBLY Rice Krispie Treats (page 118) | 1 batch | |
| Italian Buttercream (page 63) | 1 batch | |
| Marshmallow Fondant (page 118) | 1 batch | |
| Barley Roses (page 158) | 1 batch | |

⑦ Take half of the remaining egg whites and gently fold into the batter, using even strokes and turning the bowl about a quarter turn after each stroke. Work quickly but gently in order to maintain the aeration the egg whites are adding to the batter. When just a few white streaks are visible, add the remaining egg whites and continue folding into the batter until it is uniformly brown.

⑧ Divide the batter evenly among three 10-inch (25-cm) cake pans prepared with nonstick spray.

⑨ Bake for 30 minutes. Remove from the oven and allow to cool on racks.

PROCEDURE FOR THE **GANACHE**

① Place the chocolate in a large metal bowl. Set aside.

② In a large saucepan over medium-low heat, combine the cream, coffee, butter, and salt and heat to simmer. Remove from the heat.

③ Place the egg yolks in a small bowl and whisk them until they break apart. Take ¼ cup (60 ml) of the hot cream mixture from the saucepan and slowly pour it into the yolks, whisking constantly, to temper the egg yolks.

④ Add the tempered eggs to the cream mixture and return the saucepan to the stove. Attach a candy thermometer and heat to 160°F (71°C) over medium heat, whisking constantly. The cream should begin to gently simmer.

⑤ Pour the simmering cream over the chocolate. Allow it to sit, undisturbed, for 5 minutes to allow the chocolate to melt. Then, whisk the cream and chocolate together until the chocolate has completely melted and the mixture has emulsified. If you find that there are unmelted bits of chocolate, place the bowl over a gently simmering pot of water and stir until the last bits are melted.

① Divide the Rice Krispie treat mass between two 10-inch (25-cm) cake rings sprayed with non-stick cooking spray. Pat the sticky stuff down so that the treats form a compact layer. Allow to set for 1 hour and remove from the rings.

② Place your first cake layer on a cardboard cake round. Be very gentle and use a cake spatula if you have one, as the cake is terribly delicate. Coat the top of the layer with ½ cup (120 ml) ganache and place a Rice Krispie layer on top of the ganache. Place the next layer of cake on top of the Rice Krispie layer and spread with ½ cup (120 ml) ganache. Top with the second layer of Rice Krispie, then add your final layer of cake.

③ Refrigerate for at least 1 hour.

④ Ice the exterior of the cake with the butter-cream. (I like to add several drops of food coloring to it beforehand.) Make a very thin "crumb coat" first and refrigerate the cake until it is set. Then go over the crumb coat with a thicker layer of buttercream, smoothing it out with a bench scraper on the sides to make them smooth and even.

⑤ Decorate with fondant (for instructions, see page 118). Pipe beads of buttercream along the bottom of the cake to finish, and decorate with Barley Roses. Top with your sculpture of choice.

# THE MALLOW
## *of*
# THE MARSH

*If you make marshmallow look fancy, adults won't feel guilty scarfing it down.* These are gourmet vanilla shortbread cookies topped with marshmallow and covered with delectable bitter-sweet chocolate. What could be more grown-up?

IIIIIIIIIIIIIIIIIIIIIIIIIIIIIIIIIIIIIIIIIIIIIIIIIIIIIIIIII *Makes 2 dozen* IIIIIIIIIIIIIIIIIIIIIIIIIIIIIIIIIIIIIIIIIIIIIIIIIIIIIIIIII

| | | |
|---|---|---|
| all-purpose flour | 2 cups | 250 g |
| sugar | ½ cup | 100 g |
| salt | 1 teaspoon | 6 g |
| unsalted butter | 1¼ cups | 285 g |
| Don't Harsh My Mallow (page 115) | 1 batch | |
| semisweet chocolate | 6 ounces | 180 g |

① In a large bowl, combine the flour, sugar and salt. Whisk until combined.

② Add the butter in small pieces and massage it into the flour with your fingers until you have what looks like cornmeal, with no obvious butter chunks peeking through. The dough should start holding together when you pinch it.

③ Cover the dough with plastic wrap and chill for 20 minutes.

④ On a work surface lightly dusted with flour, gently roll the dough out to ½ inch (12 mm) thick. You may have to pat the dough with your hands to keep it together.

⑤ With a cookie or biscuit cutter, cut 2-inch (5-cm) rounds from the dough and place the shortbreads 1 inch (2.5 cm) apart on a parchment-lined sheet pan.

⑥ Chill the dough again in the refrigerator for 20 minutes. Meanwhile, preheat the oven to 325°F (165°C).

⑦ Bake the shortbreads for 25 minutes, or until they barely brown. Set aside to cool.

⑧ Fill a pastry bag fitted with a large star tip with the marshmallow. Pipe small mounds onto each shortbread. Allow the marshmallow to set on the shortbread for at least 1 hour.

⑨ Melt the chocolate in a double boiler over gently simmering water. Transfer the chocolate into a pastry bag fitted with a small open tip. Carefully pipe the chocolate in a zigzag pattern over each of the confections.

⑩ Allow the chocolate to set in a cool, dry place before serving.

# FLEUR DE SEL
# SPIRALS

*There is nothing more reminiscent of childhood than getting debaucherously sloppy and sticky with a fat piece of candy.* And if you're really doing it right, your teeth have gotten stuck together at some juncture of your craven candyfest. If you'd like to re-create such a moment but add a little sophisticated French flair, I suggest you get your teeth stuck on this magnificent candy beast.

*Makes approximately 20*

Fleur de Sel Caramel (page 125)  1 batch

cornstarch, for dusting

Vanilla Cream Fondant (page 130)  1 batch

① Pour the hot caramel evenly onto a sheet pan lined with parchment and liberally sprayed with nonstick cooking spray. Spread the caramel into a rough 11-by-13-inch (28-by-33-cm) rectangle on the sheet pan, making sure that it's no more than ⅛ inch (3 mm) thick. You will be trimming the edges, so at this point your goal is to approximate the rectangle. Tilt the caramel back and forth to achieve as even a layer of caramel as possible.

② Allow the caramel to cool completely. It will be very firm but still malleable.

③ On a piece of parchment lightly dusted with cornstarch, roll the fondant into a rough rectangle, smaller than the caramel rectangle. Invert the fondant onto the caramel, centering as best you can, and peel off the parchment. Gently press the fondant with your hands to cover the caramel in an even layer, making sure to leave

a gap of about ½ inch (12 mm) at the top and bottom.

④ Cut the caramel and fondant in half lengthwise. Place the sheet pan so that the longer side faces you. Starting with one of the halves, gently fold the caramel edge over the fondant on the farthest left corner and continue along the length of the caramel, just as if you were rolling a jelly roll or a piece of paper into a tight roll. Continue rolling the caramel and fondant into a log, until you have reached the midpoint where you have cut the caramel in half. Repeat this procedure with the other half, forming a second log.

⑤ Move the logs to a cutting board. With a very clean, sharp knife, cut each log into ½-inch (12-mm) slices. Make sure to clean your knife often, as the caramel will start to stick to it, making it impossible to cut through the spirals cleanly. If the caramel and fondant are too warm to cut without the fondant oozing from the center, refrigerate the logs for 10 to 20 minutes, until they are firm enough to continue.

⑥ Wrap each spiral individually in a small piece of parchment and store in an airtight container up to 2 weeks.

# GATEAU
# SINA BINA

*If you haven't already figured this out, I'm a sucker for a confection with some complicated textural properties.* I like crunchy, chewy, smooth, and silken, and I want it all in one bite. I want salty and sweet with just the right balance of nutty, and all in one bite. I want chocolate, vanilla, and almond, and all in one bite. Please and thank you.

This is such a cake: a little bit of everything I find essential to a meaningful existence, and all in one bite.

Does this cake go a little too far? Am I pushing the envelope of confectionery propriety? Hell, yes.

|||||||||||||||||||||||||||||||||||||||||||||||| *Makes 1 (10-inch/25-cm) gateau* ||||||||||||||||||||||||||||||||||||||||||||||||

| FOR THE CHOCOLATE MERINGUE CAKE | | |
| --- | --- | --- |
| cocoa powder | 1 cup | 85 g |
| almond flour | 1 cup | 140 g |
| salt | 1½ teaspoons | 9 g |
| baking powder | 1 teaspoon | 5 g |
| unsalted butter, at room temperature | 1 cup | 225 g |
| sugar | 2 cups | 400 g |
| eggs | 4 | |
| almond extract | 1 tablespoon | 15 ml |
| vanilla extract | 1 teaspoon | 5 ml |
| FOR THE ASSEMBLY salted dry-roasted almonds, chopped roughly into thirds | 1 cup | 150 g |
| Vanilla Nougat (page 121) | ½ batch | |

PROCEDURE FOR THE **CHOCOLATE MERINGUE CAKE**

① Preheat the oven to 350°F (175°C).

② In a small bowl, whisk together the cocoa powder, almond flour, salt, and baking powder. Set aside.

③ In the bowl of a stand mixer fitted with the paddle attachment, beat together the butter and sugar until light and fluffy. Slowly add the eggs, one by one. Scrape down the sides of the bowl. Add the almond and vanilla extracts and beat for a moment to incorporate them.

④ With the mixer on low speed, slowly add the cocoa powder mixture and beat until just incorporated.

⑤ Remove the bowl from the mixer. With a rubber spatula, give the batter a good stir, making sure to scrape the bottom and sides of the bowl to include any clinging butter that's refused to join the party.

⑥ Pour the batter into a 10-inch (25-cm) spring-form pan or cake ring lined with parchment and liberally sprayed with nonstick cooking spray.

⑦ Bake for 40 minutes until set in the middle.

PROCEDURE FOR THE **ASSEMBLY**

① While the cake is baking, add the almonds to the nougat and stir to combine. Set aside.

② Remove the cake from the oven, leaving it in the springform pan or cake ring. Spoon the nougat over the cake, using a small offset spatula or the back of a spoon sprayed with nonstick cooking spray to make an even layer over the entire surface of the cake. Make swirly patterns to give the top of the cake some textural interest.

③ Return to the oven and bake for 15 minutes more.

④ Allow the cake to cool completely. With a thin paring knife, cut around the rim of the cake to release the sides from the springform pan or cake ring. Remove the ring or the sides of the pan and gently slide a cake plate underneath the gateau. Serve immediately.

# The Best
# GINGER COOKIES
## EVER

*This was one of the most popular cookies at my shop in Montpelier—it's a molasses cookie with ginger aspirations.* The crystallized ginger is the "chip" in the mix, and it adds a tang and a chew unlike any other ginger cookie. The cookie itself, without the additional ginger chunks, is crisp around the edges, chewy in the center, and full of exotically spicy flavor.

|||||||||||||||||||||||||||||||||||||||||||||||||||| *Makes approximately 30* ||||||||||||||||||||||||||||||||||||||||||||||||||||

| | | |
|---|---|---|
| unsalted butter, at room temperature | 2 cups | 455 g |
| granulated sugar | ⅔ cup | 130 g |
| brown sugar, firmly packed | 1 cup | 220 g |
| molasses | ¾ cup | 255 g |
| eggs | 2 | |
| all-purpose flour | 4½ cups | 560 g |
| baking soda | 2 teaspoons | 10 g |
| ground ginger | 2 tablespoons | 12 g |
| cinnamon | 2 teaspoons | 4 g |
| ground cloves | 1 teaspoon | 2 g |
| nutmeg | ½ teaspoon | 1 g |
| salt | 1 teaspoon | 6 g |
| white pepper | 1 teaspoon | 3 g |
| chopped crystallized ginger | 1 cup | 140 g |
| sanding sugar | 1 cup | 200 g |

① Preheat the oven to 350°F (175°C).

② In the bowl of a stand mixer fitted with the paddle attachment, cream the butter, white sugar, brown sugar, and molasses until light and fluffy. Add the eggs, one at a time, incorporating well after each addition.

③ In a separate bowl, whisk together the flour, baking soda, and six spices. With the mixer on low speed, gently add the flour mixture. Be very careful not to overmix; stop the mixer just as you are positive that the flour is completely incorporated.

④ Fold in the crystallized ginger and chill the dough, covered, for a few hours or overnight.

⑤ Using a large cookie scoop, scoop the cookies and dip them in sanding sugar so that they are completely coated. Place the cookies on a parchment-lined sheet pan, spacing them 2 inches (5 cm) apart to allow for spreading.

⑥ Bake for about 15 minutes. The cookies will crack a bit but should still be soft in the middle. Place on wire racks to cool.

# THIS IS NOT
## *Your Grandmother's Mail-Order*
# NUT LOG

*The Holiday Season!* That festive time replete with joyful singing, copious amounts of alcohol, and hour-long hunts for gift receipts in the trash. How would we cope with such a divinely stressful time without processed mystery food available only from November 12th to January 2nd but with a shelf life longer than a fossilized trilobite?

The fruitcakes, the soft processed cheez-food ball, and the amorphous nut log, to name just a few, are foods most humans would ordinarily shun. Yet during the times that are the merriest, for some reason we spend precious family-bonding hours sitting in a dark corner vanquishing indestructible holiday fodder.

But have I got a surprise for you! Here's a holiday staple transformed into something so luscious and ambrosial that you can wallow in your seasonal affective disorder and family dysfunction in high style!

The maple fondant in this recipe differs from traditional vanilla cream fondant in two ways. There's the obvious: maple. Then there's the not-so-obvious: egg whites. The addition of egg whites gives the fondant filling a slightly nougat-y touch, and a little more substance.

||||||||||||||||||||||||||||||||||||||||||||||||||||||| *Makes 1 (9-inch/23-cm) log* |||||||||||||||||||||||||||||||||||||||||||||||||||||||

| FOR THE MAPLE FONDANT | | |
| --- | --- | --- |
| sugar | 1½ cups | 300 g |
| grade B maple syrup | ½ cup | 120 ml |
| water | ½ cup | 120 ml |
| egg whites | 2 | |
| salt | ½ teaspoon | 3 g |
| unsalted butter, cut into small pieces, at room temperature | ¼ cup | 55 g |
| cornstarch | 2 tablespoons | 16 g |
| FOR THE ASSEMBLY | | |
| Super-Crunchy, Salty Nuts (page 153), freshly made, unbroken, and still warm | 1 batch | |

PROCEDURE FOR THE **MAPLE FONDANT**

① In a large saucepan over medium heat, combine the sugar, maple syrup, and water, stirring until the sugar has completely dissolved.

② Brush down the sides of the saucepan with a damp pastry brush, clip on a candy thermometer, and heat to 245°F (118°C).

③ While the syrup is heating, in the bowl of a stand mixer, whisk the egg whites with the salt until they are foamy.

④ When the syrup comes to temperature, with the mixer on medium speed, carefully pour the syrup down the side of the bowl and into the beating egg whites. Increase the mixer speed to high and whip for 2 minutes.

⑤ Switch to the paddle attachment, and with the mixer on medium speed, slowly add the butter and cornstarch. Increase the mixer speed to high and beat the fondant until the bowl is cool and the fondant thickens. You'll notice that the mixture will rise and then fall with the addition of the butter. This is normal.

⑥ Scrape the fondant onto a piece of plastic wrap and shape it, as best you can, into a rough 9-inch (23-cm) log. Refrigerate for 2 hours, or until it firms up.

PROCEDURE FOR THE **ASSEMBLY**

① Meanwhile, prepare the recipe for the salty nuts, but do not break them apart. (We want the nuts in a malleable and large enough "sheet" to wrap around the fondant.) Spread the hot nuts on a sheet pan. Allow them to cool slightly.

② Place a clean piece of parchment over the nut mixture and flip it upside down so that that the underside that's been flattened and cooling on the sheet pan is now facing up. Remove any parchment that has stuck to the underside of the nuts.

③ With a sharp knife sprayed with nonstick spray, trim a large piece of the nut mixture, while it's still very warm, into a 12-by-8-inch (30-by-20-cm) rectangle. Set the yummy nut trimmings aside to scarf down later.

④ While the nut rectangle is still warm, place the maple fondant log in the middle of it. Wrap the long sides of the nut mixture around the nougat to meet in a seam along the middle. Pinch the seam together and flip the roll over. Trim the ends with a nonstick-sprayed knife; there should be about 1 inch (2.5 cm) of extra nuts on either side that can be removed. When you cut through the ends, this will seal the end pieces. Tuck under any extra bits and shape the log with your hands to keep it smooth.

⑤ Allow the log to cool completely. Serve immediately, or wrap in parchment sprayed with nonstick cooking spray, wrap again in plastic wrap, and store, airtight, for up to 2 weeks.

# VANILLA-PECAN
# SWIRL TEA CAKE
## *with Maple Glaze*

*The vanilla tea cake was a morning staple at my bakery.* It's a dense, intensely flavorful pound cake. It's buttery and smooth. It's filling and comforting. I've added a ring of moist pecan filling that brings a dash of unexpected sweet flavor, and the maple glaze is a lovely counterpoint to the luscious vanilla undertones of the cake.

*Makes 1 Bundt cake*

## PROCEDURE FOR THE **FILLING**

① In the bowl of a food processor fitted with the blade attachment, grind together all of the filling ingredients until a chunky paste forms. Transfer to a small bowl and set aside.

## PROCEDURE FOR THE **CAKE**

① Preheat the oven to 325°F (165°C).

② In a large bowl, whisk together the flour, salt, baking powder, cinnamon, and nutmeg.

③ In the bowl of a stand mixer fitted with the paddle attachment, beat the butter and sugars until light and fluffy, 4 to 5 minutes.

④ Add the eggs, one at a time, beating for 1 minute after each addition. Add the sour cream, mix again for 1 minute, and scrape down the sides of the bowl.

⑤ Add the vanilla paste, then slowly add the flour mixture. Mix until just combined; do not overmix.

⑥ Spray a 10- to 12-cup (2.4- to 2.8-L) swirled Bundt pan liberally with nonstick spray. Spoon slightly less than half the cake batter into the pan. Sprinkle all the filling on top of the layer of batter. Spoon the remaining batter on top of the sprinkled filling.

| FOR THE FILLING | | |
|---|---|---|
| pecans | ½ cup | 50 g |
| brown sugar, firmly packed | ½ cup | 110 g |
| cinnamon | 1 teaspoon | 2 g |
| salt | pinch | |
| FOR THE CAKE | | |
| all-purpose flour | 2 cups | 250 g |
| salt | 1 teaspoon | 6 g |
| baking powder | 1½ teaspoons | 7.5 g |
| cinnamon | 1 teaspoon | 2 g |
| nutmeg | ½ teaspoon | 1 g |
| unsalted butter, at room temperature | 1 cup | 225 g |
| granulated sugar | ¾ cup | 150 g |
| brown sugar, firmly packed | ¾ cup | 165 g |
| eggs | 5 | |
| sour cream | ¼ cup | 60 ml |
| vanilla bean paste | 1 tablespoon | 15 ml |

⑦ Bake for 60 to 75 minutes, until the cake is golden and a toothpick inserted in the center comes out clean.

⑧ Allow the cake to cool for 10 minutes in the pan. Invert the cake out of the pan onto a wire cooling rack placed over a parchment-lined sheet pan (trust me—there's a very good reason for this setup). Allow the cake to cool completely.

PROCEDURE FOR THE **GLAZE**

① In a large saucepan over medium heat, combine the maple syrup, sugar, salt, and water, stirring continuously until the sugar has completely melted. Clip on a candy thermometer, stop stirring, and turn the heat to medium-high. When the temperature reaches 290°F (143°C), take the pan from the heat and immediately stir in the baking soda.

② Slowly pour the glaze over the top of the cake, making a few passes back and forth. Don't pour it all out at once—you want to make sure that a decent amount adheres to the cake.

③ Sprinkle the toasted pecans on top of the glaze before it has completely set so that they stick. Allow the glaze to harden completely before serving.

| FOR THE GLAZE | | |
|---|---|---|
| grade B maple syrup | ½ cup | 120 ml |
| sugar | 1 cup | 200 g |
| water | ⅓ cup | 75 ml |
| salt | ½ teaspoon | 3 g |
| baking soda | ½ teaspoon | 2.5 g |
| pecan pieces, toasted | ¼ cup | 30 g |

# CUCKOO-FOR-COCOA
# CRÊPE CAKE

*I made this for my sweet Ray for Valentine's Day.* The cake was so pretty that he took pictures of it. And when he ate a slice, he sighed. That's better than a dozen roses, any day.

You can make this cake as high as conceivable; you simply have to make more batter if you want to stack more crêpes. This recipe makes approximately twenty small crêpes.

|||||||||||||||||||||||||||||||||||||||||||||||||| *Makes 1 (6-inch/15-cm) crêpe cake* ||||||||||||||||||||||||||||||||||||||||||||||||||

| FOR THE MOCHA CRÊPES | | |
| --- | --- | --- |
| unsalted butter | ¼ cup, plus extra for the pan | 55 g, plus extra for the pan |
| whole milk | 1 cup, plus extra if needed | 240 ml, plus extra if needed |
| cocoa powder | ¼ cup | 20 g |
| water | ½ cup | 120 ml |
| salt | ¼ teaspoon | 1.5 g |
| eggs | 2 | |
| all-purpose flour | 1 cup | 125 g |
| vanilla bean paste | 1 teaspoon | 5 ml |
| agave nectar | ¼ cup | 60 ml |
| FOR THE ASSEMBLY Bittersweet Pudding (page 46), chilled | 1 batch | |

### PROCEDURE FOR THE MOCHA CRÊPES

① In a small saucepan over low heat, melt the butter.

② Transfer the butter along with all the remaining crêpe ingredients into a blender or food processor and process until completely blended.

③ Transfer the batter to a bowl. Cover and place the bowl in the refrigerator for 1 hour to dissipate any bubbles left over from the blitzing, and to hydrate the flour and relax the gluten.

④ Pour the batter through a sieve and into a large container. (If you find that the batter has thickened too much in the refrigerator to flow freely, stir in 1 tablespoon (15 ml) milk at a time until it reaches pourable consistency.)

⑤ In a 6-inch (15-cm) nonstick frying pan over medium-low heat, melt a small pat of butter, swirling the pan to make sure it is evenly coated with butter, but not with so much that it pools.

⑥ Remove the pan from the heat. Pour 2 tablespoons (30 ml) of the crêpe batter into the pan, swirling it around to coat the pan and form an even circle. Cook over medium-low heat until the crêpe is cooked through. (I don't flip crêpes—I let them cook through over a lower heat and not brown; this keeps them tender, and the layers of the crêpe cake are guaranteed to be moist.) To ensure that the crêpe is cooked through, touch the surface to make sure that it feels dry. You can put a lid over the pan for a minute to allow the steam to cook the crêpe through and still keep it very moist (or you can turn off the heat and flip the crêpe if you're squeamish).

⑦ Repeat this process with the remaining batter, re-buttering the pan as necessary. Transfer

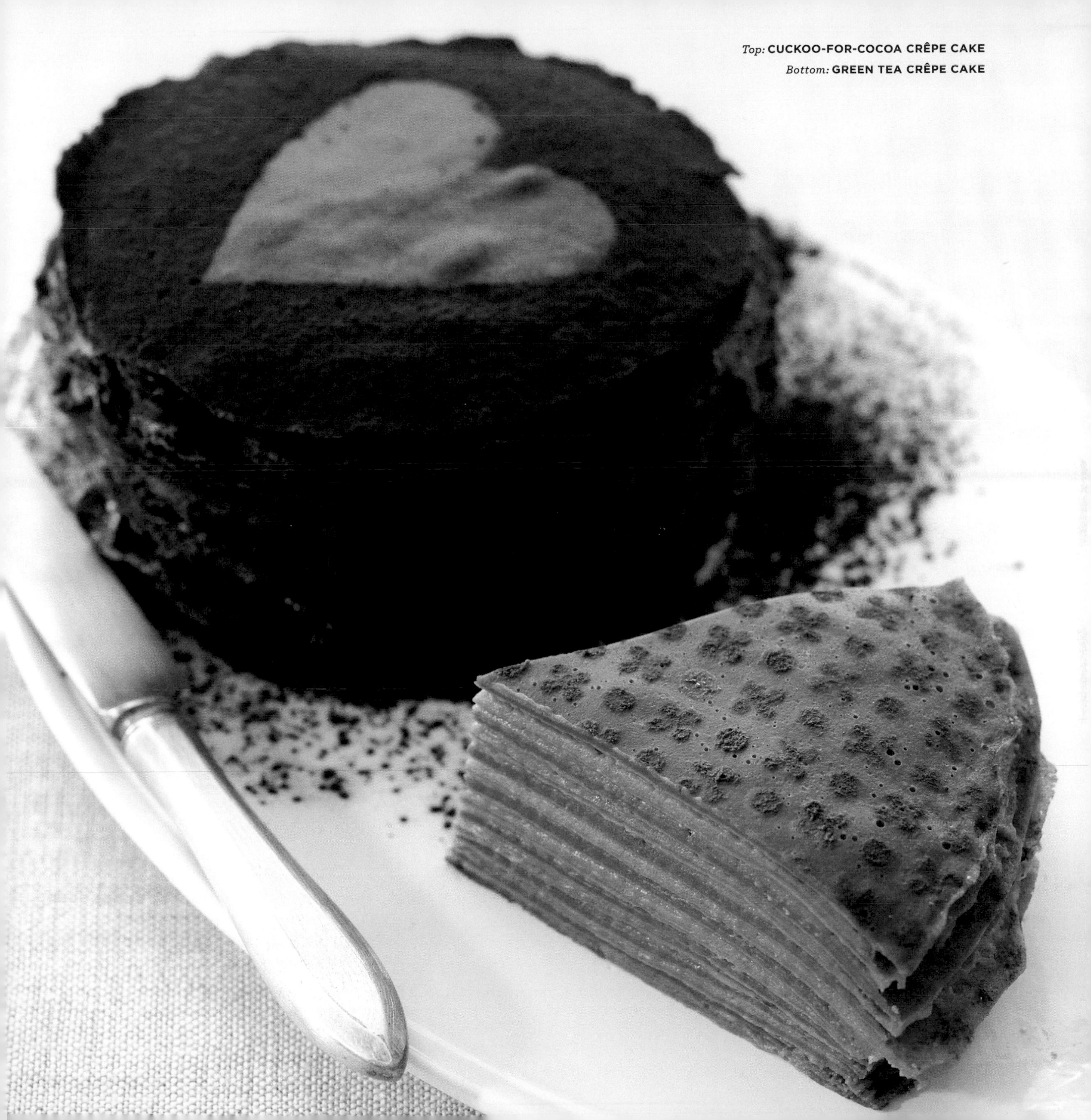

*Top:* **CUCKOO-FOR-COCOA CRÊPE CAKE**
*Bottom:* **GREEN TEA CRÊPE CAKE**

the finished crêpes to a plate, putting a piece of parchment between each crêpe to keep them from sticking together.

PROCEDURE FOR THE **ASSEMBLY**

① Give the pudding a good stir to loosen it up.

② Lay a crêpe on a serving plate. With a small offset spatula, spread 1 heaping tablespoon (15 ml) of the pudding evenly over the crêpe. Lay another crêpe on top of the pudding, and spread another heaping tablespoon (15 ml) of the pudding evenly over the second crêpe. Continue in this decadent fashion until you've used all your crêpes and all your pudding.

③ Gently cover the crêpe cake with plastic wrap and place it in the freezer to set for about 1 hour before serving. You don't want this cake frozen, but just firm enough that slicing through it with a serrated knife is easy. As an option, cut a heart shape out of parchment paper, place it on top of the cake, and dust gently with cocoa powder just before serving. To make the slicing effortless, dip your knife in scalding hot water and then wipe it dry before each cut.

# GREEN TEA
# CRÊPE CAKE

*This is a wonderfully Asian twist on the crêpe cake theme.* You can make this cake as high as you wish; simply make more batter for more crêpes. This recipe makes approximately twenty small crêpes.

||||||||||||||||||||||||||||||||||||||||||||| *Makes 1 (6-inch/15-cm) crêpe cake* |||||||||||||||||||||||||||||||||

PROCEDURE FOR THE **GREEN TEA CRÊPES**

① In a small saucepan over low heat, melt the butter.

② Transfer the butter along with all the remaining crêpe ingredients into a blender or food processor and process until completely blended.

③ Transfer the batter to a bowl. Cover and place the bowl in the refrigerator for 1 hour to dissipate any bubbles left over from the blitzing, and to allow the flour to hydrate and the gluten to relax.

④ Pour the batter through a sieve and into a large container. (If you find that the batter has thickened too much in the refrigerator to flow freely, stir in 1 tablespoon (15 ml) milk at a time until it reaches pourable consistency.)

⑤ In a 6-inch (15-cm) nonstick frying pan over medium-low heat, melt a small pat of butter, swirling the pan to make sure it is evenly coated with butter, but not with so much that it pools.

⑥ Remove the pan from the heat. Pour 2 tablespoons (30 ml) of the crêpe batter into the pan, swirling it around to coat the pan and form an even circle. Cook over medium-low heat until the crêpe is cooked through. (I don't flip crêpes—I let them cook through over a lower

| | | |
|---|---|---|
| FOR THE GREEN TEA CRÊPES | | |
| unsalted butter | ¼ cup, plus extra for the pan | 55 g, plus extra for the pan |
| whole milk | 1 cup, plus extra if needed | 240 ml, plus extra if needed |
| matcha (green tea) powder | ¼ cup | 12 g |
| water | ½ cup | 120 ml |
| salt | ½ teaspoon | 3 g |
| eggs | 2 | |
| all-purpose flour | 1 cup | 125 g |
| vanilla bean paste | 1 teaspoon | 5 ml |
| agave nectar | ¼ cup | 60 ml |
| green food coloring (optional) | 2 drops | |
| FOR THE ASSEMBLY | | |
| Green Tea Pastry Cream (page 39) | 2 cups | 480 ml |

heat and not brown; this keeps them tender, and the layers of the crêpe cake are guaranteed to be moist.) To ensure that the crêpe is cooked through, touch the surface to make sure that it feels dry (or you can turn off the heat and flip the crêpe if you're squeamish).

⑦ Repeat this process with the remaining batter, re-buttering the pan as necessary. Transfer the finished crêpes to a plate, putting a piece of parchment between each crêpe to keep them from sticking together. To learn how to make the stencil pattern on the cake as seen in the photo on page 239, go to www.sugarbabycook book.com.

PROCEDURE FOR THE **ASSEMBLY**

① Give the pastry cream a good stir to loosen it up.

② Lay a crêpe on a serving plate. With a small off-set spatula, spread 1 heaping tablespoon (15 ml) of the green tea pastry cream evenly over the crêpe. Lay another crêpe on top of the pastry cream, and spread another heaping tablespoon (15 ml) of the pastry cream evenly over the sec-ond crêpe. Continue in this decadent fashion until you've used all your crêpes and all your pastry cream.

③ Gently cover the crêpe cake with plastic wrap and place it in the freezer to set for about 1 hour before serving. You don't want this cake fro-zen, but just firm enough that slicing through it with a serrated knife is easy. To make the slicing effortless, dip your knife in scalding hot water and then wipe it dry before each cut.

# INDEX

page references in italic refer to illustrations

AND
THAT'S
*the*
SUGAR,
BABY!

I AM

NOTORIOUS

*for*

KILLING

ANGEL FOOD

CAKES

I WAS

THE ENVY

*of every*

KID

*at Woodmont*

ELEMENTARY.

I WAS

*the biggest*

CANDY CORN

ON EARTH

I SWEAR

I POPPED OUT

*of the womb*

SCREAMING

*for a*

PIECE OF

AND

*above all:*

DON'T POKE

HOT

CARAMEL

WHEN I AM

REINCARNATED

I WANT

*to*

COME BACK

*as*

ROCK CANDY

*For*

INSTANCE,

*if I could*

MARRY

PASTRY CREAM,

I WOULD

I AM

NOTORIOUS

*for*

KILLING

NO REASON

YOU CAN'T

PLAY

*with*

YOUR FOOD

*and your*

RECIPES

I SWEAR

I POPPED OUT

*of the womb*

SCREAMING

*for a*

PIECE OF

CANDY,

*a natural-born*

SUGAR BABY

I WAS

THE ENVY

*of every*

KID

*at Woodmont*

ELEMENTARY.

I WAS

*the biggest*

ROCK CANDY

*For*

INSTANCE,

*if I could*

MARRY

PASTRY CREAM,

I WOULD

AND

*above all:*

DON'T POKE

HOT

CARAMEL

THERE'S

NO REASON

YOU CAN'T

PLAY

*with*

YOUR FOOD

*and your*

RECIPES

I AM
NOTORIOUS
*for*
KILLING
ANGEL FOOD
CAKES

I WAS
THE ENVY
*of every*
KID
*at Woodmont*
ELEMENTARY.
I WAS
*the biggest*
CANDY CORN
ON EARTH

I SWEAR
I POPPED OUT

AND
*above all:*
DON'T POKE
HOT
CARAMEL

WHEN I AM
REINCARNATED
I WANT
*to*
COME BACK
*as*
ROCK CANDY

*For*
INSTANCE,
*if I could*
MARRY
PASTRY CREAM,
I WOULD

I AM
NOTORIOUS
*for*
KILLING

NO REASON
YOU CAN'T
PLAY
*with*
YOUR FOOD
*and your*
RECIPES

I SWEAR
I POPPED OUT
*of the womb*
SCREAMING
*for a*
PIECE OF
CANDY,
*a natural-born*
SUGAR BABY

I WAS
THE ENVY
*of every*
KID
*at Woodmont*
ELEMENTARY.
I WAS
*the biggest*

ROCK CANDY

*For*
INSTANCE,
*if I could*
MARRY
PASTRY CREAM,
I WOULD

AND
*above all:*
DON'T POKE
HOT
CARAMEL

THERE'S
NO REASON
YOU CAN'T
PLAY
*with*
YOUR FOOD
*and your*
RECIPES